KICKING AGAINST
THE PRICKS

KICKING
AGAINST
THE PRICKS

A Theatre Producer Looks Back

The Memoirs of

OSCAR LEWENSTEIN

NICK HERN BOOKS
London

A Nick Hern Book

Kicking against the Pricks first published in Great Britain in 1994
by Nick Hern Books, 14 Larden Road, London W3 7ST

Copyright © 1994 by Oscar Lewenstein

Oscar Lewenstein has asserted his right to be identified as
author of this work

A CIP catalogue record for this book is available from
the British Library

Typeset by Country Setting, Woodchurch, Kent TN26 3TB,
and printed in Great Britain by Mackays of Chatham PLC

ISBN 1-85459-171-1

Contents

	Introduction *by Keith Waterhouse*	xi
Part One	Doors Open *at the Royal Court and in the West End*	1
Part Two	Flashback *to where I came from*	41
Part Three	Second Flashback *to Unity, the people's theatre*	65
Part Four	The Long and the Short and the Tall *with Wolf Mankowitz in the West End*	85
Part Five	The Ghandi of Threadneedle Street *or the knack of surviving despite doing my own thing*	105
Part Six	The Living Theatre *epic theatre at the Roundhouse*	131
Part Seven	I Become Artistic Director of the Royal Court *Fugard's African season and Orton's trilogy*	145
Part Eight	After Words	177
	Appendixes	183
	Index	203

For
Eileen, Mark and Peter

Illustrations

Oscar's grandfather
Oscar's father
Oscar's mother, with her children
Oscar on leave from the army, 1942
Ted Willis as a young man, photo courtesy Lady Willis
Oscar and Eileen, 1953, photo Kevin MacDonnell
Cover for *New Theatre*, April 1941
Cover for *Smoke*, September 1941
Women of Twilight, photo Houston Rogers
Robert Mitchell, photo courtesy Evelyn Garratt
Original programme cover for *Mother Courage*
John Craxton's front cloth for *The World of Sholem Aleichem*
Oscar and Wolf Mankowitz, photo Tom Blau
Orson Welles in *Moby Dick*
Look Back in Anger, photo Houston Rogers
The Party, photo David Sim
A Taste of Honey, photo David Sim
The Long and The Short and The Tall, photo John Cowan
The Hostage, photo John Cowan
Rhinoceros, photo John Timbers
Oscar promoting *Billy Liar*, photo *The Tatler*
Billy Liar, photo Lewis Morley
Baal, photo Lewis Morley
Luther, photo Sandra Lousada
Hotel in Amsterdam, photo Zoe Dominic
The Living Book of the Living Theatre (cover)
Semi-Detached, photo David Sim
St Joan of the Stockyards, photo Morris Newcombe

What the Butler Saw, photo Angus McBean
Athol Fugard
Brian Friel
Keith Waterhouse and Willis Hall, photo *Yorkshire Evening Post*
What the Butler Saw, photo David Montgomery
Sizwe Banzi is Dead, photo John Haynes
The Girl with Green Eyes, photo *The Tatler*
Oscar, Tony Richardson and John Osborne at Acapulco
Tom Jones, photo BFI, courtesy Samuel Goldwyn
The Knack, photo BFI, courtesy United International Pictures
Rita, Sue and Bob Too, photo BFI, courtesy Mainline Pictures
On the set of *Rita, Sue and Bob Too*
Oscar and Jeanne Moreau on location for *The Bride Wore Black*
Oscar and family
Oscar, 1993

Acknowledgements

My title is taken from the Bible, Acts of Apostles, Chapter IX, Verse 5. I must thank the late Margaret Ramsay, who in 1966, when I was depressed following the failure of the film *Sailor from Gibraltar* and an attack of jaundice, proposed to me that we should do a series of tapes in which she would ask me questions about my life and career. Peggy put a lot of time in, coming round to my house in Hove each Sunday morning for about ten weeks. I was considering at the time whether I wanted to continue to work in the theatre and films and Peggy thought the idea of the tapes might clear my mind. It helped to do that, but when the tapes were typed, we agreed that the only thing to do with them was to put them away in a cupboard. They proved useful twenty-four years later when I began writing this book.

The book was suggested to me by Keith Waterhouse, whose early plays I had produced and whom I met again after many years at a party given by Victor Spinetti. Keith spent a large part of the evening telling me I must write this book and ending by promising to read it and give his comments as I went along. This he did and I certainly would not have undertaken it without his encouragement.

Nick Hern, my publisher and editor, to whom I gave the book at a time when his business was being reorganised, a circumstance which caused him to be rather slow in responding to my various drafts and to which, I fear, I was not as sympathetic as I should have been. He gave me many useful suggestions and the book would have been much worse without them.

I should like to thank the many critics from whose notices I have quoted in this book. Heaven knows, there is little to say in favour of the critics. Too often they have failed to recognise a new talent when first faced with it and yet as Irving Wardle in his recent book says, the future reader's knowledge of what it was like on the first night of Brook's *King Lear* or Olivier's *Oedipus* depends almost exclusively on what the reviewers made of it. He quotes Ken Tynan as saying that his role was to give permanence to something impermanent and Brecht as saying about critics: 'What they say about my plays doesn't matter, my plays will survive the critics, but what they say about my productions matters very much because what they write is all that posterity will know of the subject.' So, since many readers of this book will not have seen the plays discussed, I am using these quotations to fill in the gaps as best I can.

I must thank my secretary, Caroline Sutcliffe, for so patiently helping me with the typing of the various drafts and my secretary from earlier days, Elizabeth Lomas, and Sarah Woodcock of the Theatre Museum, for helping me track down the various illustrations.

Lastly I must thank my wife, Eileen, for her constant encouragement.

Introduction

Time magazine got the wrong epithet for the now frequently-maligned Sixties. Swinging? Swinging suggests snorting and swigging and – well, swinging – the decade away. Wasting it. Frittering it, like the Roaring Twenties, as if killing time while waiting for a war or some such calamity to happen.

In truth the Sixties – and let's date them properly, from the late Fifties – were wonderfully productive, a powerhouse of energy and talent. Were they still going on – what a pity that a decade has such a limited lifespan – we should be in better shape.

It didn't just happen, of course. Nor was it exactly or entirely the consequence of the social passing show, the aftermath of the war and all that. The 1944 Butler Education Act establishing the right to secondary education for all had produced an upstart generation who instead of becoming factory fodder had come up through the grammar schools and redbrick universities and was now ready to take the world on.

By every train into Kings Cross and Euston and Paddington, it seemed, writers, artists, actors came pouring into London. The artists brought images the south-east had only read about, the writers wrote about the working class and the lower middle classes as if D.H. Lawrence hadn't been a one-off after all, and the actors no longer spoke in anyone-for-tennis accents.

At that time, it seemed, you could not climb over a slag heap without encountering two film directors squabbling over who had logged the chimney-stack horizon extreme long shot first. Major film companies were buying movie rights in old tram tickets. For those born on what had up to then been regarded as the wrong side of the tracks, the world was their oyster washed down with champagne. And in one respect at least Time magazine was right: life was a party.

On the periphery of all this activity – for he was never a party man – the observer looking in on this exuberant tableau would have noticed a slight, beaky individual, who looked as if he might have come along to audit the books. All that champagne, all those oysters: who was paying for it all? This was the impresario Oscar Lewenstein, and he had most certainly not come to perform any such mundane task as looking at the books – although you may be sure he kept a sharp eye on them – but for a piece of the action. The Sixties were happening and Oscar wanted some of them.

He was an eminently suitable candidate, a political animal who had, however, the predatory nose of a commercial animal. Emerging, improbably, from the Glasgow Unity Theatre, he became Artistic Director of the Royal Court Theatre Club, as it then was, just as the Fifties were tuning up to become the Sixties. Having, somewhere along the way, launched Sandy Wilson's *The Boy Friend* on its stupendous career for a return to his own pocket of just £30, he thought to become a producer on his own account. The rest is the history that may be read here.

From the Unity to the Royal Court, from Osborne to Orton, from *Billy Liar* to *Baal*, from *A Taste of Honey* to *Tom Jones*, Oscar Lewenstein was from the start a big player in that heady game of chance that was the late Fifties and Sixties. He was hard-headed but never hard-hearted – while he would not be inclined to put on a sure loser for the hell of it, he would nurse along, or anyway help along the way, a limping candidate because he believed in it. Whatever his private political inclinations, his loyalty and enthusiasm were to the theatre as theatre, with perhaps the main chance thrown in (why else, one asks, would the producer of *The Three-penny Opera* have put on the *Punch Revue* and a show based on the writings of Art Buchwald?)

Like us all, he made misjudgements (he was all for turning down Osborne's *The Entertainer*). Like us all, he has a memory that occasionally plays tricks on him; it is not true that Willis Hall and I sold the film rights of *Billy Liar* to Joe Janni because we did not want Lindsay Anderson to direct it: we sold them because Joe came up with a handsome two-picture co-production deal (the other being *A Kind of Loving*) and because there was no other deal on the table. Nor, since John Schlesinger's film continues to be screened regularly to this day, is Oscar entitled to call it 'a film which was not a real success'. Also, it is a typically austere Lewenstein judgement to dismiss our 1962 Royal Court double bill *Squat Betty* and *The Sponge Room* as 'a disaster'. I would have settled for a success teetering on failure, or a failure teetering on success.

There is no luvvies tittle-tattle in this volume: indeed, there is an exasperating lack of it. 'During *The Charge of the Light Brigade*, for which John Osborne wrote the first draft script and which I was producing, both of us fell out with Tony Richardson, and each of us for his own reasons resigned from the project and from future Woodfall activities . . . ' Yes? And? Answer comes there none.

But for the serious student of the period it is all here, or at least some of it is here – what made those Sixties, or the theatrical division of the Sixties, tick. Oscar Lewenstein is a reluctant recorder of his times, indeed he brings diffidence to a fine art – but do not be deceived by that (we never were when he was practising it in person); this is a fascinating stretch of the tapestry as it is unfurled.

KEITH WATERHOUSE

Part One

Doors Open

at the Royal Court and in the West End

It was 1952. The Royal Court Theatre had been standing on the east side of Sloane Square for 64 years when I first read the announcement. At the time, not only had I never been to it (for I had only come to live in London in 1933 and the Court as it was then called closed down in 1932), I wasn't even aware of its fame. There, during the great seasons of 1904-1907, Granville Barker, with his partner, Vedrenne, presented the plays of Euripides, Schnitzler, Hauptmann, Yeats, Galsworthy, his own plays and no fewer than eleven plays by Shaw. Later the theatre had fallen on hard times, closing in 1932 and being badly bombed in the Second World War.

In 1952 I was living in a semi-basement flat in South Hill Park Gardens, Hampstead, with my girl friend, Eileen Mawson. Since being demobbed from the army in 1946, I had been working with Unity Theatre, first as the National Organiser of its local amateur groups, which at that time existed in most big cities and in many London boroughs. Then I became the Manager of Unity Theatre, Goldington Street, London and was there when Ted Willis formed his short lived professional company. After that, at Robert Mitchell's invitation, I became General Manager of Glasgow Unity Theatre. In addition to its amateur companies, a first rate professional company had been formed from amongst its best actors, which toured Scottish plays first in Scotland, then in England. Eventually they came to the West End under the auspices of Jack Hylton to present their most successful, if not their best play, *The Gorbals Story*.

Afterwards the company often visited the Embassy Theatre, Swiss Cottage, London, at first with Scottish plays and then with a series of Jewish American plays. At the same time, I edited the leading theatre magazine of the day, *New Theatre*, published by Unity. However, all these ventures were under-financed. Glasgow Unity, despite its success, never obtained an Arts Council subsidy and had folded by the end of 1951. On a part time basis I was helping Tony Hawtrey find plays to present at the Embassy. Eileen and I, after living together for five years, were thinking about having a baby and therefore getting married. In those days the second decision automatically followed the first. We had no savings and our financial prospects were not bright. I wanted to continue to work in the theatre and to be involved in the presentation of progressive plays of social and contemporary interest, as I had at Glasgow Unity. Eileen was a potter and had started a pottery in Baker Street with her friend, Brigitta Appleby, despite my warning that it would not be viable. 'Briglin', as they called it lasted over forty years, first as a partnership between the two girls, then run by Brigitta alone when Eileen decided some years later to concentrate on her own individual pots and set up a studio in the house to which we had by then moved. An early example of my powers of prophecy. Anyway, although Briglin survived, it did not provide Eileen with more than a minimum wage. I was earning very little at the Embassy and wondering what to do next when I saw an announcement in the newspapers to the effect that the Royal Court in Sloane Square was to re-open as a Club Theatre. I wondered whether there might be an opportunity for me there, so I rang Alfred Esdaile, the leaseholder of the theatre, and arranged to see him. Mr. Esdaile's office was in Park Lane, a street I had not visited before except as part of a demonstration on its way to or from Hyde Park Corner. In this capacity I had marched down it many times protesting against fascism and war, urging support for the Spanish Republicans, supporting the hunger marchers in the thirties, protesting against the Atom Bomb and in general demonstrating for all the good causes espoused by the Left in the years between 1935 and the day I visited Mr. Esdaile.

As befitted successful property developers, Mr. Esdaile and his partner and brother-in-law, Arnold Klausner, had offices in an elegant town house. Esdaile was a plump, perky, brisk little man. He was dressed in what I supposed was a smart city suit; he wore spats and sported a monocle. I was very thin at that time, and my clothes must have seemed rather shabby. However, Esdaile was not a snob and made me feel welcome. He had a quiet confidential way of speaking, as if he was about to tell you something important that other people didn't know. There was something of the music hall both in his voice and in his appearance. Though I did not know it at the time, he had had a long and interesting history in the theatre. He had been a pioneer of non-stop variety and was the inventor of the microphone that comes up out of the floor. He had built the Prince of Wales Theatre in Coventry Street in 1937 and had now acquired, as part of his property business, leases of the Royal Court and Kingsway Theatres. He must have been about 50 years old when I met him. I was 35. We got on well.

I told him about my career to date and he said he was sorry we had not met earlier, but that he had now appointed Giles Playfair to be his Artistic Director, that Mr. Playfair had chosen a Board to support his work and that his first season was due to open quite shortly. I thanked Mr. Esdaile for his interest and said goodbye, thinking that that was that.

Eileen and I proceeded to get married at the Hampstead Registry office. It was not a grand affair. Eileen's mother and father came. We had somehow or other managed to keep our living together a secret from them – I rather think with their co-operation – and I hardly knew them. My mother came. She lived up the road and knew all about our life of sin. She did not approve but I do not think it worried her too much. She was a woman who could find acceptable compromises in most situations. Thus she would not eat pork but was quite happy to eat bacon, and she ate a little less than usual on Yom Kippur. She said that she would rather have half of my father than the whole of any other man and that is what she got. The only other witness at our wedding was Brigitta.

We went off for the first time in our lives for three weeks in the South of France. Back in London, almost the first thing that caught my eye was a newspaper report to the effect that Giles Playfair had resigned as Artistic Director of the Royal Court Theatre Club and that the whole of his Board had resigned with him. I telephoned Mr. Esdaile. He said, 'Come over, boy.' I went over to the Royal Court Theatre and for the first time in my life entered that building which was to play so important a part in my future. Within about fifteen minutes I was installed as Artistic Director of the Royal Court Theatre Club at, for me, the handsome

salary of £20 per week, with the proviso that I could put on any programme I wanted, as long as 'it did not lose any money'.

The Royal Court is a small theatre. Nowadays it seats just under 400;
when I first arrived it seated about 420. Before it closed in the thirties it
had seated 600. Most of the lost seats were in the back of the Upper
Circle where a space has been created for offices and for a lighting box.
Other seats have been lost since, through reconstructing a downstairs bar
and making the stalls more comfortable. The box office was typical of the
times, a little rabbit hutch in the foyer, in which sat Albert Rouse, a long
time employee of Alfred Esdaile, who survived all the changes for many
years. I do not think Albert ever saw the plays or was particularly interested in them. He spent most of the day in that little hutch or in the pub
next door. Since I do not drink, I never got to know him socially, nor
did I get to know his views on anything beyond his work in the Box
Office, but I do not think he was in sympathy with the type of plays we
put on, except during the brief period when the theatre had a long
running success.

I took over the staff I found working there on my arrival, settled into
one of the small offices and got down to finding a show that could come
into the theatre quite quickly. The Playfair regime had presented a play,
The Bride of Denmark Hill, about Ruskin's wife, which they transferred for
a short run in the West End and had arranged for another play, Miss
Hargreaves with Margaret Rutherford, which had just opened when I
arrived. After that, nothing.

I was lucky. Rupert Doone, director of the Group Theatre, which had
put on Auden and Isherwood's plays in the thirties, wanted a theatre for
his production of The Comedy of Errors, and this opened at the Court on
27th August 1952, the first play of my first season. I call it 'my season'
but in fact my choice was limited to productions which either had small
casts and were already in being and thus had no production expenses, or
came with their own finance, as was the case with Comedy of Errors. The
theatre was running under club conditions because Esdaile in his refur-
bishing the theatre had not satisfied the London County Council that it
qualified for a public licence. So everyone had to become a member at
least 48 hours before buying a ticket. Membership theatres did not come
under the same fire regulations as public theatres, nor did their plays

have to be licensed by the Lord Chamberlain, members thus being free both to see uncensored plays and to burn whilst watching them.

This restriction on our audience plus the small capacity, made our chance of breaking even remote. No subsidy was available for Club Theatres, and very little money had been spent on a campaign to win members. Despite these difficulties, this first experience of running a theatre was invaluable to me, and I managed to put on six more or less interesting productions during my period as Artistic Director of the Club.

We opened with *The Comedy of Errors*. The cast was headed by Ernest Milton, who had played in Glasgow Unity's production of *The King of the Schnorrers*. A young actor, John Garley, also appeared, who I thought was going to have a great future, and who became a close friend, as did his wife, June Brown, now famous as Dot in *East Enders*. The play was charmingly set in Edwardian costume and was generally liked. We were lucky to get it. The second play was *Ebb Tide*, strongly adapted from the Robert Louis Stevenson story by Donald Pleasence, who also appeared in it. The third production was *Lord Arthur Savile's Crime* adapted from Oscar Wilde's story by Constance Cox. Claude Hulbert played the lead and also directed it. It opened on 7th October, but, unfortunately for its future prospects, another adaptation of the same Wilde story opened at the better known Arts Theatre on the 23rd. On 29th October we opened *The Long Mirror* by J.B. Priestley. This we had put on ourselves, and it ended in disaster. My old associate from Unity days, the director André Van Gyseghem, was married to the brilliant actress Jean Forbes Robertson. Jean unfortunately had a 'drink problem'. I had asked André if there was any play in which Jean would feel so confident that we could safely put it on. He had suggested *The Long Mirror*, which she had played many times all over the country. The play has one set and a cast of only five. It seemed a safe bet. On the first night the curtain went up, Jean had to say her first line – and couldn't speak. We had to bring the curtain down, put on the understudy, my young friend June Brown, and I don't think Jean ever played again. She was said to have been the greatest Peter Pan ever.

I quickly brought in a production of Genet's play *Les Bonnes* performed in French, that I had seen at the Mercury Theatre. The cast was bi-lingual and later played it in English. We were not satisfied that the English translation by Bernard Frechtman did justice to the original so I tried to get Dylan Thomas to translate it, but without success. It was the first production of Genet in England and was directed by Peter Zadek, later to become a famous director in Germany. The last production opening on 20th November was *A Kiss for Adèle*, in an English adaptation by Talbot Rothwell and Ted Willis of a French comedy. Fortunately it was guaranteed against loss by Jack Hylton, as a couple of weeks into the run down came the worst fog that London had experienced for years, the last of the real pea soupers. One evening, in the fog, not a soul came. I suppose this must have happened before in the history of the theatre but it was the end. Out of it came some good, because Alfred Esdaile decided to do the work on the building that was necessary to get it a public licence.

Whilst the necessary building work was being done, the theatre was closed. It was agreed that when it re-opened as a public theatre it should be run as a small West End theatre, bringing in other people's shows, charging them a rent and hoping they would have a long run. It must be understood that putting on shows at the Embassy or the Royal Court for runs of two, three or four weeks could not possibly be profitable unless some of them transferred to the West End for a long run. Only a subsidised theatre could afford to adopt such a policy, so Alfred Esdaile, who was running his theatre as a business, could only make it viable by letting the theatre. On re-opening, I was to be General Manager and my task was to find successful shows to bring into the theatre on a normal West End rental basis. I fortunately found that Laurier Lister, a producer of intimate revues, had a new show he wanted to open in the spring. So I arranged that *Airs on a Shoestring* should come to the Court. A delightful show starring Max Adrian, Moyra Fraser, Sally Rogers and Betty Marsden, it opened on 22nd April 1953 and was an immediate success with the critics and the public. It ran for nearly two years and gave me the opportunity everyone hopes for and so few get; to do my own thing.

In June of that year, our son Mark was born. Eileen soon went back to work at Briglin Pottery and Rosebud, June Brown's sister, came to live with us and look after the baby. The flat was very small and Mark had a little room scarcely bigger than a cupboard. Eileen painted golden stars on the blue ceiling, which made it seem higher, but she could not increase the floor space, so we decided to look for a bigger flat. We had bought a piece of land opposite us, backing on to the Heath, where there was a project to build eight houses. But when we came to try to get a mortgage we were refused everywhere on account of the uncertainty of both our incomes. Unlike the situation today, when you are encouraged to take up unnecessary loans, then you could not get necessary ones. Fortunately we found a house at Park Village West and my in-laws, with great generosity since they could ill afford it, loaned us the money we needed to buy a crown lease. We moved there the following June, just in time for Mark to try out movement possibilities without undue constraints.

Whilst *Airs on a Shoestring* ran at the Court, I had for the first time the chance to think and plan for the future. I was receiving my salary each week and, apart from keeping an eye on things at the theatre, had very little to do. There was obviously no point in thinking about the next show to bring into the theatre, for whilst the current show was filling the seats, we had no right or wish to terminate the run and nor had Laurier Lister. I began to think how I could have a production company of my own.

In June, I saw a one-act play at the Arts Theatre Club by Wolf Mankowitz, *The Bespoke Overcoat*, an adaptation into a Jewish milieu of Gogol's story. The two leading parts were brilliantly played by David Kossoff and Alfie Bass, both ex-Unity Theatre players. I was very impressed by the play and shortly afterwards met its author, who at that time ran the Wedgwood shop 'Gered' in Piccadilly Arcade and was best known for his column in the Evening Standard written under the name of Mr. Fat. We got on well and I encouraged Wolf to write another play to form a double bill with *The Bespoke Overcoat*. Meanwhile opportunities for production came up at the Embassy Theatre. This theatre, where I had worked before going to the Royal Court, was, at that time, together with the Q, near Kew Bridge, the main try-out theatre in London for new plays. In the winter of that year, Tony Hawtrey of the Embassy was not well and asked me if I would help by finding and setting up productions to play in the theatre for a few months. Thus it came about that Bob Mitchell (until recently Glasgow Unity Theatre's director) returned to the Embassy and directed there Noah Elstein's play, *Israel in the Kitchen*, with a cast including Meier Tzelniker, Eveline Garratt, Jack Stewart and Ida Schuster, all of whom had played in earlier Bob Mitchell productions. This was followed on 17th November by *Dance Dress*, a play about deprived young people by Michael Voysey, again directed by Bob Mitchell.

Then, at the beginning of the December I brought in Sandy Wilson's *The Boy Friend* from the Players Theatre, who had been trying without success to arrange a transfer to the West End. I thought the show was quite exceptional and, with Tony's bedridden agreement, arranged for it to play the Embassy for six weeks, one of the conditions being that if it then transferred to the West End, the management would pay the Embassy one per cent of the takings throughout the run of the play in the West End. It proved an enormous success at the Embassy and did indeed transfer to Wyndhams on 14th January 1954, where it ran for more than five years. It was subsequently produced on Broadway, made into a film by Ken Russell and revived many times. It was quite the best and most original small scale English musical in my lifetime, rivalled only by the Rocky Horror Show twenty years later. The first production was brilliantly directed by ex-Unity Theatre player, Vida Hope.

I received £30 for my part in all this, £5 per week for each week The Boyfriend played at the Embassy. This sharply increased my feeling that it was time I became a producer on my own account. The next show into the Embassy was Wolf's double-bill of *The Bespoke Overcoat*, this time directed by Bob Mitchell with the original cast, and his new one-act play *The Boychick*. After it had opened, Wolf and I decided to form a company to produce plays. The plan was that I would work at it full time and he would give me help with money-raising, advice and ideas, whilst continuing with his own work. This was the first fruit of the time to think and plan given to me by the success of *Airs on a Shoestring*.

One day soon after Christmas 1953, I was visiting the Embassy Theatre when the Box Office Manageress called out to me quite casually, 'Did you know your wife had died?' At first I thought she was talking about Eileen, the only wife I had and who had been alive half an hour before to my certain knowledge. Then she explained she was talking about my first wife, Clare, who had left me during the war and from whom I had been divorced since 1946. I was shocked. I had not seen Clare for some time but we were on friendly terms and still met from time to time. She was two years younger than I was, we had married when I was 21, we were both in the Young Communist League, both lived in the same street and both came from the same Jewish/East European background. We had that in common, otherwise I do not think we were particularly well matched, but she was my first love, and sexual passion made us blind to our differences. I was a totally dedicated Young Communist at the time, almost a fanatic, certainly a prig. My attitude to Clare was expressed in the the verse, 'I could not love thee half so much, loved I not honour (i.e. the Party) more.' I couldn't really blame her when, whilst I was in the Army editing a magazine for the smoke screen companies, I received a letter ('one of those' as Jimmy Porter was to call them some years later) saying that she had decided to live with someone else – in fact a man who was almost the exact opposite of me in every way. I was sad and sorry for myself but not broken hearted. We divided up our possessions, mostly records and books, quite amicably, and I spent the remainder of my leaves staying with my friend Ted Willis. There was a sequel to this incident shortly afterwards. One evening I was in the bar of Clement Freud's restaurant at the top of the Royal Court Theatre, the old rehearsal room where Shaw was said to have met Ellen Terry and now the Theatre Upstairs, when a man I did not know started apologising to me for Clare's death. It appeared that he was her last lover, that he had left her on the morning of Christmas Eve or Christmas Day and not come back until the following morning when he found she had gassed herself.

After *Airs on a Shoestring* had been running for a year, Laurier Lister decided that he could not afford to pay my salary. Under his contract he was responsible for paying all the salaries of the Royal Court staff. As Esdaile did not want to pay it either, I got the sack. Thus these two friends gave me a prod to get on with my own plans, for which I should have been more grateful than I was at the time.

Some time in 1953 I met Ronald Duncan. In the period immediately after the war he had had considerable success as a playwright. *This Way to the Tomb* ran for nearly a year at the Mercury Theatre and transferred to the West End. He wrote the English adaptation of Cocteau's *The Eagle has Two Heads* and the libretto for Benjamin Britten's opera *The Rape of Lucretia*. Now in his fortieth year, he had hit a bad patch.

No one was interested in producing his plays, but Ronnie was a man of many parts. He was the main inspiration behind the Devon Arts Festival, he was involved with the English Opera Group and regularly wrote a countryman's column, 'Jan's Journal', for the *Evening Standard* and occasional pieces for *Punch*. He ran a farm in Devon. He seemed to know everyone, from Ezra Pound to Gandhi. He brought me his play *Don Juan*, because he hoped it might be produced either at the Royal Court or the Embassy Theatre. Much to my surprise, since I had not been in sympathy with his earlier work, I rather liked the play, and although I was unable to help him get a production for it at the time, we became friends. Outwardly we had little in common. Politically I should say that Ronnie was a right wing anarchist. Class: English upper middle. Religion: High Church. However, we both considered the British theatre to be in a woeful state and, as we found out quite soon, we both wanted to do something about it. I went down to stay with Ronnie and in our many talks, walking along the sand, we came to the conclusion that what was needed was a non-commercial company dedicated to the production of the best contemporary plays both English and foreign. A company concerned with the truthful presentation of such plays, selecting them for their merit alone, not for their suitability for stars. We wanted their designs to serve the plays and not the plays to be backgrounds for the designs. In fact a Playwright's theatre, a theatre in which the play came first and everything else, director, designer and actors served the play. This went right against the current prevailing style of the West End, where Tennents, the most powerful producers of the day, dominated the scene and, under the direction of 'Binkie' Beaumont, produced plays which were vehicles for their stars in elaborate decor, often by Beaton or Messel.

Yes, we needed such a Company but where was the money to come from? Subsidy was in its infancy and although we might hope to get some support from the Arts Council, it would certainly be on a small scale. I was probably more aware of the difficulties than Ronnie, for I had had the experience of Glasgow Unity and the Embassy Theatre, both worthwhile theatrical enterprises which had failed through lack of money. Ronnie was optimistic. He had been involved in the successful launch of the English Opera Group. 'Get a bicycle,' he said, 'and someone will come and ride on it.' So this is what we did. And they did.

We decided to start by forming a non-profit distributing Company and drew up a short list of possible supporters. Most of them were friends of Ronnie: Lord Harewood, possibly his closest friend at that time, Edward Blacksell, Headmaster of a Devon school, (both of them were associated with Ronnie in the work of the Devon Festival), Greville

Poke, recently editor of *Everybody's Magazine* and a keen amateur actor, Viscount Duncannon, playwright and politician and Sir Reginald Kennedy Cox, Chairman of the Salisbury Repertory Theatre. Introduced by Ronnie, I went round to see each of these gentlemen, explained our project and each agreed to become a member of the first Council. With Ronnie's agreement, I also invited Alfred Esdaile, owner of the Royal Court Theatre, to join. This group, together with Ronnie and me, became the first Council of the English Stage Company, which was the name we quite soon took. We had at first wanted to call ourselves 'The English Stage Society' but the original and very distinguished 'Stage Society' objected and 'The English Stage Company' was chosen instead. We met at the offices of our solicitor, Isadore Caplan, who was also the solicitor for the English Opera Group. Leslie Periton was our accountant and also the accountant for the Opera Group, whose constitution was the first model for ours. Greville Poke agreed to be Honorary Secretary, and now we had to decide upon a Chairman. Lord Harewood was invited to take this on but refused. He later said that this was the best thing he ever did for the English Stage Company, for if he had accepted, Neville Blond, who became our first Chairman, would not have joined us. Before I tell of the strange chance which led to Neville joining us, I must say a further word about Lord Harewood. When Ronnie proposed that we invite him to join our venture, I thought that perhaps he would be worried about being associated with a Company in which I, an active member of the Communist Party, would be playing a leading part, and I said that he should be told about this problem and if the connection disturbed him, I would be willing to resign. Happily and characteristically, George Harewood was not at all worried, in fact according to Ronnie he said that if I was a Communist I could be counted upon to work hard for the common cause. I hope I did not disappoint him. For his part, George gave wonderful, wise and steady support to the E.S.C. during the many years in which he was associated with it, always a sane and liberal voice in the middle of the many storms that beset us.

Neville Blond, a semi-retired businessman – married to Elaine, a sister of Simon Marks, founder of Marks and Spencer – was a strange man to become the Chairman of a progressive, combative and committed theatre. His own taste in theatre was towards the West End. He was in no sense a radical. He was introduced to us by Edward Blacksell, the

Devonshire Headmaster, who had met him during the war in connection with Neville's work for the East Grinstead Hospital for wounded servicemen needing plastic surgery. Blacksell was a sergeant on duty at the hospital. Taken to lunch by Ronald Duncan, Neville agreed to become our Chairman, provided we would take a London Theatre. Agree to take a London Theatre! Not much persuasion was necessary. How to find the money? Neville said not to worry, he would find it alright.

Why did Neville agree to join us? The invitation came at exactly the right moment. For now after a busy life, he had some time on his hands. He was attracted by the prospect of being connected with a Company in which the Queen's cousin, Lord Harewood, was playing an active part and perhaps he sensed the Company was starting at the right time. And of course, its future artistic and social policy was then vague to all of us, only becoming clearer as the work progressed. At the time of Neville's appointment we all saw ourselves simply as an arts theatre in the business of presenting the best new plays we could find.

We needed an Artistic Director and a London theatre. Up until that time Ronnie and I had thought that we would try to raise sufficient money to present a season of plays from time to time in London and on tour, particularly serving festivals such as the Devon one. We had obtained the rights of a few plays with this in mind. Arthur Miller's *The Crucible* had been presented at the Bristol Old Vic, but no manager had been interested in taking up the rights to present it in London, and when I told Miller's agent that I wanted to do so, there was no problem. Brecht's *The Threepenny Opera* had been performed in Berlin in 1928 and had a very successful run in New York in 1954, but no one apparently had wanted to present it in England until I came along. The only difficulty here was that the rights were a little bit tangled and the royalties had to be paid into escrow until Brecht and someone in dispute with him had sorted their problems out. A few hundred pounds was all that had to be paid as an advance against royalties to secure the rights on these two important works. Ronald Duncan's *Don Juan* and its companion piece *The Death of Satan* were the only other plays for which we held the rights. For these last two plays Sir Reginald Kennedy Cox had agreed to put up £2000 provided we would use George Selway, a young actor from the Salisbury Rep whose work he admired, in the cast. We had so far raised no money for the other two plays which I had optioned.

Now, following Neville's appointment as Chairman, we started to discuss possible Artistic Directors. I remembered that a year or so before, George Devine had come to see me and Alfred Esdaile to discuss the possibility of taking a lease on the Royal Court Theatre for a new company which he and Tony Richardson were hoping to form with aims something like our own. This came to nothing, because the backer they had hoped for did not come through and the Royal Court found *Airs on a Shoestring*, which ran for a long time. Siobhan McKenna, the Irish actress, with whom I was friendly, had confirmed that George and I were thinking along the same lines. I put his name forward at one of our meetings and it was agreed that I should sound him out. None of us knew George Devine well and yet I can remember only one other name being suggested, E. Martin Browne, who had directed many of T.S. Eliot's plays and *This Way to the Tomb*. I think it must have been Ronnie Duncan who mentioned his name but without any great enthusiasm. I was not in favour of the idea and certainly no one fought for it. Looking back, it seems strange that no one had a convincing suggestion for this very important, all important role. But then, apart from Ronnie and to a very limited extent myself, no one on the Council had much experience of the London straight theatre. None of the directors who had worked with me at the Royal Court or the Embassy seemed right for the job. Without there being any other strong candidates in the offing, I went to see George Devine.

George was playing Tesman in a production of *Hedda Gabler* which had opened at the Lyric Theatre Hammersmith, but by the time I went to see him it had transferred to the Westminster Theatre. Peggy Ashcroft, who was to play a prominent part in the history of the English Stage Company, was playing Hedda, and Rachel Kempson, Michael Redgrave's wife and another long time future associate of the E.S.C., was playing Mrs. Elvsted. I met George in his dressing room between the matinée and evening performance. I told him about our Company and asked him if he would be interested in becoming our first Artistic Director. Since our plan was, at least in outline, so similar to the project he and Tony Richardson had tried and failed to realise, George had to be interested, though it came from such an unlikely source. I say 'unlikely' because George Devine's career had been at the centre of English theatrical life. Starting off as President of O.U.D.S., he had worked with all the great names: Laurence Olivier, Peggy Ashcroft, Michael Redgrave. Although there had always been an unconventional side to his character, he was basically an 'insider' whereas we of the E.S.C., even Ronnie, were theatrical 'outsiders'. George Devine belonged to the central magic circle, we did not. What a fortunate piece of luck for the theatre that some kind of intuition – it was certainly not a decision based on knowledge – made me propose this man, and the rest of the Council support the suggestion.

After a series of meetings, George Devine accepted our invitation on the understanding that Tony Richardson would be engaged as his associate. Probably none of us realised at the time what a vital decision had been made. We agreed with George Devine that no play should be produced that both he and the Artistic Committee appointed by the Council did not approve. This Artistic Committee in the early days consisted of George Harewood (Chairman), Ronald Duncan and myself plus George Devine and Tony Richardson, both ex officio without a vote. This Committee had the task of preparing for and setting up the first season.

Meanwhile, Alfred Esdaile had offered the Company a lease of the old Kingsway Theatre, bombed during the war, which he proposed to rehabilitate. We accepted and the first press conference announcing the new company and its plans was given amidst the rubble of the old theatre. Not long after, however, Alfred Esdaile changed his mind about the Kingsway and offered us instead a lease of the Royal Court Theatre. Everyone was very happy to accept and Neville Blond set about finding the money to finance it. More by luck than judgement, we had found both the right theatre and in Neville Blond a man who was able to perform the miracle of keeping the E.S.C. afloat. His energy, drive, generosity and connections, plus the good fortune of finding *Look Back in Anger* so early, kept the company solvent when it seemed impossible that it could survive. The idea for such a company had come at the right time and the unlikely combination of personalities gathered together under its banner established it against all the odds.

I cannot tell its story here, only my own part in it. When Ronnie and I walked along that Devon beach, and when George and Tony had discussed their plans for a Contemporary Playwrights Theatre, we could of course only discuss the writers who then were known. Important foreign writers we considered neglected in England, novelists who might be encouraged to write plays and any British writers we felt were being neglected. In the first group came Brecht, Beckett, Gorky, Strindberg, Lorca, Wedekind etc. We all had these names on our lists and initially these seemed likely to form the backbone of our programme. When it came to British writers things became more difficult. Ronnie was interested in Eliot, Whiting, Fry and Ustinov. George Devine, Tony and I were less than enthusiastic about these but did not have many alternatives to suggest. In the end our first programme was a compromise. We planned to open with *The Mulberry Bush*, a play by the novelist Angus Wilson, which had in fact been produced at the Bristol Old Vic. (This was probably George Devine's suggestion.) Then came Arthur Miller's *The Crucible*, also previously produced at Bristol, of which I owned the London rights. I passed these over to the E.S.C. Then Ronald Duncan's two plays, *Don Juan* and *The Death of Satan*, which George Devine persuaded him to cut down to make two halves of a single evening. After this, John Osborne's *Look Back in Anger*, which had come through the post in response to the Company's publicity. Lastly, a play commissioned from the novelist Nigel Dennis, based on his novel *Cards of Identity*, initiated by Tony Richardson. This season was followed by Brecht's *The Good Woman of Setzuan* and Wycherley's classic *The Country Wife*. A Company was assembled to perform these plays in repertory. This brings me to the second important point of policy, upon which we were all agreed at the outset. We all wanted to have a permanent company and perform plays in true repertory, more or less as the National Theatre and the Royal Shakespeare Company do now, though neither of these organisations have a long-term permanent company on the Continental model. It is strange looking back that no one, not even George, seems to have realised the implications of this policy for a company dedicated to new plays and working in a theatre with only 400 seats.

The acting company of the first group of five plays included Gwen Ffrangçon-Davies, Rosalie Crutchley, George Devine, Michael Gwynn, Kenneth Haigh, Rachel Kempson,Keith Michell, Mary Ure, Alan Bates, Robert Stephens and Joan Plowright. The Company was due to start operations in April 1956. During the previous year of preparation I was not employed by the Company but, like the other members of the Council, was giving my help on a voluntary part-time basis. A General Manager was employed, but I cannot remember where we found him.

He did not make an important contribution to the work of the Company, the administration of which was, in general, undertaken by George Devine. Neville put in some money himself, persuaded the more prosperous members of the Council to donate or lend money and the Arts Council to make its first small grant, £5000 I think it was.

Meanwhile, Wolf Mankowitz and I planned to produce a series of plays on a commercial basis, i.e. by raising capital from 'angels' for each play and presenting it on tour and/or in the West End or at some other suitable theatre.

Hy Kraft, whose play *Café Crown* Glasgow Unity had presented at the Embassy Theatre, helped me in all manner of ways to get started. He it was who first told me about *The World of Sholom Aleichem*, an entertainment based on Jewish stories, presented with great success in New York. Through his introduction to Arnold Perl, the deviser of the evening, I acquired the rights, and Wolf and I decided to present it at the Embassy Theatre. *The World of Sholom Aleichem* was a good choice for our first production. We were both Jews, although I have never been comfortable with that description. I am, like Isaac Deutcher, 'a non-Jewish Jew' and even more so than Deutcher, for he was brought up in a Jewish community, whilst I, although I had orthodox Jewish grandparents, had parents who were agnostics and did not keep up the Jewish customs and were not part of a Jewish community. I went to two schools, in the first of which there were two other Jewish children and in the second I was the only one. I do not speak Yiddish or Hebrew. I am an atheist. The only Jewish religious services I ever attended were in the Army where, in answer to the question of what was my religion, I put Jewish, since I did not want anyone to think I was denying it. Later I was rewarded, because I was detailed to attend the Jewish services, whilst non-Jews had to do P.T. So what am I? If I am asked that question in England I say 'A Russian Jew born in England'. If I'm asked it when I'm abroad I say (because I become much more English then), 'English of Russian Jewish parentage'. Because English is my only language, I suppose I must be more English than anything else, but I'm aware that I'm not a real Englishman despite my love of English literature. I have an equal love of the great Russian writers. Chekhov means as much to me as Shakespeare does. And I felt equally at home, but not more so, in *The*

World of Sholom Aleichem. The truth is I'm a rootless cosmopolitan and must make the best of it.

The capital for *The World of Sholom Aleichem* was £2,000, which we raised from about ten people including Hy Kraft, and a number of Hy Kraft's friends and contacts amongst the victims of the McCarthy era in the U.S.A., who were now refugees in London. Wolf and I knew the Jewish actors in London well and we gathered together a first rate cast led by Meier Tzelniker – who had been in the earlier Jewish plays presented by Glasgow Unity at the Embassy and Saville Theatre seasons – Alfie Bass and David Kossoff – who had played the two parts in Wolf's *The Bespoke Overcoat* – and, from the more conventional theatre – Miriam Karlin and Mark Dignam, who happened also to be a friend from the Communist Party. Sam Wanamaker agreed to direct and Bernard Sarron, another Unity Theatre graduate designed. Miriam Brickman, who was then my secretary, played an angel. She later became a famous casting director, first for the English Stage Company and then for films. She, too, had previously been associated both with Unity Theatre and the Embassy.

The play had an unfortunate first night. For one of its three parts, *Bunche Sweig*, a lot of the action was performed to music, which was played on tape. The tape broke and the action had to continue without its proper accompaniment. However, the production had good notices and good audiences, mostly from the Jewish public, probably because its title was off-putting for other people. It ran for twelve weeks at the Embassy but did not transfer and did not recoup all its capital.

Our second production was *Moby Dick* adapted by Orson Welles, who also directed it and played Captain Ahab and, not content with that, the Rev. Marples as well, a part he later played in John Huston's film. The cast was impressive: Patrick McGoohan played Starbuck, Gordon Jackson Ishmael, and other parts were played by Kenneth Williams and Wensley Pithey, whilst Joan Plowright made her first West End appearance as Pip, the negro cabin boy. Billy Chappell was responsible for movement and Hilton Edwards for lighting.

Orson had recently played Othello for Laurence Olivier's company at the St. James and, following this, had approached several West End managements with his proposal to produce *Moby Dick*. His script, originally titled *Moby Dick Rehearsed*, imagined a company at the end of the 19th century performing the last run through of a play based on *Moby Dick* before the dress rehearsal. Thus only a minimum of sets and props were needed, some of the actors wore costumes appropriate to their part in *Moby Dick*, others wore normal 19th-century dress. Pip, the negro cabin boy, did not need to black up. The set consisted of a few rostrums, flats and ropes hanging from the flies, such as might be found in any theatre before the sets for the play arrived, and with these scant resources Orson conjured up the great storms and mighty seas in which old Moby Dick and Ahab fought.

Orson had no luck with the West End managements, possibly because of the uncommercial nature of the play, perhaps because he only wanted to present it for a season of four weeks, or because his reputation frightened them. Whatever it was, one day Orson was in Wolf Manko- witz's office in Piccadilly Arcade lamenting his problems, when Wolf suggested that Orson should let us produce the play. Orson agreed. Where Wolf thought the money was going to come from I don't know, because a four week season with Orson was obviously not an economic proposition to put to our angels. However, Orson introduced us to two New York producers, Henry Margolis and Martin Gabel, who agreed to put up all the capital required in return for a share in any of the unlikely profits and an interest in the T.V. film that Orson proposed to make of the production. Luckily for us, Wolf and I were not invited to be involved in the film production.

Rehearsals went well, except for one detail. Orson himself never rehearsed with the other members of the cast, always using a stand-in for his part, which he learnt away from rehearsals. He only joined in rehearsing with the other actors in the last few days. This naturally caused everyone to be nervous, as did his reluctance to sign his contract in the early days of the project, so that it reached a point where the contract for the Duke of York's Theatre was ready to sign and we still had no contract with the writer, star and director. I remember a very emotional scene in Orson's hotel when I explained to him that I couldn't and wouldn't sign the theatre contract unless and until he signed his. He considered this to show a lack of confidence in him, which I suppose it did, but I couldn't risk the white whale Orson sinking our frail craft at that early stage in its career, and I stuck to my guns. Eventually, with a very bad grace, Orson signed, pretending not to have read the contract. I said this would not do and finally got him to read it and agree everything. I got to know Orson well at this time and even better later when I worked with him on a production of Ionesco's *Rhinoceros*. The fact is that on both occasions he worked within a very tight budget and brought the productions in without any extravagances, taking very little for himself. The main problem in working with him was that he was very secretive. He was usually working on several things at once and you always had the uneasy feeling that he might not be there when needed, since he would not reveal what his other commitments were. A lot of this elaborate secrecy appeared to have no practical purpose or benefit to anyone, including Orson, but was simply second nature to him. I think he also had a great reluctance to finish a project. He had to finish in the theatre where a first night forced rehearsals to come to an end. But he was always unready for the first night, usually making last minute changes on the night itself. When it came to making the T.V. film of *Moby Dick*, which was shot at the Hackney Empire, he never completed it, never shot his own part, so that Henry Margolis and Martin Gabel were never able to take delivery of the film that might have made their investment in the play pay off. As it was, they lost a little money, which I know that Henry felt was well spent. And *Moby Dick* without an Ahab lies rotting, who knows where?

I thought the production was quite stunning, but London was slow to respond and we only did good business for the last week. Strangely enough, Orson's name was not a draw with theatre audiences. Kenneth Tynan wrote, 'British audiences have been unemployed for too long. If they wish to exert themselves, to have their minds set whirling and their eyes dazzling at sheer theatrical virtuosity, Moby Dick is their opportunity. With it the theatre becomes once more a house of magic.' But even the last week was not sold out.

Our third production was also suggested by Wolf. It seemed like a brilliant idea, a Revue based on *Punch* and its writers. Malcolm Muggeridge, *Punch*'s editor, was enthusiastic. The owners of *Punch* agreed to co-operate and put up 40 per cent of the required capital. Vida Hope, another Unity Theatre personality agreed to direct (she had played the Fairy Wishfulfilment in Unity's most famous pantomime *Babes in the*

Wood and more recently had directed the enormously successful musical *The Boy Friend*). Ronnie Duncan was also engaged to help compile the material and through him Benjamin Britten was persuaded to compose one or two pieces for us. But alas, it turned out that the *Punch* writers on the whole could not write good revue material and the revue writers, like Geoffrey Parsons from Unity's pantomimes and revues, did not write the kind of material that went well with the *Punch* idea. The result, despite a goodish cast, was an undistinguished production, which ran a few weeks, came off and faded from memory. Our first real failure.

Our fourth production was the Brecht/Weill *Threepenny Opera*, which we had taken over from the English Stage Company. George Devine did not think that this work would fit in with the rest of his first programme, so the rights were taken back by my company and we agreed to give the English Stage Company a small percentage when we produced it. We spent a long time setting this up. First we had to raise more money than for our other productions and we could not get this from our regular angels, so we needed a partner. We approached Tom Arnold, who at that time (1955) was one of London's leading impresarios, mainly in the field of musicals, pantomimes and circuses. He had originally been an accountant and that was the impression he still made on us. A complete contrast to Jack Hylton, and I cannot now remember why we did not go to Jack with our project. Anyway, after considering the matter carefully, Tom told us that he had decided against coming in with us on it. But as Wolf and I were leaving his office, to our surprise and delight, Helen, Tom's wife, said she would be happy to be our partner in presenting *The Threepenny Opera*. So, much against Tom's wishes, this charming, intelligent and energetic woman became our partner in a company we called 'Peachum Productions Ltd', through which we produced *The Threepenny Opera*. Helen herself had had a successful career on the musical stage before marrying Tom and later, after Tom died, took over his theatre business and ran it very successfully before passing it over to their son Tom, the Tory M.P. Having found a financial partner, we were able to go ahead and prepare for the production. Our rights were to present the Marc Blitzstein version, which had recently been running very successfully in New York, where Lotte Lenya played Jenny. We did not know then that Brecht was not too happy about this version. Sam

Wanamaker was invited to direct and he and I went over to Berlin to discuss the production with Brecht. Sam could only stay a short while but in that time we agreed to put back into the script certain scenes and bits of dialogue that Blitzstein had cut. It was also agreed that Caspar Neher, who had designed the original production, would design it for us, though quite differently from before. Brecht proved himself to be anything but dogmatic, recognising that different times and different places required new approaches. His theories about theatre have suggested to many a certain humourlessness and rigidity. But we found that Brecht was the least dogmatic of men and he encouraged Sam and me to find the best way to produce *The Threepenny Opera* in London in 1956. That was his sole concern.

When Sam left for England, I stayed on for a few days in West Berlin with my assistant, Renée Goddard, and together we went each day over to the Berliner Ensemble to discuss further outstanding matters. When necessary, Renée translated, but, as Brecht and most of his close colleagues spoke English, having been refugees in America during the Nazi period, this was not often necessary. And so, on my last day it was arranged that Renée would stay in West Berlin and I would go over to East Berlin on my own. There was no problem at that time about going from West Berlin to East Berlin, no Checkpoint Charlie to go through. The Berlin Wall had not yet been built. It was only one stop on the S. Bahn. I spent the day in discussions at the Ensemble and in the late afternoon set off for West Berlin. We were to fly home later that night. I saw the train coming in the right direction and boarded it as usual. Alas, when it reached my station, the next on the line, it didn't stop. I wasn't worried. I thought, when it stops I'll go back over to the other platform and take the next train back. However, it went on and on, passing station after station without stopping. At last it stopped. I got out intending to cross over and take the next train back. I had just time to notice that no one else was getting out at that station, when I was arrested by some East German soldiers. I tried to explain what had happened but as I spoke no German and none of the soldiers spoke English, we made no progress. I was made to wait on the platform until some Russian soldiers arrived and I was passed over to them. They didn't speak English either. Eventually I was told by signs to get in the back of an army truck and, surrounded by a group of young Russian soldiers, off we went, destination unknown. Siberia? I realised that my train had gone right through West Berlin and out the other side and that the first stop was in East Germany proper, probably not a zone open to foreigners. After a while I was handed over to a Russian officer who indicated that I should get into his car. We two then set off. Night was falling and we were driving through the country when the car had a puncture. I helped the officer/driver change the wheel and we continued, arriving at length back in a city which I took to be Berlin and at a building which I learned later was the Russian Commandantura. I was now not worried that I would land up in Siberia but about what Renée would do when I did not turn up in time for the plane back to London. I need not have worried. When I did not turn up she said she realised what had happened and knew that either I'd be back the next day or, in the unlikely event of the Russians wanting to make something of it and holding me, there was nothing she could do about it. I didn't altogether agree with this analysis because I thought that if I had not got back the next morning at the latest she should have called the Berliner Ensemble for help. Anyway, it wasn't necessary. By the time I got to the Russian Commandantura it was late at night. Eventually, someone who could speak English was got out of bed. He asked me a number of questions as to why I got out at the platform where I was arrested. I told him my story and suggested he rang Brecht's associate, Elizabeth Hauptmann, for corroboration. He apparently did this but Elizabeth, being woken up in the middle of the night, did not clear things up. The result was that I had to sleep there and next morning, after a foul breakfast, someone came and asked me all the same questions and then, having signed a form to say that I had no complaints, I was taken by car to the nearest S. Bahn and so back to West Berlin and thence back to London. Apparently when the people at the Berlin Ensemble heard the story they all thought it very funny. I did too, but only after I was safely back home.

The Threepenny Opera opened at the Theatre Royal Brighton at the beginning of 1956, the year of Suez, the Hungarian Uprising and the birth of our second son, Peter, and after a week with a typically hostile Brighton audience, came into the Royal Court Theatre, which we had leased from the English Stage Company for a six week run from the 9th February. Bernard Levin wrote that after it, the British theatre would never be the same. Brecht gave us one piece of very good advice which unfortunately we were unable to take. He said that in every theatre production there should be one sensational element. It might be in the casting of a character or the staging of a particular scene. Our production of *The Threepenny Opera* I think was good but it did not have this one sensational element which might have made it the talk of the town. The result was that, although it ran for just under six months, first at the Royal Court, then at the Aldwych and finally at the Comedy, it was not a financial success and only recouped two thirds of its capital. However, there is no doubt that *The Threepenny Opera*, together with the production at the Arts Theatre of *Waiting for Godot* in the previous August, more truly heralded the new dawn in the British theatre than *The Mulberry Bush*, the English Stage Company's lack-lustre first production which followed *The Threepenny Opera* into the Royal Court.

Strangely enough, I might have had the honour of producing *Waiting for Godot* as well as *The Threepenny Opera.* Donald Albery had the rights of *Godot* and asked me if I would be interested to produce it. I did not really understand it but thought that with wonderful casting it might work. I offered it to Wilfrid Lawson, who thought it was an elaborate joke. Donald Albery approached other distinguished actors, who all turned it down, until Peter Hall directed it at the Arts with a good, but certainly not a 'sensational' cast. I have to confess that when I saw it on the first night I was bored out of my mind. I did not see a production that I really enjoyed until Nicol Williamson played it in Anthony Page's production at the Court in 1964. Perhaps in 1955 my own political and social outlook would not have permitted me to enjoy any production of that play. By 1964 I had become less narrow-minded and could app-reciate both Beckett and Brecht.

The Threepenny Opera not only prepared the way for the new drama that was to appear on the stage of the Royal Court, it also prepared the stage itself, introducing the forestage that has been a feature of the Court ever since. The cast included some ex-Unity players as usual. Mack the Knife was played by Bill Owen, Warren Mitchell played Crookfinger Jake, and George Tovey Bob the Slasher. Renée Goddard was Coaxer. Two actors from Theatre Workshop joined the cast: Ewan MacColl was the street singer (in the early days of Theatre Workshop he was their principal playwright and later became a famous folk singer) and George A. Cooper was Tiger Brown. Georgia Brown made her first appearance on stage as Lucy, and the French singer Maria Remusat played Jenny very brilliantly. At the end of the run of *The Threepenny Opera*, Wolf and I had staged four productions, three of them could fairly be called 'succés d'estime' and one was a flop. Our backers had lost money, and most of them decided that they had lost enough. The English Stage Company reckoned that they needed a General Manager more in sympathy with their aims than the one they had, and asked me if I'd go and work there. I was pleased to accept and so, taking Miriam Brickman with me as my secretary, I moved back to the Royal Court. So ended the first phase of my career as an independent commercial producer.

Sometime during 1954, Gerry Raffles and Joan Littlewood of Theatre Workshop, with whom I had become friendly when they had presented MacColl's *Uranium 235* at the Embassy Theatre, told me that they had obtained the rights to produce Brecht's great play *Mother Courage*. I suggested to Ronald Duncan that Wolf and I should present *Mother Courage* and Shakespeare's *Richard II* with the Theatre Workshop Company at the 1955 Devon Festival. He agreed and Joan and Gerry were delighted.

Shortly after I returned from my visit to Brecht in Berlin, Joan and Gerry came to see me and told me that the rights for *Mother Courage* had fallen through because they had only been granted them by the translator and not by Brecht. They asked me if there was anything I could do to help them get Brecht's permission and I agreed to go back to Berlin to see what I could do. Their intention was that Joan Littlewood should play the part of Mother Courage as well as directing the play and, whilst in general I don't think it is a good idea for the same person to direct and play a leading part, in this particular case I thought Joan might make a wonderful Mother Courage, and she obviously had to direct. So I went to Berlin, saw Brecht and persuaded him, on the basis of Theatre Workshop's record and my description of Joan, to let them go ahead. Not only that, he offered to send one of his young assistants, Karl Weber, to help them and also said they could use any music or designs from his own production that could be of use to them, knowing how tight their budget would be for such a production. I returned with this good news and Joan and Gerry took Eileen and me out for a special meal to celebrate.

Sometime later they went into rehearsal. Karl Weber arrived and I introduced him. Everything seemed to be going well. Then Karl rang me in a great state and told me that he had been forbidden to attend rehearsals. Then we heard (we were not told by Joan or Gerry) that Joan had retired from the part of Mother Courage and an unknown actress had been put in to replace her. We were given no satisfactory explanation. Karl and I reported the position to Brecht, who was then in Paris with the Berlin Ensemble preparing for the International Festival there. Brecht was furious. He wrote insisting that Joan went back into the part or the production be cancelled. Joan went back into the part but it was too late. *Mother Courage* opened at the Devon Festival in July 1955. It was a disaster. Ken Tynan in his review wrote: 'Joan Littlewood plays it in a lifeless mumble, looking over-parted and under-rehearsed . . .The result is a production in which discourtesy to a masterpiece borders on insult.' I felt very guilty for having given Brecht what had turned out to be such bad advice. I loved the play and thought Joan would rise to the occasion. Perhaps I underestimated its difficulties. Perhaps her temperament did not suit her for Brecht's plays. Certainly, after that she never directed one. Perhaps the greatest artists when they fail, fail most disastrously. There is a feeling of improvisation in Joan's best productions, there is nothing of the kind in Brecht. It was a long time before any English director really mastered the Brecht style, indeed I can say that I did not see a truly great English production of Brecht until I saw Deborah Warner's production of *The Good Person of Setzuan* with Fiona Shaw at the National Theatre in 1989. 'Nevertheless,' wrote Harold Hobson, 'even in the lamentable proceedings of that only half rehearsed first night it was evident that *Mother Courage* was a work of quality', and in his preface to his book *Theatre in Britain: a Personal View* he writes, 'the theatrical revolution usually associated with the name of the Royal Court Theatre, but which really began in the Queens Hall, Barnstaple, Devon with the first British professional production of a play by Brecht.' In other words Joan's production at the Devon Festival of *Mother Courage*. So whether we accept the view that the revolution started with *The Threepenny Opera* or *Look Back in Anger*, or Hobson's more eccentric view that it started with Joan's production of *Mother Courage*, I can claim to have had an equal hand in it. Hobson cites four plays, *Mother Courage*, *Waiting for Godot*, *Look Back in Anger* and Harold Pinter's *The Birthday Party* as being 'the watershed of modern British drama. From them all great rivers flowed.' Surely *The Threepenny Opera* was part of that.

To return to the early days of the English Stage Company. During the preparations for its first season and during most of that season itself, I was involved only in a voluntary unpaid capacity, as a member of the Council and its two sub-committees, the Management Committee, which met very frequently under the Chairmanship of Neville to watch over the business affairs of the Company, and the Artistic Committee, which approved the programme of plays and discussed the artistic policy matters that concerned the Company. During those early days harmony reigned. We all approved of the first programme though, in fact, George Devine and Tony Richardson did not like Duncan's plays and only included them because they felt they had to, that it was a debt that had to be paid in recognition of the part Ronnie had played in setting the Company up. George should probably not have agreed to direct the double-bill himself, feeling as he did about the plays, but he did it as a misguided gesture of goodwill. When the plays failed, Ronnie realised that George had not had his heart in the project and unfairly blamed him for the failure.

From that time onwards there was a deep division within the Artistic Committee between Ronnie on the one hand and the rest of us on the other. This division became wider when the success of *Look Back in Anger*, which was a choice enthusiastically supported by all of us, led to the Company finding and producing the work of a number of new writers with whose work Duncan was not in sympathy. Duncan was also out of sympathy with the theatre's enthusiasm for Brecht, although he had been a great admirer of *The Threepenny Opera*. He later wrote: 'I felt like a python who had given birth to a mongoose. But stayed on, hoping in vain to influence rather than withdraw. It was a mistake. When you realise a bus is going the wrong way, you save time if you get off immediately.' In fact Ronnie took more than ten years to get off that bus and it was not until shortly after the death of George Devine in 1966 that he resigned. In the meantime he constantly and savagely attacked Devine and his artistic policy. It was a bitter experience for Ronnie to have done so much to build the company and then find no welcome there for his own works. I should probably have felt the same had the Company chosen Martin Browne for its first Artistic Director instead of George Devine. I did not have a particularly close relationship with George, though we worked together over a number of years in a friendly and co-

operative way. I always felt that he was a bit of a snob and that in his
eyes I was a second class citizen. I think that he may have had this effect
on a number of people working at the Court. His close relationship with
and admiration for Tony Richardson excluded most of the other people
working there from feeling that they were welcome as colleagues in
decision making. On my side, I think I undervalued George when he
was alive, just as I believe he came to be overvalued after his death. He
was not a brilliant stage director, but he was a fine artistic director of the
Court because, unlike most theatre directors he got as much pleasure
from the success of the younger colleagues he helped to promote, as
from his own successes.

George was 45 years old when the first season opened in 1956, but
his hair was already white. He was a handsome man and the very image
of a father figure for the young writers, directors and actors who came to
the theatre. George was also a splendid actor and I still remember with
pleasure many of the performances he gave for the English Stage Company over the years, particularly Father Golden Orfe in *Cards of Identity* –
'I stink therefore I am' – Mr Shu Fu in *The Good Woman of Setzuan*, The
Old Man in *The Chairs*, Baron Von Epp in *A Patriot for Me* and, above all,
as Dorn in *The Seagull*, a part which seemed to be an extension of his life
at the Royal Court. George was, however, a complicated man and I do
not think I really understood him. Apparently in his younger days, he
had been a fat, jolly man. At the Court he was not fat and certainly not
jolly. He was splitting up with his wife, Sophie Harris and was about to
live with Jocelyn Herbert, who was to become the most brilliant and
influential of the Court designers. Sophie Harris was one of the Motley
sisters design partnership so she also worked at the theatre, since the
firm of Motley had designed the permanent surround in which the first
season of plays was presented. Sophie, whom I did not know well,
seemed to me the saddest woman I had ever seen, the image of all the
women who have been wronged by men throughout the ages.

George had a lot to put up with. He was treated by Neville Blond as if
he was a foreman in one of Neville's factories or an N.C.O. in one of his
charities. Neville shouted at George in front of other people, rudely cut
him short when he was delivering a public speech and in all sorts of
ways failed to treat George with the respect he deserved. For the good of
the English Stage Company and because he realised that Neville with

all his faults was necessary to it, George valiantly put up with this treatment. For that alone he deserves our gratitude. I could not have borne it.

What a strange pair they were, Neville so insensitive and basically unsympathetic to the work we were doing, yet totally loyal to the Royal Court and on the side of its artists when they were under attack. George, devoted to serving the interests of the playwright, yet capable of cutting out one of the principal characters in *The Crucible* without consulting the author or indeed informing him, and having to be threatened by the author's agent that the play would not be allowed to go on, before reluctantly putting the cuts back. Although the suggestion may have come from his co-director, Tony, George must have agreed and gone along both with the cutting and the failure to discuss it with the author.

Look Back in Anger came in through the post in response to an advertisement for new plays issued by the Court. Of the 675 plays so received, this was the only one accepted. I think it was first read by Tony Richardson and then by George and then submitted to the Artistic Committee, all the members of which responded with the same enthusiasm. I remember George and Tony reporting on their first visit to John on the house boat on the Thames in which he was then living. The play had been submitted to many theatrical agents and theatres and been turned down by all. The first night audience was completely divided by the play, some sitting in stony silence whilst others laughed and clapped with happiness and relief hearing at last their own voices, hopes and fears expressed so eloquently upon the stage. The critics were also divided, but not as generally hostile as the myth has it. However, it only became a real success some time later after an excerpt had been seen on television. Before the season started, Tony and I had sat one day in a nearby café and written down how we thought the various plays would do. We both thought that *The Crucible* would be the biggest success of the first season and that Look Back would be lucky to cover itself. The last play of the first group, *Cards of Identity* by Nigel Dennis, a brilliantly funny Jonsonian comedy, did not do particularly good business despite excellent performances, including one from the author of *Look Back*, who had joined the Company. It is surprising that it has never been revived. It should be.

This, then, was the first group of plays all performed with the same company of actors and in the permanent surround designed by Motley. They were produced in repertory usually two plays a week: one play being performed from Monday to Wednesday and another from Thursday to Saturday. They played until 31st October when Brecht's *Good Woman of Setzuan* was brought in for a straight run of six weeks. Many members of the first 'permanent' company stayed on for this, but the leading part was taken by Peggy Ashcroft, the first of the great stars to appear with the English Stage Company. I had originally spoken to Brecht about the possibility of doing this play in London, and George Devine, quite separately, had also spoken of it when he had visited the Ensemble for the first time towards the end of 1955, during a tour of his production of *King Lear* with John Gielgud. I dealt with the contractual side for the E.S.C. when I returned there as General Manager in the autumn of 1956. George Devine directed *The Good Woman of Setzuan*, as it was then called, but despite splendid designs by Theo Otto, an old Brechtian designer from Zurich, and a good cast it was not a success. Peggy Ashcroft was not really right for the part of Shen Te or the hard hearted Cousin. The translation by Eric Bentley, the only one available then, was without much theatrical life, the direction rather unsure of the new ground it was treading. The best performance was by George, who seemed to be able to do himself what he could not inspire the other actors to do.

We followed Brecht with our first classical revival, William Wycherley's bawdy comedy, *The Country Wife*, in which Joan Plowright, who had been making a reputation for herself as a fine actress in our other plays, was given her first leading part, and Laurence Harvey was brought in to play opposite her. George Devine directed and also played Pinchwife and this was by far his best production of the season. It was an immediate success and afterwards became our first West End transfer when I was able to work out a deal with Jack Hylton, whereby he presented the English Stage Company at the Adelphi Theatre, taking the risk of the costs of the transfer, and sharing the profits. It had played to over 90 per cent capacity at the Court.

Earlier my Company with Wolf acquired the rights of Carson McCuller's play *The Member of the Wedding*. The flow of new English plays had not yet begun and my colleagues at the Court suggested that it should be produced there to begin with. If successful, both companies would transfer it together. Tony Richardson agreed to direct. It was through this play that I first met the black American jazz singer, Bertice Reading, and we remained close friends until she died tragically young in 1991. Bertice came to England with *The Jazz Train* and it was Tony's idea to audition her for Ethel Water's part of the Housekeeper. She was a small roly poly barrel of dynamite – a wonderful actress who made her mark in several stage productions – she should have been used more on the legit stage. She was the success of the production. Geraldine McEwan played Frankie, the young girl. She had problems with the part and was not helped by her coach, Iris Warren, from whose destructive, if well meant advice I tried my best to protect her. I thought the play was well worth doing but it was not a success. It followed *The Country Wife* into the Court and played its run of 37 performances at an average capacity of 41 per cent and then was replaced on 11th March by a revival of *Look Back in Anger* with Richard Pasco now playing Jimmy Porter. This production ran until 3rd April, thus completing our first year of operation. Since I was the General Manager and on the Management Committee, I was particularly relieved that, in spite of all our ups and downs, we had almost broken even that first year. We had received £7,000 in grants and guarantees from the Arts Council, £8,505 as profit from transfers and had taken £56,680 at the box office, making a total income of £74,185. Against that, production costs for our eight productions had totalled £10,587 and our running costs had come to £65,160, a total expenditure of £75,747. Our first year had ended with a deficit of just £1,562. Not bad for a start? Not bad? A miracle.

Before the end of our first season we were in the midst of negotiations with New York producers in connection with the New York presentation of our two successes, *Look Back in Anger* and *The Country Wife*. Both David Merrick and Roger Stevens, then probably the two most active Broadway producers, were interested in *Look Back*, but eventually we made a deal with David Merrick, who agreed to take over the entire London cast and production. David was a difficult man, tough and mean, who enjoyed his reputation as a hard unscrupulous bastard and in many ways played up to it. However, he was an excellent promoter, the best fighter for a play I have come across and, providing one stood up to him, as Tony Richardson always did, the worst results of his rather penny-pinching nature were avoided. I negotiated the deal with David Merrick and enjoyed the challenge. It was the first of many. Roger Stevens was not really the man for a play like *Look Back in Anger*. Later the head of the Kennedy Center in Washington, he was a respected financier and establishment figure. He produced *The Country Wife* in a production which George Devine directed, without the original London cast.

Writing about deals reminds me that it must have been about this time that John Osborne asked me one day if I could recommend a solicitor to him. He wanted to get a divorce from his first wife in order to marry Mary Ure, who was playing Alison in his play. I suggested Oscar Beuselinck, who had been my solicitor since my days at the Embassy, when he worked from Jack Hylton 's offices. I thought Oscar's rather unusual personality would appeal to John and I was right. Oscar was, or seemed to be, obsessed by sex, which he expressed in an extrovert way, rather unusual, I thought, for a solicitor. If he had an appointment with you, on arrival at your office, always late, he would call out, by way of greeting, 'How many times have you had it off today?' Without waiting for an answer, he would then inform the secretaries in the outer office of his own real or imaginary sexual exploits. He was a modern version of Frank Harris but instead of writing a book about his life and loves, he gave you a running commentary as he went along. I was right in thinking that John would enjoy this eccentric but brilliant solicitor and, in fact, some of his characteristics made their way into the character of Bill Maitland, the solicitor in *Inadmissible Evidence*.

It was during this period that I got to know some of my colleagues at the English Stage Company properly. On many evenings I would sit in Joan Plowright's dressing room at the Adelphi and try to convince her that she would be wonderful — which indeed she was — as the Old Woman of 94 in Ionesco's *The Chairs*. This was her next part, and she was very apprehensive about it. I admired Kenneth Haigh enormously as Jimmy Porter. I still think his was the best performance I have seen in this part. I used to meet him quite often in the Bistro just behind the Royal Court. It was run by an eccentric woman, Elizabeth Furze, who only served you if she liked you. Milton Shulman was in there night after night, as were a number of Sloanes. It was not a place to go if you wanted to be left to yourself. Several Royal Court people used to go there but gradually stopped going. Elizabeth was surprised when I introduced Eileen to her as my wife, because it wasn't my habit to order Eileen's meal for her without asking what she wanted to eat. Apparently most husbands did this.

It was at this time that Tony Richardson and I began a working relationship and friendship which lasted for about ten years and covered, I think, one of the most fruitful periods of both our working lives. I wasn't around very much when he directed *Look Back in Anger* or *Cards of Identity* but from *Member of the Wedding* we worked together on many plays mostly, but not always, for the English Stage Company, and later on a number of films. I had not been impressed when I first met him briefly in Esdaile's office when he came there with George Devine to enquire about the possibility of leasing the Court. On a first meeting his strange voice and very tall thin appearance made the biggest impact. It was only later that I appreciated his immense drive and energy, his sharp intelligence and sense of humour and his ability to bring enthusiasm and leadership to any project that caught his imagination. I do not think he was ever a great director, in the sense of having a total artistic vision which he was able to achieve. I think he was, however, a wonderful impresario, a great caster of actors and a good practical director, and that is saying a lot. He loved work and made working with him fun. Unfortunately, he was a manipulator of his friends and colleagues and, although a very generous man, wanted to own the souls of those who benefited by his generosity. Unlike Mephistopheles in his dealing with Faust, Tony's deals were not usually spelt out. When I first knew him, Tony always kept his friends apart. Later when his confidence grew, he no longer found this to be necessary. Gradually, many of the people who had worked with him most closely ceased to want to work with him, could not feel that confidence in him which is necessary to a working relationship. They left him feeling that he had been treated badly by those to whom he had given a lot. He never seemed to realise why his friends could not trust his friendship. A vivid picture of the impact he made on his colleagues is given in Osborne's play *A Hotel in Amsterdam*. Of course, like all works of art, this play is not a simple picture, but a montage made up from many memories of incidents and people, some real, some invented, all linked together by the playwright's imagination.

It shows the enormous part Tony Richardson played in the life of his friends and closest colleagues. Whilst I was writing this book, news came through from Los Angeles of the tragic early death of Tony from Aids. He had always felt happier living away from England, in France and particularly in America. I think he always wished he'd been born American but in fact he was inescapably English. We had not seen each other for nearly twenty years, but I shall never forget him or the fun and inspiration it was to work with him in those ten years, from the time the English Stage Company was formed in 1955. I can hear his braying laugh now neighing out over the set and then his strange voice calling 'Action.'

We were now actively preparing for our next season and our preparations began with the first real split on the Artistic Committee. Laurence Olivier had been to see *Look Back in Anger* and, so it is said, had not been very impressed. Then he went again with Arthur Miller and was bowled over by the play and John's talent. He told George that if ever there should be a part for him in a play by John he'd be keenly interested. Osborne at this time had already started work on what was to become *The Entertainer* and George, with John's agreement, showed the first act to Larry. Who flipped. Said he'd do the play, and George announced it to us as a triumph, as indeed it was. But Ronnie and I had started the English Stage Company determined that it should not be a theatre for stars: not that it should exclude stars, but certainly not be a theatre that would agree to do a play before it was finished, because a star wanted to play the leading part. And when the play was finished, neither Ronnie nor I liked it very much, both of us thinking it much inferior to *Look Back in Anger*. I think disappointment with the play, plus thinking that George, by giving it to Larry, had by-passed the Artistic Committee, made us make what I am now quite sure was a foolish mistake. Even if it was not such a good play as *Look Back*, was it not a play which we should have been excited to receive from a new author? Why should we have to think each author's play must be 'better' than his last one for it to be worth doing? I still think the play has many weaknesses, particularly in the last act, but it has many virtues apart from containing a wonderful leading part, and we were absolutely wrong to oppose it. But it was a kind of honourable puritanical opposition, which was probably not a bad thing – a mistake in the right direction. Fortunately, we were overruled by the Chairman, advised by George Harewood, George Devine and Tony.

After that experience, George insisted that the Artistic Committee should only be advisory. Ronnie and I were not pleased at this but, again, I am sure George was right and the Council right to support him. So *The Entertainer* was scheduled to open on 10th April 1957, but before that on April 3rd we brought in for one week Samuel Beckett's play *Fin de Partie* together with his short mime play *Acte Sans Paroles*. *Fin de Partie* was the French title of the play later known as *Endgame*. It was given in French, directed by Beckett's friend Roger Blin, and I believe the production was available for the Court because it had had some problem in finding a theatre in Paris. This was Sam Beckett's first visit to the Royal Court. From then on, most of his plays were premiered there and George Devine and Jocelyn became two of his closest friends and colleagues. *Fin de Partie*, like most of Beckett's plays after *Waiting for Godot*, was not a success with the public or critics when it was first presented. This one, which has two of its characters living in dustbins, caused an uproar. The 'dustbin' drama had arrived to join the 'kitchen sink' as part of the Court's myth. Sam Beckett was not, I think, a Court writer in the sense that that expression is generally used, probably because he was already established as an important playwright before he came to us and also because he was older than most of the Court writers and inspired a certain awe. When you were with him he immediately put you at your ease, he had great charm. But he was a severe man and people walked about the Court on tiptoe when he was around.

Tony Richardson directed *The Entertainer*, which played to capacity. Some of Olivier's friends were astonished to find him playing an unsuccessful, immoral, broken down music-hall comedian in a theatre associated in their minds with kitchen sinks and dustbins. They were not too happy about it, but he was as happy as Larry. The play transferred to the Palace Theatre after its run at the Court; later it went on tour and to New York for a season and, like *Look Back in Anger*, was made into a film by Woodfall, the Company that Tony and John Osborne formed with Harry Salzman. During the negotiations which were necessary to arrange for the West End and Broadway runs, I got to know another important figure in the theatre of that time. Cecil Tennant was Managing Director of M.C.A., then the leading Theatrical Agency and also Managing

Director of L.O.P. Ltd, Olivier's Company, who were partners in the venture with the English Stage Company. Cecil, who became one of my best friends in the theatre, gave the Court and Woodfall and my other theatre activities great help and support over the next years. He was an enormously tall, friendly, very English type of man, married to Irina Baronova, the Russian ballet dancer. Cecil was another of those friends I met in the theatre who had nothing whatever in common with me as far as background and social views were concerned, but with whom I nevertheless established a close relationship based on common sympathies and interests which overcame the social and political barriers.

We (The English Stage Company) arranged to present *The Chairs* by Eugene Ionesco (a Rumanian who wrote in French and lived in Paris) and *The Apollo de Bellac* by Jean Giraudoux, which Ronald Duncan translated for us. Donald Watson translated *The Chairs*, which gave me the opportunity for the first time to meet Margaret 'Peggy' Ramsay, who became by far and away the most important playwrights' agent, and a good friend of mine. Before that, if an author arrived at the Court without an agent, we would usually suggest he considered going to Margery Vosper, whom we knew because she was Ronald Duncan's agent. After we met Peggy, we usually suggested authors try her and many of them did, some successfully, others not. Peggy on her side introduced us to a number of playwrights over the next years. In 1957, however, we were still for the most part relying on established writers.

Following the French double bill, we scheduled *The Making of Moo*, a new play by Nigel Dennis, which Ken Tynan called 'a milestone in history: the first outright attack on religion ever to be presented on the English stage.' I loved it. Not a perfect play by any means, it gave just the sort of offence that is a sign of health. The cast, directed by Tony Richardson, was led by George Devine and Joan Plowright, also included John Osborne and John Wood. It was followed by *Purgatory* by Yeats and *How Can We Save Father*, two plays that we had produced initially to present at the Taw and Torridge Festival. After that, another revival of *Look Back* before it was taken by my company to the Moscow Youth Festival for a short season at the Moscow Arts Theatre. It received a very appreciative reception there from an audience who mostly spoke English and it had a good press which came out some time later. I think all of us, except John, who made far too much of petty difficulties like the lack of plugs in the basins, were impressed by the atmosphere of enthusiasm we met with. I remember our set was built in a day in the theatre's workshop and put up in an hour by the very efficient staff. When we arrived we were given rather inconvenient accommodation in a youth hostel but after some days I got us transferred to an hotel in Central Moscow. John, not enjoying his visit, went home earlier than the rest of us. Lindsay Anderson caused one of our young girl interpreters to cry because he praised the old wooden buildings he saw and did not like some of the modern ones. On his return to England, Tony Richardson phoned Eileen and said she must never, ever let him forget how wonderful the whole experience had been.

This was 1957, not long after the 20th Congress of the C.P.S.U. where Khrushchev made his famous speech denouncing Stalin. I had by this time left the Party, for I felt I had either to spend more time in it fighting for an understanding of what the Stalin revelations really meant for us, or else leave it. My work in the theatre left me little time for Party work. I was not disillusioned, I still supported the same social ideals that had made me join the Young Communist League in the first place, but I realised that Khrushchev's explanation of the 'the Cult of the Individual' was superficial and that some fundamental thinking had to be done to explain in terms of the social and economic conditions of the Soviet Union what had gone wrong, and I felt there was a reluctance to do this. So I quietly left. But I had many emotional meetings and discussions in Moscow with Russian comrades who had lived through the Stalin years. With them I mourned the death of so many honest Communists who had died falsely convicted of being criminals and traitors by their own comrades. No death, I thought, and think, could have been so bitter.

Directed by Tony Richardson, The Chairs was Jocelyn Herbert's first opportunity to design for a Royal Court production. From then on, she was the designer that our directors most wished to work with. I went into the circle one night whilst the dress rehearsal was in progress. There was a most wonderful atmosphere of silence and tension as the Old Man (George) and the Old Woman (Joan) waited for their unseen guests to arrive and placed the chairs out for them. Finally the Orator came, who was to deliver the Old Man's message – the wisdom of his life's long experience – to the packed room of chairs and unseen guests. The Orator opened his mouth and alas was dumb. I turned to Jocelyn and remember saying, 'This is the real thing,' and she agreed.

After another revival of *Look Back*, we presented *Nekrassov* by Jean Paul Sartre. Wolf and I had acquired the rights of this play, which was translated by Sylvia and George Leeson, and had previously been produced succesfully at London's Unity Theatre. Now I was working at the Court full time and George wanted to direct the play, we made the same arrangements as for *Member of the Wedding*. The English Stage Company agreed to present the play initially at the Edinburgh Festival in the autumn of 1957. I introduced George to several actors I had known in the past: Harry H. Corbett, who had been one of the leading actors at Theatre Workshop, Roddy McMillan, who had been one of the leading actors in Glasgow Unity and Martin Miller, who had played in several of our Jewish plays. They were all cast in *Nekrassov* and Robert Helpmann played the name part. However, the play – which was a farce about a conman pretending to be a Soviet defector – was not a real success, probably because it went against the prevailing cold war climate of the times. It had a respectable run of 46 performances and played to an average of 56 per cent.

In the spring of 1957, we presented the first of our Sunday night Productions without Decor. These were given on the main stage, usually after two weeks rehearsal but with no scenery, costumes or special lighting. They became a very important feature of the Court's work, enabling us to present a number of plays we could not otherwise have shown and to offer opportunities to new directors and other theatre workers. I can't remember who thought of the idea. Sometimes I think I did, at others I'm not so sure. At a theatre such as the Court was then, ideas came from all sides and were picked up and passed along. But it certainly came at the right time to enable the work of some new young writers and directors to get started. These Sunday night productions were only open to members of the English Stage Society, which was a supporters' organisation for friends of the Royal Court. The first production was *The Correspondence Course* by Charles Robinson. I do not know what happened to him subsequently but the play's director was Peter Coe, later well known as a theatre director, though not associated with the Court. After that came *Yes and After* by Michael Hastings, who was still writing for the Royal Court into the 1980's. The director was John Dexter, introduced to the Royal Court by John Osborne. This was the first of Dexter's many productions at the Court and he became one of its first associate directors. Osborne had met him in weekly rep in Derby and he was to have a long and distinguished career in the theatre, associated particularly with the Court, then the National Theatre and later with the New York Met. The third Sunday production in June, *The Waiting of Lester Abbs* by Kathleen Sully, introduced Lindsay Anderson as director, whose relationship with the Court was to last for nearly twenty years. The last Sunday night production in 1957 was probably the most important. While I was working at the Embassy Theatre, I had produced a stage version of Louis Golding's *Magnolia Street* and had got to know the author. Some time later Louis told me he had been a judge of a radio drama competition in the North of England and thought that one of the plays might interest me. I asked to see it and so got to hear for the first time from John Arden, who sent me a play about King Arthur. I did not think I could do anything about it but was impressed enough to ask him if he had written anything else. He sent me *Waters of Babylon* which I thought an extremely interesting piece of work. I showed it to my colleagues at the Court and they offered John a Sunday night production. He accepted and it was directed by Graham Evans. Arden went on to become one of the most important writers of George Devine's period as Artistic Director of the Court.

Meanwhile the main bill continued with Faulkner's *Requiem for a Nun*, featuring Zachary Scott and his wife, Ruth Ford. Tony Richardson directed and Bertice Reading was in the cast. The play, which I remember principally because Bertice tried to combine her work in the play with concert performances – not always with happy results – was not much to my taste, but it played to 89 per cent capacity and transferred to the West End and later to Broadway.

Our second bawdy classic for Christmas followed: *Lysistrata*, from the Oxford Playhouse directed by Minos Volonakis, with Constance Cummings in the leading role. This was an even greater success playing to 98 per cent capacity and transferring to the Duke of York's Theatre. Between them on a Sunday night, came the first play of another famous Court writer, N.F. Simpson's *A Resounding Tinkle*, directed by the third of the

Court's new associate directors, William Gaskill. Gaskill, like Anderson, had known Tony Richardson at Oxford: indeed, he had known him earlier in their home town of Bradford. Both had been introduced to the Court by Richardson. *A Resounding Tinkle* had won a prize in the *Observer* Play Competition which was how the Court had heard about it.

After *Lysistrata*, we put on *Epitaph for George Dillon*, a play John Osborne had written with Anthony Creighton before writing *Look Back*. It was directed by William Gaskill, his first production in the main bill, and starred Robert Stephens. Although it did not do particularly well at the box office, it transferred to the West End and later to New York.

The last play of our second year was *The Sport of My Mad Mother* by another Observer prize winner, Anne Jellicoe. Anne was to become one of the Court's most important writers but *Sport*, which she directed with George Devine, was only the second play to be presented in the main bill by a completely new and unknown playwright and was a financial disaster. It played to only 35 per cent seat capacity and 23 per cent box office capacity. It was reluctantly decided that it had to be withdrawn after only 14 performances.

The Court finished its second year with a surplus. It had an Arts Council grant of £5000, box office takings of £65,289 being 63.8 per cent of capacity and income from transfers of £39,631, making a total income of £109,920 against expenses of £92,067. The Arts Council grant was less than the previous year, because part of that grant was a guarantee against loss. We tried to budget in such a way as to make it possible to break even if we played to 50 per cent capacity. George and I used to prepare the budgets which we would present to a meeting of the Management Committee, which met usually once a fortnight under the Chairmanship of Neville Blond. George was free to present the programme he wanted, provided he could do it within the tight budget. Many of our most important plays were financial failures and in many cases we knew that they would be, but it was the presentation of those plays that made the Court essential to the theatre of its time. Beckett, Arden, Jellicoe: all financially disastrous. Of the new playwrights only John Osborne was both an artistic and financial success.

So in our first two years we had produced the first work of four important new English writers: Osborne, Arden, Jellicoe and Simpson. Also plays by three of the leading avant garde writers based in Paris: Beckett, Ionesco and Sartre, and three leading American contemporary writers, Arthur Miller, William Faulkner and Carson McCullers, and the first production of Brecht's *Good Woman of Setzuan*. We had found four exciting new directors in Tony Richardson, John Dexter, Lindsay Anderson and William Gaskill and a magnificent new designer in Jocelyn Herbert. Looking back, it seems a wonderful beginning, but at the time I think we were more aware of the problems facing us than the successes we had achieved.

When I had accepted the proposal that I should return to the Court as General Manager, I had asked for a salary of £30 per week, which was £10 more than provided for in the budget. Neville Blond had agreed to contribute the extra £10 but instead of paying it to the English Stage Company and the Company paying me, he had insisted on paying me the £10 himself. After I had been doing the job for about a year, I had some disagreement with Neville, I forget what it was about, but I am sure it was not anything very important. This prompted him to stop paying me the £10 per week and to say that if I wanted to continue to work as General Manager, I must resign as a member of the Council, a position I had held since the formation of the Company. To his surprise, I said I would prefer to remain a member of the Council. I resigned as General Manager and began the second phase of my work with Wolf as a West End producer.

But before I tell the story of my life as a West End producer, I go back to the time when my mother and her family first arrived in England.

Part Two

Flashback

to where I came from

About the year 1892, my mother, Mary Convisser, then a child of eight, arrived in England with her parents and three younger sisters. The family had come from Moscow by way of New York, where they had failed to make a living. On arrival in London they had walked to the East End and arrived unexpected at the door of some relatives who took them in.

My father, Arthur Solomon, arrived in London some fifteen years later, a deserter from the Russian army.

Both my parents came from orthodox Jewish families and were refugees from anti-semitism. My father was stated to be Polish on his Nansen passport, he had been born in Lodz, a part of Poland then included in the Russian empire. He always considered himself to be Russian and, although he lived in England for the remainder of his life, he never applied for British naturalisation.

My mother's father had been a bookbinder in Moscow, binding books for Tolstoy and other leading Russian writers of the time. It was very unusual for Jews to be allowed to live in Moscow, which would have been essential for my grandfather's work. I can still remember the hand printing presses, guillotines and other fascinating machinery of his trade that I saw in the basement of his house in London. But there was no bookbinding work for him in London, so my grandfather worked as an inspector of the ritual killing of meat for the Court of the Chief Rabbi; the Beth Din.

My father must have had some knowledge of the English language when he arrived or else been able to learn enough very quickly, because he became the Russian correspondent for Robert Crooks of Moorgate Hall in the city, who imported timber from Russia, and was their General Manager in 1919 and 1920. At that time, apart from their timber business, they were selling boots to Kerensky's army, and I found amongst my father's papers an uncashed cheque for 11,000,000 roubles in this connection. From this it appears they had some difficulty in getting their cash and it is not clear if they ever received it. They backed the wrong side with their boots and perhaps paid the price for this.

My father and mother had very different temperaments. My mother was shy and rather inhibited, physically undemonstrative, not at all vivacious but intelligent and witty in a quiet way. My father on the other hand was sociable, charming and entertaining, a lover of women, work and whisky. He was well read, particularly in the Russian classics. I remember sets of books in Russian by Chekhov, Gogol and others and a Tolstoy collection that later provided a little welcome money for my mother. She thought Father was the most wonderful and brilliant man who ever lived and apparently never had an opinion differing from his except on family matters. Only after my father died did my mother's rather original personality show itself.

My father and mother were married in 1916 and I was born in a nursing home in Queen's Down Road, Hackney on 18th January 1917. My father was my mother's uncle.

I was named Silvion Oscar. To this day, I don't know why. I have only come across the name Silvion in Marie Corelli's novel *Wormwood*, which my father might have been reading about that time . . . But why name his son after the handsome, evil Catholic priest who brings about the downfall of the book's hero and is murdered by him? As with so many other questions, I never asked him and he never told me. Nor do I know why Oscar was chosen as my second name but Oscar Wilde and Oscar Slater were in the news at the time.

I always felt that in giving me these two names, my parents had started me in life with a great disadvantage. By the time my sister and brothers came to be named, they had calmed down. For the first eight or nine years of my life I was called Sonny – afterwards Oscar and at home

Ossie. For the first years of her life my sister Natalie was called Neenie. Afterwards Nat or Nassie. Paul was called Possie and David Dassie.

In the middle of 1917 we left London and went to live first in Regency Square, Brighton and then at Seaside Villas, Hove, where I live now, though in a different house and after a gap of 50 years.

My father spoke English with a strong Russian accent. He always mixed up v's and w's. Thus 'Don't vurry, let's go to Wentnor'. My mother had no trace of a foreign accent.

By the time I was four years old my father was quite a successful business man, managing a plywood factory for Vickers. We had a nurse and an under nurse. As my father's business was in London, he spent a great deal of time there, living at the Waldorf Hotel and coming down to us at week-ends. If we disturbed my father in any way he would shout 'to the nursery' and there we would go to be looked after by Nanny. My memory is that we saw a great deal more of Nanny Green than of my parents, and I have few memories of my mother from those early days. I do remember that she couldn't cook and never tried to. We didn't have the sort of food usual in most Jewish families. In fact we were not really part of the Jewish community, though it seems to me that most of our family friends were Jewish. Neither of my parents kept the Jewish holidays and, of course, we didn't keep a kosher house.

My friends, before I went to boarding school, were few. Natalie, Paul and I played on the beach together and with Eric, who lived next door and was the son of my father's accountant and Boy Garman, son of the local works foreman, who lived in a nearby black hut on the beach.

At different times we had as neighbours Lord St. Oswald, J.R. Clynes, Home Secretary in the second Labour Government, Arthur Bouchier, the actor, and Arthur Prince, the ventriloquist. I used to play tennis with Mrs. Prince, who told my mother I was a very bad loser. I cannot say that she was wrong. I think it ran in our family because I remember my father telling me that when the team from one of his factories came off the field after a sporting event, if they looked miserable it meant that they had won and if they looked happy they had lost. He found this difficult to understand, as did my friend, David Tutaeff, when at school he and I were upset at being defeated in a vote for prefect, whilst the other boys did not appear to care when they were in that position. We all concluded that it was a question of the English character.

When I was in my teens, I had quite a bad stammer, not helped by my father advising me to speak more slowly and think before I said anything, which is just the way to make a stammer worse. It disappeard gradually when I was in my early twenties.

When we lived in Hove, my father regularly and my mother occasionally went riding on the Sussex Downs and, when I was 9, I was given a birthday present of twelve riding lessons. This paid off when I was in the Army and I used to go riding, either by myself or with a group of friends from the local riding stables, when I was stationed in or near the country. I didn't continue with this sport, nor with any other, after the war was over. I was too busy trying to change the world.

When I was nine my father had a quarrel with Vickers and was given a golden handshake of £10,000. My mother insisted on him using part of it to send Natalie and me to Dunhurst, the Junior School of Bedales. Unlike the traditional Jewish family, my parents had no strong feelings about stinting themselves to give their children the best education possible. Certainly my father didn't. He had made money fairly easily at first and also had a natural aptitude for spending it. When he was with Vickers he saved nothing. We never owned a house but always rented one and my father tried to live up to the standard of his colleagues at Vickers, whose family fortunes and backgrounds were completely different, a fatal folly as it turned out.

Although we had not liked the idea of going to boarding school, my sister and I had scarcely been there an hour when we felt so thoroughly at home that we could hardly find time to say goodbye to our parents. We were only at the school for a year, because my father decided he could not afford to keep us there any longer, but that year was one of the happiest and most influential of my life.

Bedales was a really free and progressive school. Certainly at Dunhurst we were encouraged to spend a lot of our time doing things that particularly interested us. Re-reading my letters home, I was surprised to find how keen I was on the theatre even then. I saw my first Shakespeare production there, *Romeo and Juliet*, and still remember a fragment of a song we sang from a piece about the Greek heroes: 'No siren or monster our quick craft shall stay, To Ithaca's island we shall find out the way.' Dunhurst also gave me my first realisation that I was a Jew and therefore in some way different from other people. My sister and I and one other

student were the only three Jews in the junior school. We had to stand
out in front of the class and sing a song which went something like this:

Once upon a time there were three Jews
And the first one's name was Abraham
Abraham ham ham ham ham
Abraham ham ham ham ham
And the first one's name was Abraham.

And the second one's name was Jacob
J-ay-cob cob cob cob
J-ay-cob cob cob cob
And the second one's name was J-a-cob.

And the third one's name was Isaac or Moses, I'm not sure which, but
I was Abra-ham-ham-ham, I remember that.

I have a programme 'printed by the Dunhurst press', probably by me, for
I spent a great deal of time printing in those days. It is for an evening of
excerpts of plays in The Dunhurst Theatre. *The Treasure of the Garden* by
Jack B. Yeats. Act III Scene 1 from *The Merchant of Venice* with apologies
to WS. Scene and costumes by Oscar. Four Tableaux: (1) The Nativity
by Jenny, Beth and Jill. (2) Scene from *Treasure Island* designed by Peter
and John Wheeler (3) *The Shepherd* designed by Sheila (4) *Old Mother
Hubbard* designed by Jean Hicks.

Peter and John Wheeler were my best friends at Dunhurst. About ten
years later, all of us were members of the Hampstead Branch of the
Communist Party.

I see from my letters that it was during my stay at Dunhurst that I first
fell in love. I wrote to my mother 'I'm in love with Jenny Crow but don't
tell anybody.'

When I was ten I left Dunhurst, and that same year we also left Hove
Seaside Villas with a lot of rent owing. We moved for a few weeks to a
tiny house nearby and then to a rather splendid rented house with a large
garden on top of the cliffs at Sandown on the Isle of Wight. My father
had now started up a plywood factory on the island for Saunders Rowe.

On the wall in one of the living rooms was a framed illuminated text of Kipling's poem 'If'. My father urged us children to learn this by heart and rewarded anyone who achieved this with half a crown. I can still remember most of it and I often wonder whether my father's enthusiasm for the poem in any way affected his own actions.

I now went to Ryde Grammar School, a small private school for boys. I never ceased telling the very liberal headmaster how much better Dunhurst had been. But I learned to enjoy English, History and Mathematics. I was the only Jew in the school but I came across no anti-Semitism. I don't think most of the boys knew what a Jew was.

Mention of religion reminds me that during my last half term at Ryde School, when I was boarder, I attended church on Sundays, because otherwise it meant staying in school on my own. There were, of course, no arrangements for a Jewish service. I went to the service of a different denomination every week. I enjoyed the hymns but otherwise the services made no impression on me other than to wonder how people could believe the things they taught there. The only religious experience I can claim was that about that time, I was just on sixteen, I dreamt that I was in love with the Virgin Mary. I can't remember if she was in love with me.

There was one Russian boy, David Tutaeff, with whom I became very friendly. We once had a great cricket partnership and were dubbed 'Trotsky and Oscar'.

David told me many lurid tales about how his family had been tortured by the Bolsheviks. Despite this, I was already thinking of myself as a Communist at the age of 14, although I had almost no knowledge of that movement beyond that gained by reading a book, *Lenin the God of the Godless*, a work whose extreme right wing opinions were intended to have the opposite effect on its readers.

David, in spite of his family background, was a good deal more in sympathy with the aims of the Labour Movement than I was. I remember him explaining to me the reasons for the Hunger Marches, about which I knew nothing. My Communism was of a quite non-political kind, a dream of a perfect egalitarian society, influenced by a romantic idea of Russia given to me unwittingly by my father, who was all in favour of Communism for Russia but totally opposed to it for England, where it 'would be bad for business'. However, our daily newspaper was the *Daily*

Herald, then the paper of the Labour Party, and my father's favourite English authors were Shaw and Wells. When I won a school prize one year and was asked which book I would like, he suggested Wells' *Men Like Gods*, which the school thought a strange choice but which they gave to me none the less.

We moved after a year in Sandown to a house just above Shanklin Chine. It was an old house, with a tower and a very wild and rather romantic garden running along the top of the Chine. On Regatta days my father allowed a band to play in the garden, which was lit up with fairy lights. As David Tutaeff and I walked along the cliff tops he would plan an invasion of Shanklin from the sea.

About a year before leaving Hove, my paternal grandfather had arrived from Moscow with one of my aunts and her two children, Iussick (Joe) aged about 20 and his sister Bella aged 16. My aunt and her children went back to Russia after a few months' holiday and I lost touch with them. My grandfather stayed with us. He couldn't speak any English and we couldn't speak any Russian, Yiddish or German, so he remained a distant, even mysterious figure. I remember him in his prayer shawls with his phylacteries (which were small leather boxes tied on to his head) saying his prayers in Hebrew, another language we didn't understand. Although I was circumcised by a Rabbi, that was the beginning and end of my Jewish education and the same went for my brothers. Looking back, I'm grateful to my parents for leaving me free to choose my own religion or none at all.

When we moved to the Isle of Wight, grandfather of course came with us, and, as he was very old, he had to have a nurse to look after him. For this task my father appointed a series of beautiful young women from Germany or Scandinavia. This was only one of several indications of a tendency to live his sex life outside the confines of his marriage.

The first liaison discovered by my mother was in about 1925, when my father was still living away from home during the week. He fell ill in his flat in the Waldorf and was taken to hospital. My mother, taking Natalie and me with her, went up to town and found signs of another woman living with him, who turned out to be my father's secretary. My father begged my mother not to do anything until he was out of hospital. She agreed and never left my father, though his relationship with Miss H.

continued for the rest of his life. He even had a son by her, whom I regret I have never met.

During our stay in Shanklin I can remember many rows between my parents. Shouting by my father, tears from my mother. We did not understand the cause of these rows but I always took my mother's side and blamed my father, unfairly as I now think. It got to such a point at one time that I persuaded my brothers and sister to send my father to Coventry. How long we kept this up I don't remember, nor how my father reacted. The most serious of these quarrels arose through my father falling in love with one of grandfather's nurses, Ria, a tall, beautiful German woman in her early twenties. My mother eventually dealt with this emergency with great resource. She introduced Ria to Harold Fairhurst, the violinist of the local Concert Party, and they fell in love. My father was furious, turned Ria out of the house, and she and Harold went to live in a tent on the cliffs. Ria remained a friend of my mother's for many years.

This story reminds me that most of my early theatrical experiences were of the concert parties that visited Sandown and Shanklin. There I saw Clarkson Rose, Ronald Frankau, and Arthur Askey, amongst many others whose names I have now forgotten.

At some time during our seven years on the Isle of Wight, my father quarrelled with and left Saunders Rowe. He then made an arrangement with Cootes of Chingford to start a business, Flexo Plywood Industries. Cootes was mainly concerned with making cork products. My father, whose business reputation had been mainly as a salesman, became interested in the technical side of things and developed uses for applying metal, cork and eventually plastics (Bakelite) onto plywood. The association with Cootes did not last long and when it came to an end in 1932, my father was completely broke. He had a deep-seated reluctance to go bankrupt and did avoid doing so, but at the cost of having no money at all. So my parents with my brothers and sister went to live in the basement of my maternal grandparents' house in Osbaldestone Road, Stoke Newington. It was arranged that I would stay at Ryde School as a boarder, but at half term I was told that my father had unexpectedly sent me a rail ticket to go home for the half term holiday. I was surprised and, not without reason, apprehensive. On arriving at my grandparents, my father told me that my school fees had not been paid and that, as a consequence, I could not go back to school. He had not wanted me to get the news of my leaving from anyone but himself.

Before my family left the Isle of Wight, the old grandfather, as we called him, died. His body had to be taken to the mainland because there was no Jewish cemetery on the island. We children did not attend his funeral.

For one term I went to the Central School in Hackney but I couldn't settle down there. So I left school without taking the matriculation, the School Certificate or any other exams, and went to work as an office-boy with my father and two of his friends. I was just 16.

At this time my father was sharing a city office with two other men who had been successful and had now fallen on hard times. Mr. J., who owned the office, had been a big wheel on the foreign exchange. Mr.M. had been an important stockbroker, who had been sent to prison and had now opened an office as an outside broker, i.e., a broker outside the Stock Exchange. These two gentlemen and my father each agreed to pay me five shillings a week, or a total of 75 pence in today's money. Unfortunately my father didn't pay me his share because he hadn't got it. And Mr. J. didn't pay me his share because my father hadn't paid him the rent. Only Mr. M's five bob was left to pay for my lunches and fares, and even so there was a little bit over for my mother and me.

After a while, Mr. M. took larger offices and I went with him on the full princely salary of 15 shillings a week, though I did not stay long.

My father found some people who were prepared to back his plastic covered plywood on a small experimental scale. A very small factory with a couple of presses was provided, and I was engaged as foreman at a small wage. Sheets of paper were impregnated with resin, placed over plywood boards and pressed in the heated presses. The papers usually had the appearance of polished wood surfaces but could have many other patterns. It was called Plyrock. It could be used for table tops or panelled walls, for furniture or trays. Eventually my father obtained an order for the panelling of a Cunard liner but the factory to which the job was given (ours was too small to undertake it) botched the job, I don't know how or why, and this small venture collapsed.

I must go back to the time when I left school. My mother, who had suffered the most through the ups and downs in my father's fortunes, wanted me to have a steady job. Her ideal was the Civil Service but, that being out of the question because I had no academic qualifications, the Co-op seemed to her the next best thing. I was not keen on that and, perhaps for that reason, failed in this direction also. Then my mother set her hopes on the Houndsditch Warehouse and I went for an interview there. No luck again. She then urged me to master shorthand and typing. I wasn't keen but agreed to attend evening classes in these skills.

At home, conditions were pretty bad. The six members of my family, or more usually five, since my father frequently stayed away, lived in two basement rooms in my grandparents' house. Apart from my grandfather and grandmother there were three maiden aunts and Uncle Morrie. All of these disapproved of my father and thought he had got his rightful come-uppance. Only the grandparents were kind and welcoming. I particularly remember one day when my father and I were playing chess on the table in the grandparents' sitting room, evidently taking up more space than Morrie wanted to let us have. He made the situation so unbearable we had to abandon our game, and it was so humiliating for my father that he walked out of the house.

I never liked my Uncle Morrie. He was a narrow, self-righteous pecksniff of a man, but I was very fond of my maiden aunts. They had given me my first two grown up experiences of the theatre, taking me to the West End to see Sybil Thorndike in Bernard Shaw's *Saint Joan* and Dennis King in *The Vagabond King*. 'Sons of toil and sorrow, will you yield tomorrow, and bow down to Burgundy? We shall bring salvation to a starving nation and to hell with Burgundy.' I must have been about nine years old when I heard Dennis King as Francis Villon lead the chorus of beggars in this song.

Later in life I could never forgive my aunts for their coldness to my father when he was down. My grandmother and her sister Aunt Nookeh were married to two brothers and this added to the confusion caused in our minds by my father's being my mother's uncle. This latter relationship was never spoken about and we children didn't ask about it, because I suppose we sensed that it was in some way taboo.

Now for the first time since her marriage, my mother went out to work in a local factory. I was horrified at the thought that she, a woman of nearly 50, which seemed very old to me, should have to do this. At this time I still had little idea of how the other half lived.

At my evening classes I used to discuss the affairs of the day with the other students. I still considered myself to be a Communist and still had no real idea of what the Communist Party stood for. One day a fellow student suggested I join the Young Communist League. He gave me the address of the local branch. The meetings took place in a fairly large room in a private house. The room was packed with about 25 young people ranging in age from 17 to 30. I was particularly impressed with a couple called Esther and Johnny, who appeared to be the oldest and most experienced of the comrades. The women smoked and swore – a new experience for me. I did neither and, although my father smoked and drank, my mother did not, and the general attitude in our family and in that of my grandparents was rather puritanical. My father was certainly the odd one out, intellectually, sexually, in fact in every way. None of mother's three sisters ever married, nor do I think they ever had a relationship with a man. Uncle Morrie remained a bachelor until he was over 40.

I loved and admired my father but was rarely at ease with him and certainly did not enjoy working for him. I never felt that my work satisfied him, and indeed how could he be pleased, since my interest in the work couldn't possibly compete with my interests in the Y.C.L. But my father was a difficult, divided man. He was a Victorian where the family was concerned and a modern man outside it. One incident illustrates this. I became very friendly with Esther and Johnny, who lived together and seemed to me to be a model of a modern couple. They had no children and one day, talking with my father about them, he said he supposed they used something disgusting to avoid Esther becoming pregnant. Sometime later he asked me if I knew how he could obtain an abortion for 'a friend'.

After about a year living at my grandparents, when my father obtained the backing for the small experimental factory I have already mentioned, we moved out and took a shabby flat on the first floor of a house in Evering Road, Hackney.

Through living in this street and going to the Y.C.L. I met Clare, who became my first lover and my first wife. Clare came from an East European Jewish family. Her father, when I first met her, was a foreman on building sites – later he became a Bradford millionaire. Though not as deeply involved in the Y.C.L. as I was, she shared many of my views. On the other hand, she was more sexually experienced than I. She slept in a room adjoining the back door of her house and we used to go in there when her parents were asleep. I would creep out of the house again in the early hours. One day when we had thought her parents were safely in bed, we were in bed ourselves when we heard the back door open and her parents enter the house. Someone turned the door handle. Fortunately, Clare had put a chair under it. When her mother called out, she was reassured to learn that Clare was safely in bed and said goodnight. At which point I emerged from underneath the blankets.

This was the time of the rise of Hitler, of the appearance of Mosley's Blackshirts and of mass unemployment. War threatened. The Y.C.L. was involved in all these political struggles. 'Hitler and Mosley, what are they for? Thuggery, buggery, hunger and war.' Thus we chanted on our almost weekly demonstrations in Hyde Park or Trafalgar Square, or sometimes just to Ridley Road in Hackney to break up some Blackshirt meeting. Finsbury Park and Tottenham Speakers' Corner were other places where the North London Y.C.L. fought their battles against fascism and war and unemployment and the means' test. At our branch meetings we arranged speakers for outdoor meetings and sellers for the *Daily Worker*, the newspaper of the Communist Party and *Challenge*, the weekly paper of the Y.C.L.

The Marxist classics were read and studied and discussed. If a member said he or she couldn't attend one of these activities, it was necessary to explain why. Every member in those days was dedicated and active, both in the work I've just described and in his or her union branch, co-operative society or other organisation which we sought to influence. It was heady stuff for a young man. Probably the Militants in the Labour Party today have something of the same feeling. We believed that Capitalism was on its last legs and that it was only a matter of a few years before its inner contradictions, together with the activities of the masses, led by the Communist Party, would bring it crashing down in ruins, and Socialism would triumph over the whole world.

'Then forward you workers, freedom awaits you, o'er all the world on the land and the sea. On with the fight for the cause of humanity. Forward you workers and the world shall be free.'

So we sang and so we believed. I had found my niche in life, and I was blissfully happy, despite conditions at home.

In fact, I was scarcely ever at home, for in addition to our political work, our social life also was catered for by the movement. Often on Sundays, if there was no demo to attend, we went hiking with the Progressive Ramblers in Epping Forest or Hertfordshire. It was at this time too, between 1936 and the outbreak of war, that I began to go more often to the theatre. Most Saturday nights my friends and I would queue up for the gallery of Sadler's Wells or the Old Vic to see opera, ballet or Shakespeare. We also went regularly to Unity Theatre productions, first in Britannia Street, where I saw Clifford Odets' *Waiting for Lefty*, *Where's That Bomb?* by Herbert Hodge and *On Guard for Spain*, by Jack Lindsay, and later in Goldington Street, where the plays I particularly remember were *Plant in the Sun* with Paul Robeson and Alfie Bass and the brilliant political pantomime *Babes in the Wood* by Robert Mitchell, Geoffrey Parsons and Berkeley Fase, with Vida Hope wonderful as the Fairy Wishfulfilment. 'My best friend is Godfrey Winn, Castlerosse is my enchantment, Beverly Nichols is my sin.' Of course at that time I had no idea that one day I would work there, nor at that time did I have any thought of doing so.

I went to work in the world outside the family as some kind of office worker. I could type with four fingers and that was about the limit of my commercial abilities. First I worked at a Tin Plate Merchant's office in the city. I was supposed to write up the books, but my handwriting was so atrocious that I didn't last long. Then I worked in the gift book department of the *Daily Mail*. By this time I was an active young communist and brought into work a copy of the satirical 'Marina Special' published by the *Daily Worker* on the occasion of Princess Marina's marriage. For this crime I was dismissed. I had quite enjoyed my few weeks at the *Mail* and at least the money was better. My next job was at Simpson's tailoring factory in Stoke Newington. Here I had my first encounter with homosexuals.

Simpson's was then a non-union shop. A group of us, Communist and Labour Party people working in the factory, decided to start a campaign to unionise it. We issued leaflets, held meetings and engaged in all the usual activities connected with unionisation. We had a group, whose names were kept secret, working with this objective within the factory, helped by sympathisers outside it. Gradually one by one the members of our groups got the sack, until only three of us, all Jews, were left. It was clear that one of the three was giving away the names to the bosses. At a meeting to discuss this, one of the young men broke down and confessed that he was the lover of one of the directors of the firm and that he'd given away the other names. The director was Jewish himself and on this account had spared me and my colleague.

I was an invoice typist in that company, not a job I wanted to stay at, particularly now our Union plans were in ruins. I was offered a job at the Workers' Bookshop in Farringdon Road, distributors of the Left Book Club. Here at last was something I wanted to do and I was happy in a job for the first time.

I started at the Workers' Bookshop in 1936. It was the main wholesale distributing centre for left-wing and Marxist literature and was controlled, if not owned, by the Communist Party. In addition it undertook distribution of the Left Book Club, a popular front project launched by the publisher, Victor Gollancz. With a panel of book selectors composed of John Strachey, Harold Laski and Gollancz himself, it was completely independent of Communist Party control. My job was to deal with queries from members who had not received the books they had ordered or had received the wrong books. Not a particularly interesting job in itself, but the satisfaction lay in the fact that I was working on one of the most successful progressive projects of the time and with a group of people all sharing the same ideals. In his book *The Fellow Travellers*, David Caute says that, by 1939, the Club claimed fifty seven thousand members, representing an actual readership of about a quarter of a million for each title. It is unquestionable that the Left Book Club played a large part in forming the climate of opinion that led to the formation of the influential Army Bureau of Current Affairs (A.B.C.A.) and subsequently to the election of the Labour Government of 1945.

The Manager of the Left Book Club section of the Bookshop was Nelly Lansbury, daughter of the Labour leader, George. Her secretary was Ivy McMillan, always called 'Mac'. She and her husband, Peter Venning, who also worked in the Bookshop, became my closest friends. Peter was the son of a Ceylon tea planter. He had been a medical student at Oxford, where he became a Communist. He was very active in the anti-colonial struggles of the time and dropped out from university so that he could give more of his time to political work, much to the fury of his parents, who more or less disowned him. Peter's decision was unusual, for the Party's policy was for its students to remain at university and do well in their studies. Peter remained a life-long friend.

In 1937 Clare and I decided that we wanted to get married. I was 20 years old and Clare 18. My father refused to give us permission. So we decided to live together and we moved into a flat in Clissold Road, Stoke Newington, vacated by a comrade who had gone to fight in Spain.

Clare's parents were furious and ostracised her. However, when a wedding was about to take place in her family circle, they thought that Clare's absence would be suspicious, for they had not told anyone of the dreadful thing their daughter had done. They asked Clare to come home for a few days and bribed her with the promise of some new clothes. We agreed that she should go back for a few days, but when the wedding was over they tried to stop her from returning to our flat. I consulted our Bookshop Solicitor, and he explained that they had no right to detain her. She was released and returned to our love nest.

On 19 February 1938, just after my 21st birthday, Clare and I were married at the Hackney Register Office. The only members of our families present were my mother and one of Clare's aunts. A couple of friends came along but there was no celebration and I don't think we regarded it as a landmark in our lives, except in so far as it was a declaration of independence from my father. We had been living as man and wife for a year and nothing was changed by our wedding except that it enabled us to have a divorce nine years later.

It was in 1936 that an attempt was made to unite all the British anti-fascist forces in a popular front. In France and Spain Popular Front governments had taken power, and in Spain the Spanish Civil War had begun – 'The Last Great Cause', as it has been called, a cause which fired the enthusiasm and idealism of my generation. The Y.C.L. was very active in all areas of work for the Spanish Republic. Many of my friends went to fight in the International Brigade. I did not go because my comrades and I agreed that I would not make much of a soldier and could best serve the cause by continuing my work at home. That the International Brigade had not lost much by my absence was confirmed later, when I spent six years as a rather unsoldierly soldier in the British

Army in World War II. One of the activities was the sending of the Spanish Youth Foodships. In this work we were joined by many members and indeed whole branches of the Labour Party League of Youth (L.L.Y.), who were fed up with the right wing policies of the Labour Party leadership and sympathetic to the idea of a united front with the Y.C.L. It was suggested to me that I should join the L.L.Y. and help our friends there. As a result I came to know and work with a group of people, three of whom are among my closest friends to this day. The first of these was Ted Willis. When I first knew him he lived in Tottenham and was a worker on London Transport. He has written about this early life in his volume of autobiography, *What Ever Happened to Tom Mix* and tells there better than I can the story of those early days when we used to hold our meetings in a small upstairs room in his parents' house. Then there was Alec Bernstein, now the writer Alexander Baron, whom I introduced to the Movement. Alec was a year or two younger than I was and had just left school when we first met and found that we shared an enthusiasm for the works of Dostoevsky, Tolstoy and other Russian writers. And thirdly there was Doreen Williams, a young shop assistant, who, when we first met, was living in the dormitory of Bradley's, a large department store in Westbourne Grove. She worked in the blouse department, which was known as 'the bolshy blouses', because she and her colleagues were trying to unionise the shop.

I thought of Ted in those days as a real working-class hero. He was an inspiring public speaker and organiser. He took the lead in all our activities. He initiated the publication of *Advance*, a magazine of the left section of the League of Youth, which rapidly became the majority of that organisation and elected Ted as Chairman, and a National Committee consisting entirely of *Advance* supporters. Ted it was who, together with John Gollan, the brilliant leader of the Young Communist League, and Gabriel Carritt, Secretary of the League of Nations Youth, took the initiative in forming the British Youth Peace Assembly and the Spanish Youth Foodship Committee, of which Ted was the first Secretary and Organiser. These organisations were supported a by broad sweep of youth organisations ranging from the Young Communist League to the Y.W.C.A.

I myself took a part – but not a prominent one – in all these activities. I had not the confidence to play a very public role. I could make a report to the branch meeting but did not speak in public. When I was a child of about two or three, my father used to say I looked like Hamlet because of my pale face, black hair and rather solemn old-man expression. But I saw myself rather as playing Horatio to Ted's Prince. So, whilst I worked at the Bookshop during the day, I was a liaison between the Y.C.L. and the *Advance* group in the L.L.Y. in the evenings. I was also active in helping with the work of the Spanish Youth Foodship Committee, which had the task of raising money to send food to the struggling people of the Spanish Republic. Many relief organisations functioned at this period, raising large sums for those days. They would have been much larger but for the failure of the Labour Party to really throw its full weight into the struggle. Nevertheless, many branches of the Labour Party were actively supporting the relief organisations, as were many Trade Unions both nationally and locally. Sir Stafford Cripps, Aneurin Bevan and other Left Labour M.P.'s also gave their support. Bevan and Cripps led a campaign which concentrated on three main political objectives: the creation of a united front of all working class parties and men of goodwill to force the Chamberlain Government out of office and replace it with a Popular Front Government; full support and the supply of arms to the Spanish Republican Government; the creation of a system of collective security in Europe led by Russia, France and Great Britain with the aim of stopping Nazi aggression. Cripps formed an alliance with the Communist Party to fight for this programme and approached the League of Youth for support. Ted went on a national speaking tour with Cripps and George Strauss M.P. and with well known communists. *Advance*, which had achieved a circulation of some 50,000 monthly played a prominent part in the campaign.

After I had been at the bookshop for about two years, Ted asked me to work full time at the Spanish Youth Foodship Committee as the National Organiser. This I was very happy to do, as it was a more direct way of participating in political activities than working at the Bookshop. I travelled all over the country setting up local, broadly-based Youth Foodship Committees, raising money and food for Spain.

Later, when the Civil War ended and thousands of refugees fled to France, some young socialists and communists from Spain, Czecho-slovakia, Germany and Austria came as refugees to England, and we changed the name and function of the Foodship Committee to the Relief and Refugee Council of the British Youth Peace Assembly.

Among these refugees were many gifted musicians, singers and dancers, and one of our ways of raising money and giving publicity to the cause was to put on concerts given by these young artists, sometimes with and sometimes without the addition of English sympathetic performers, often from Unity Theatre.

Early in 1939 the Labour Party Executive suspended the National Advisory Committee of the L.L.Y. and cancelled its annual conference. Then as now they wanted that impossible combination, a successful but tame League of Youth. Willis resigned and called upon all members of the League to follow him into the ranks of the Young Communist League. As he says in his book, most of the leaders of the League and some of the rank and file responded to his appeal. I had no need to for I was already a member of the Y.C.L.

War came as I was walking along Deansgate, Manchester, on my way to another appointment to encourage support for our work for the young refugees. As far as I remember I went on that day as if nothing special had happened, but that I got much response to my efforts I doubt.

My work for the Relief and Refugee Council culminated in the organisation of a grand concert at Sadler's Wells with the participation of the youth groups from Spain, Austria, Germany and Czechoslovakia, professional musicians from these countries and, as star of the evening, Sybil Thorndike.

I was called up in the Royal Fusiliers at Buckingham Gate on 5 March 1940 for 'the duration of the emergency'. My Soldier's Service and Pay Book describes me as follows: Height 5ft 5 and 1/8th inches. Weight 108 lbs. Maximum chest 30 ins. Complexion sallow. Eyes brown. Hair dark. My medical category or grade was said to be A1.

Almost immediately we went down to Bognor for our initial training. I did not enjoy that first period of army life. I was not much good at drill and had very little liking for shining my boots and brass buttons and badges. However, I was not bad at taking a machine gun apart and putting it together and got on well enough with my fellow recruits. At Bognor we lived in private houses that had been taken over by the Army. At first we slept with blankets on bare boards but we soon had paliasses.

This was the phoney war period and when training came to an end after about three months, we were sent to an army camp near Canterbury to defend our coast against possible invasion. Fortunately the invasion did not take place, for I cannot think that we would have made much of a stand against the panzer units we should have faced.

I was drafted to a key position, clerk in the Company office, but after a short time, for some reason was medically regraded 'C' (I never discovered why) and was sent to the more strategic post of G.H.Q. Home Forces in London. Here I cooled my heels week after week waiting to be given something to do. My wife took a furnished flat nearby and I was given a pass to sleep out. Some air raids were taking place, but otherwise things were quiet. Finally, without explanation, I was transferred to the Pioneer Corps and to a Company which was to specialise in putting up smoke screens over industrial cities.

Here I again worked in the Company Office and in my spare time started a Wall Newspaper called *Smoke*, which consisted of a number of typed and drawn pages pinned to a wall. It had news, stories, cartoons, etc. created by the men of the unit. I was lucky in my Commanding Officer. He liked the paper and arranged that I should go with him to an Army school which was starting up, with him as Commandant, to train soldiers in the use of the Haslar smoke-making machines. I was to produce a duplicated newspaper for all the smoke companies.

Naturally I was delighted by this prospect, and on 13th September 1941 the first fortnightly issue was 'published by the Smoke School Pioneer Corps, by kind permission of the Commandant, Major C.E. Hoare, Editor O. Lewenstein. Price 2d'. The magazine was well supported by officers and men and came out regularly from the Smoke School at Compton Verney, Warwickshire, until the editor was transferred to Smoke Unit 808 Coy. Pioneer Corps based in Birmingham. There *Smoke* came out with rather less regularity until May 1943.

The first issue of *Smoke* came out just two months after the Nazi invasion of the Soviet Union. Up to that time the Communist Party and its supporters had declared the war to be an imperialist one and had called for a People's Peace. It would have been more difficult in that period for me to have produced a magazine, or at any rate, since I accepted the Party line, I should have had to confine it to uncontroversial issues. By the time it came out, Russia was our ally and the C.P. was staunchly, if critically, supporting the war effort. *Smoke* enthusiastically played its small part in this.

Throughout the magazine's life, around one third of it was written by me, another third by a small group of people who helped me to get it out and the final third by a miscellaneous assortment of the magazine's readers.

There is another piece of information on the first page of my Service Book. Trade on Enlistment: Organiser of Refugee Committee. During my time in the army there were occasions when I felt that the army's knowledge of my past associations affected their decisions concerning me, but, as with many things about the army, there was no consistency in their attitude.

In the spring of 1943, I went on a course to qualify as an instructor at a school for illiterates. Having passed, I was promoted to Acting Sergeant and posted to Command Education Centre, Wootton Hall, Wootton Wawen, Warwickshire, where one of the first army schools for the illiterate was established. Here I spent an interesting year teaching soldiers who, for various reasons, had not learned to read and write before joining the army. Of course, this put them at a big disadvantage and most were glad to come for a six week course, when in any case they would escape normal duties. Many had missed out because they had not been sent to school or because they had sat at the back of the class and could not see the board. For such soldiers our six weeks' course gave them a sufficient start to ensure that they would be able to read. For some who had failed to learn because of having a low I.Q., only a little progress could be made, and sometimes students in this category were given an extra period at the School. I think it can be said that almost all the soldiers who came there made some progress, and it convinced me that everyone was capable of learning to read and write if given enough time and attention. We also taught arithmetic and I remember a gypsy who could add up but couldn't take away when he arrived. He was a quick learner.

Wootton Hall, where the school was based, is a large dignified mansion built in 1687 situated in the centre of the village of Wootton Wawen, not far from Stratford-upon-Avon. We took advantage of this by arranging parties to see Shakespeare plays at the Memorial Theatre, as we had done when I was at the Smoke School in Compton Verney. Many of them had never been inside a theatre before and they accepted the plays as being absolutely real. Margaretta Scott was the leading lady at Stratford at the time and we all thought she was smashing. Certainly I did not think that I should ever mix with such immortals.

After about a year at this School, during which my work appeared to be considered satisfactory, I was told that I was being recalled to my unit. No one knew why. I found myself back in a Pioneer Company in Birmingham, stripped of my rank. I may only have been 'Acting Sergeant' whilst I was teaching, but now I was a private again, shovelling coal.

I applied for an interview with the Colonel and whilst I was waiting to be granted one, I was given the job of medical orderly. One day I went into the medical hut. It was very cold and all the medicines had frozen, so I got a bowl of hot water and put the medicine bottles into it. The medicines unfroze of course, but unfortunately all the labels came off the bottles. I thought this was a catastrophe, since I had no idea how to get the right labels back on the right bottles, but to my surprise the M.O. took it quite calmly and said that no great harm would come if a mistake was made, and indeed I never heard of anyone suffering as a result of being given the wrong medicine.

When eventually I saw the Colonel, he gave me no clear explanation for my transfer from the School but said that I was going to be given another job in Army Education but that there must be 'no religion or politics'. With that I was put in charge of the educational programme for a number of Pioneer Companies in the Birmingham area. There we have an example of the strange army mind. If it was my communist past that had put me under suspicion and led to my removal from the School, then surely the job of organising education throughout a number of units would only put me in a better position to undertake my political work than had I been left teaching illiterates.

Anyway in Birmingham, I helped to initiate educational activities, such as play readings, debates, film societies, lending libraries and various classes, all of which formed a good preparation for the Army courses in which I was involved as an instructor during the last year of the war. Every soldier had to take a certain number of classes each week while waiting to be demobbed.

In March 1944, whilst I was stationed in Birmingham, I had a telegram from my mother saying that my father was very ill in hospital. I applied for compassionate leave, but by the time I reached London he had died. He was 57 years old. The last few years of his life things had been a little better financially. In 1938 or 1939 he had made an arrangement with a financier whereby the production of his Plyrock was to be undertaken and my mother and father had moved from Evering Road to a flat in South Hill Park Gardens, Hampstead, near where Clare and I were living. Then the war came and the financier had decided that it was not the right time to set the business up, but paid my father a retainer so that they could go ahead when the time was right. Unfortunately that time never came. By the time the war was over, not only was my father dead, but plastics had made great advances and outstripped his invention. I had not seen my father for about the last three years of his life because, coming home on leave shortly after being called up, I had had a violent quarrel with him on some stupid point concerning the army. As usual he couldn't bear to be contradicted by one of his children and in a dramatic gesture had banned me from the house for five years. I was too stupid and stubborn to find a way of appeasing him and used to visit my mother when I knew he was not at home. After he was dead I began to realise how alike he and I were in many ways and to regret more and more that we had not been better friends. My poor father. During the last twelve years of his life he had had one disappointment after another. And he didn't have a good relationship with any of his children which might have softened the blows. When he died, the nurse at the hospital who had had most to do for him, said to my mother, 'He never really grew up did he?'

In 1945 I took another course to become a Sergeant Instructor at the Garrison Education Centre at Donnington, Shropshire. Here I remained until I was demobilised in April 1946, taking classes in Current Affairs, Economics, Politics and any other subject under the sun where I could be a couple of pages ahead of my class. I had a certain aptitude and liking for this work and could make the classes interesting and entertaining. The Army Bureau of Current Affairs produced some excellent pamphlets to guide this work, and the mood of the soldiers at the end of the war made the discussions and classes, sometimes over 100 strong, stimulating and rewarding. How excited we all were when the Labour Government was elected in 1945. Even though I knew that Social Democracy was not to be trusted, I thought we were at the dawn of a new age. And so in a way we were, for the Labour Government with all its weaknesses did introduce the Welfare State which, until the advent of Mrs. Thatcher, was supported by all parties.

Looking back over my six years in the Army, I realise how much it taught me. Up until then I had lived a rather protected life, at first in my family and then in the Communist movement. When I was in the Army I was amongst strangers, people with whom I shared neither a common background nor common ideals. But I found that I could function quite well in this situation, that I could get on and work with people of all kinds. This gave me a confidence in myself that I had not previously had. The army also gave me time to extend my reading in English, Russian and French literature that I might have studied had I gone to University. Of course my reading was not structured, but it was extensive and enjoyable and no doubt gave me the confidence to make my own decisions about plays and films when I came to produce them.

Part Three

Second Flashback

to Unity, the people's theatre

When I was demobbed from the Army, Clare was living with her bald-headed engineer and had given up the flat in Tanza Road, Hampstead, where we were living when I was called up. So I had no home to go back to. After Clare left me, I stayed with Ted Willis whenever I came to London on leave. Ted, who had been called up in the early days of the war, had quite soon been discharged from the army and had started to write plays, as a result of which he had become active in Unity Theatre, where he became quite rapidly both the director of the theatre and its leading playwright.

In the months before I was demobbed, I heard from Ted that Unity were about to revive the theatre magazine *New Theatre*, which they had published before the war. I applied for the job of Editor, which, not unnaturally, considering my total lack of experience either of the theatre or of professional journalism, I did not get. However, I was offered a temporary job for three months as Organiser of London groups of Unity Theatre. At that time, apart from the Unity Theatre at Goldington Street, London, there were groups in most of the London boroughs and in many of the cities throughout the country. They were all linked in the Unity Theatre Society Ltd., a non-profit distributing Co-operative Society, whose purpose was: 'To foster and further the art of drama in accordance with the principle that true art, by effectively presenting and truthfully interpreting life as experienced by the majority of the people, can move people to work for the betterment of society.'

My first duties were to visit the London Groups and help them with advice on organisation and repertoire. I also gave assistance to people who wanted to set up new branches of Unity. All this was not dissimilar to the work I had done with the Relief and Refugee Council of the British Youth Peace Assembly before the war. Ted also brought into Unity another old comrade of ours, Alec Bernstein, also recently demobilised. My 'temporary' status did not last for long. Soon Ted, Alec and I were acting as a team again as we had done in the youth movement before the war. I became at different times, and sometimes at the same time, manager at Goldington Street, secretary of the National Society, business manager of the Glasgow Unity when it went professional, and executive editor and editor of *New Theatre Magazine*. Alec became Chairman of Unity, Goldington Street, editor of *New Theatre* and producer of Unity's short lived film company, Crescent Films.

My first period of duty with Unity Theatre was, as I have said, as London Organiser of the Society's branches. At the end of that period, I was asked to take over as Secretary of the National Society. I continued to work with branches throughout the country in this capacity in the same way that I had previously worked with the London branches. I was also responsible for the production of material at the National Office, in particular, publicity pamphlets and leaflets and a National Play Service, which we initiated in August 1946.

In May 1946, Unity had just under 7,000 individual members with 190 affiliated organisations and 36 branches, two of which, in London and Glasgow, were partly professional, i.e., they had a professional company but also continued to do amateur work. In the summer of 1946 we launched a membership campaign, and by May 1947 the National Society peaked at 10,000 members (about 2,000 of whom were active), more than 3,000,000 affiliates and 50 branches. I was very actively involved in this and produced a pamphlet, 'Unity Theatre Presents', illustrated by the *Daily Worker* cartoonist, Gabriel, and a four-page leaflet, which on the front page, over a large photograph of the actors, said, 'Sybil Thorndike and Lewis Casson say, We wish you the best of luck. Bless you and Hurrah for Unity!'

To coincide with the first Edinburgh International Festival, in the summer of 1947, I organised, on behalf of the National Society, a

Summer School to run for three weeks in Edinburgh under the artistic direction of Bob Mitchell, the director of Glasgow Unity. That company also planned a season in Edinburgh to run at the same time as the Festival; and this turned out to be the start of the Fringe. To help with the organisation of the school I had a student on vacation from Trinity College, Dublin, Helen Hackman. When I was managing Unity Theatre, Goldington Street, I used to put a leaflet in the programmes asking people to volunteer to help in the work of the theatre either backstage or front of house. In that way I met Helen and my future wife, Eileen Mawson, who volunteered to help by illustrating an internal bulletin that we circulated to our members. The bulletin was duplicated, and Eileen illustrated it by drawing on the stencils with a stylo, exactly as we had done with the *Smoke* magazine years before. The Unity Play Service Scripts were produced in the same way. I remember Eileen's appearance the first time we met. She was wearing a black tailored costume and, although she had wonderfully bushy brown hair, she gave the appearance of fantastic efficiency. My memory has always been that she described herself on the form as being 'A Company Director', which she denies. She was, in fact, one of six partners in a pottery in Southwark, so perhaps she put herself down as 'Partner'. We didn't get together right away, but that is when we first met, and after that we kept in touch with each other, both through our work at Unity and through Eileen's work as a designer of sets for North West London Unity.

The formation of a professional company and the expansion of Unity took place against a background of fierce argument basically between Ted and a group of Unity members who had been there in pre-war days. The arguments were on two fronts, organisational and political/artistic. Colin Chambers, in his history of Unity, quotes a good example of the differences: 'The battles within Unity intensified as pre-war veterans were demobbed; threatened prestige, the burden of previous sacrifice and genuine political and artistic disagreement came together in opposition to Ted's plan and spilled over into conflicts concerning the running of Goldington Street. When Ted, for example, directed *Juno and the Paycock*, a strong body of opinion felt that it was too pessimistic, showing the working class as divided and weak just after winning the most important war of modern times and that had put socialism on the agenda across Europe. Ted had made his position clear. 'A great play,' he said, 'can never be untimely or out of date' and, with reference to the professional company, 'we do not intend to repay the Labour Movement and the working class for their support by putting on plays which make propaganda for their point of view in a narrow sense or which portray the working class as a class of angels . . . '

Alec and I supported Ted in most of these fights. He saw that the new times presented new opportunities for making a leap forward in the theatre in this country and that Unity could play a leading part in this. This leading role was performed very successfully through the medium of *New Theatre* magazine, but Unity Theatre at Goldington Street had neither the financial nor the artistic resources to become a successful professional theatre. Given an auditorium as small as Unity's (300 seats) it is doubtful if anyone could run a professional theatre without subsidy. Unity had no subsidy, but also no really first rate directors and not a very strong company of actors. Certainly they had nothing like the artistic strength of Glasgow Unity when it turned professional, and even so, Glasgow was only able to keep going for four or five years, the last years only sporadically.

Ted's fault was not that he was devious in organisation, nor that his ideas on a suitable repertoire for Unity were wrong, but that he was over-enthusiastic and inexperienced as a man of the theatre. Alec and I were the same. The heady atmosphere of the time resulting from victory in the war and the Labour victory at the polls, taken together with our arrogance as young Marxists (we thought that with Marxism as our guide there was nothing we could not do) led us to make the kind of mistakes that wisdom and experience could have avoided.

After their first production, Eugene O'Neill's *All God's Children Got Wings*, the Professional Company staged the British premiere of another American play, *Casey Jones* by Robert Ardrey, author of the successful *Thunder Rock*. The third piece, *The Shepherd and the Hunter*, was the first new play produced. It was written by David Martin, literary editor of *Reynolds News* and was set in Palestine in the 1940's where Martin had worked on a kibbutz. The play made a plea for Arab Jewish friendship. None of these productions did well at the box office. The fourth was yet another American play, *Boy Meets Girl* by Bella and Sam Spewack, a satire on Hollywood. This did a little better, and Ted Willis followed it with the professional company's greatest success, a revival of Sean O'Casey's *The Star Turns Red*. A success by Unity's previous box office standards, but not good enough to save the company from financial disaster. After the O'Casey, the Company went on a tour of the South Wales coalfields sponsored by the South Wales Miners' Union and the Arts Council. The play they took was Clifford Odets' *Golden Boy*, which the Group Theatre had brought to London so brilliantly before the war. *Golden Boy* came back for a short run at Goldington Street and then, by May 1947, the professional company collapsed, leaving debts of about £3,000, a tidy sum for the theatre to find. During the period of the professional company's brief existence, I had had nothing to do with artistic decisions. My main work was to obtain block bookings, party bookings of blocks of seats by organisations affiliated to Unity. We got 75 of them for *The Star Turns Red*. I was also trying, as far as I could, to heal the rifts amongst the theatre personnel. When I was not applying myself to the routine work of running the theatre, I was attending an endless succession of meetings. Membership meetings, meetings of the management committee, meetings of the Communist Party members working in Unity. These meetings never seemed to change anyone's mind but were extremely bad tempered and passionate. Ted, Alec and I wanted to give Unity a broader appeal, but Unity's most loyal supporters tended to be the Communist Party branches and individual members who wanted the old Unity Theatre's sharper, leftist political line. We thought it had been right in the political situation before the war but it did not take account of the new situation in which the Communist Party gave critical support to the Labour Government. Perhaps if the artistic standard had been higher, the audience would have responded to the broader policy and the dissident members might have been won round. That was the hope but it did not happen. Ted Willis had been in pursuit of a dream: the dream of a permanent company with a united approach to acting and production, playing in a repertoire of social significance, presented to a broad public not limited by the expense of seats or inhibited by social habit. It was a dream shared by many of the people I was to meet during the course of my life in the theatre, many of whom made attempts to make it a reality. In my experience, Ted was the first of these.

In August 1947, Ted Willis and I went to the World Youth Peace Festival in Prague, invited by the Czechs to study Czech theatre. When we arrived we found that most of the regular theatre companies were away for the summer so instead we went to see the many international companies that had gathered there. Most of these had very little relevance to our own work, being folk song and dance companies, the most outstanding of which was the Mongolian troupe. We did, however, see a quite conventional Czech production of *The Importance of Being Earnest* at the Realist Theatre and were taken to a castle in the country, where Emil Burian, the country's outstanding theatre man, was rehearsing his company in a new play without benefit of costumes or clothes of any kind. It is my most vivid memory of our visit.

Returning from Prague, I went straight up to Edinburgh to our Summer School and the Festival and then went to St. Ives for my first holiday with Eileen.

Whilst I was up at the Unity Theatre Summer School in Edinburgh, Robert Mitchell, the Director of the Glasgow Unity Theatre, asked me if I would take on the job of General Manager of the Glasgow professional company. This company had been formed the previous April, it had secured the backing of the Scottish Arts Council and had made a brilliant start by presenting a new Glaswegian play, *The Gorbals Story*, by Robert McLeish, which had been an enormous popular success at the Queens Theatre, Glasgow, an old music hall theatre where it had played for five packed weeks. The run had to end only because the theatre was already booked for pantomime. Then Glasgow Unity, after calling unsuccessfully for a Scottish Company to be invited to the first International Festival in Edinburgh in 1947, had decided to go to the Festival itself, whereupon the Arts Council had withdrawn its grant, stating that its standards had fallen, though there appears to have been no basis in the accusation. Saved at the last minute by an anonymous businessman with a gift of £800, Glasgow Unity had gone to the Festival anyway with *The Laird O'Torwatletie* and its Glasgow version of Gorky's *The Lower Depths*. Both productions scored a tremendous artistic success and drew full houses and standing ovations throughout their stay. In a glowing tribute in *Tribune*, Miron Grindea summed up their achievement: 'By a strange set of circumstances, the most significant theatrical event [of the Festival] was sponsored by Glasgow Unity Theatre, which, although considered by some people in authority as below international festival standards, was greeted by critics and public alike as the best group of players in the Festival.' Despite this success, Glasgow Unity was faced with the difficult task of keeping a company going with no theatre of its own, no grant and no reserve funds. It needed some help, and I, after discussing the matter with my colleagues in London and securing their agreement to release me from my work there, agreed to go up to Glasgow to see what I could do.

Glasgow Unity had been formed in 1941, some years after London Unity. It did not have a theatre of its own, but in 1945 an opportunity occurred to rent the Atheneum on a semi-permanent basis. Unity took it for a season, playing every Thursday, Friday and Saturday. They also took central club rooms in Sauchiehall Street. Their first production at the Atheneum was *The Lower Depths*. It was translated by Bob Mitchell into the Glasgow idiom, the actors using their own accents and speech rhythms. 'The command of the piece was firm and sure, and play and actors merged beautifully to produce a work of force and strength.' So wrote the historian, John Hill, whose article on Glasgow Unity in *Theatre Quarterly*, Vol. VII No. 27 1977, has reminded me of much that I had forgotten. By the time I arrived in Glasgow, Unity had formed a professional company from about twenty of its members in April 1946 but had been refused further use of the Atheneum by what Hill describes as 'the perverse and probably political decision of the Governors of the Royal Scottish Academy of Music' and was once more homeless. It had discovered three new Scottish playwrights in Robert McLeish (*The Gorbals Story*), Ena Lamont Stewart (*Starched Aprons*) and the novelist James Barke (*Major Operation*). Apart from the professional company, Unity had what it called the part-time company, which played in and around Glasgow and whose members often augmented the full-time professionals. Following that first Edinburgh Festival, when I was asked to join them, the plan was to tour *The Gorbals Story* in the twice-nightly music-hall theatres and undertake a tour of the Scottish coalfields. The part timers now had in their repertoire *Men Should Weep* by Ena Lamont Stewart, a powerful play of Glasgow slum life, better structured than *The Gorbals Story*, though it was never as popular, probably because it did not have as much humour. There was also Henry Saunders' *Hell and High Water*, about a Highland village in the grip of commercialism, and Robert McLeish's second play, *A Piece of Milarkey*, a farce which failed to match the success of his first play.

Robert Mitchell was a short, thick-set man, with the face of a middle-aged cherub and with very poor eye-sight, so that he had to wear thick lenses in his spectacles. He was divorced or separated from his wife and living with Evelyn Garratt, the only non-Scottish actress in the Company. Evelyn was a Jewish girl from London with long, black, uncombed hair, very intelligent and intense. She and Bob formed a united front on all matters to be decided in Unity. Bob was an electrician by trade and during the war had been the shop stewards' convenor in one of the largest factories in Glasgow, so he was an experienced political organiser. He was also an experienced director in the amateur theatre. In Glasgow there were not quite the same intense political and artistic differences as there had been in London, although there were disagreements and jealousies. Most of the members of the professional company did not think Bob deserved the praise and recognition he was getting. Bob on his side did not seem to give full credit to the worth of the company members. Because the company was a real collective, with no stars or 'star' performances, critics were apt to say, as Miron Grindea did in his review of *The Lower Depths*, 'We cannot enumerate the players – all were excellent – but Robert Mitchell, the producer, should be congratulated . . . ' Bob became a little swollen-headed, the players a little fed up. Political questions took second place. Bob was certainly a Communist: how many others were I do not know, but somehow in Glasgow it did not seem to matter so much. Communists were just another strand of the Labour Movement, and there were certainly nothing like the same number of meetings, partly perhaps because everyone was so busy with theatre activities. There was also a better atmosphere between the full-time and the part-time players. Perhaps the very names imply this. This is not to suggest that Glasgow Unity was in any way less closely involved in the Labour Movement and its struggles than London Unity was.

When Glasgow Unity first brought *The Gorbals Story* to the Queens Theatre in Glasgow, 'The first night', says Hill, 'on 2nd September 1946 caused a storm, adroit showmanship only serving to add fuel to an already explosive play. Whilst Glasgow's Lord Provost and numerous civic and literary dignitaries sat in the stalls, above in the circle as guests of honour were a large contingent of squatters from the Glasgow suburbs, whose leader, Peter Colin Blair McIntyre, was allowed to harangue the audience from the stage before the rise of the curtain. The

play made its own bitter comment on the housing situation of the time
. . . it was not surprising that for one observer it was perhaps the nearest
Scotland has come to a riotous evening at the Abbey.'

We could not get bookings in the regular straight theatres controlled
by Howard and Wyndham and so had to play either in the twice-nightly
music-halls or in town halls and other multi-purpose buildings. In these
circumstances, it proved more and more difficult to find continuous
work for the Company. The tour of one night stands in the coalfields
was excellent work and enthusiastically received but could not be
continuous. Something more was needed. I spoke to William Galt, who
booked our company into the twice-nightly houses and asked him if he
knew of anyone in London who might be interested in taking us down
there, thinking that a success in London might open more doors to us in
Scotland. He gave me four names, all of whom I discovered later were
variety agents and therefore quite unlikely to have the contacts we
needed. However, one of them, Hymie Zahl, turned up trumps. He came
to see *The Gorbals Story* on a bitterly cold, rainy night in the small town
of Irvine, liked the production and said he would introduce me to Jack
Hylton. Hymie was as good as his word and not long after his visit I was
in Jack Hylton's London office. Hylton said he would come and see the
show if we brought it to a theatre somewhere in the North of England, so
Hymie Zahl fixed us a date in West Hartlepool. One Monday night a
month or two later, Jack Hylton sat with me in the front row of the circle
in an almost empty theatre in the god-forsaken town of West Hartlepool.
At the end of the performance he turned to me and, to my astonish-
ment – for there had been very little reaction from the sparse audience –
said, 'I'll do something with this.' And so he did.

Jack Hylton had been a famous band leader between the wars, and by
the time I met him had become one of the foremost London producers,
best known for musicals and the Crazy Gang shows, but also with a
reputation for presenting a certain type of play of the common people,
such as was not usually presented in the West End at that time. Examples were *No Room at the Inn*, a sensational story of evacuee children
and their suffering at the hands of an unscrupulous landlady, the Irish
play, *Happy as Larry*, and the black American play, *Anna Lucasta*. *The
Gorbals Story* fitted into this pattern, and Hylton was genuinely
enthusiastic about it. Despite his success, Hylton was a man who had

kept the common touch. He was not patronising to the bunch of scruffy ex-amateurs he was going to bring to London, nor, although he was an exceedingly hard businessman, was he tough on this occasion. He gave us a very fair, not to say generous deal, which guaranteed us against any loss, gave us an assured small profit and a larger profit if we were a success. On 19 February 1948, 'by arrangement with Jack Hylton and Jack Buchanan', the Glasgow Unity Theatre presented *The Gorbals Story* by Robert McLeish, at the Garrick Theatre in the heart of London's West End, the first Scottish repertory theatre to perform a Scottish play in the West End. The notices were excellent for the Company but rather mixed for the play, which did not surprise us, since most of the Glasgow Unity people realised that the play, whilst having considerable virtues in the way of good dialogue and lively characters, was rather formless and without the depth or poetic quality of *Juno and the Paycock*, a play in a similar milieu. Alan Dent in the *News Chronicle* was enthusiastic, writing: 'Playgoers who are – as they should be, a little weary of The Mayfair Story, The Chelsea Story and the Home Counties Story – should go to see Mr. McLeish's play and get a profound shock and a strange thrill. For this is Glasgow, the slummy, swarming core of it, presented with honesty, frankness and verisimilitude.

'A baby is born. Its mother dies. A young unmarried couple make love. Young married couples seek a home, hopelessly. An old drunk comes close to fortune and then discovers he has forgotten to post his pools coupons. Nothing – as we say – happens. It is all a mere matter of life and death.

'But let me declare that the middle hour of this play, the heart of it – after its slow beginning and before its arbitrary conclusion – is the very stuff of human drama.

'This is the music of humanity, not still and sad as the poet declared it, but rich, raucous, clamant, tingling, coarse and thwarted. There is no sentimentality here. Its sheer avoidance makes the single love-scene all the more poignant.

'The pair envisage that halcyon impossibility, a home of their own. The young tough (with his razor in his pocket) is drunk enough to imagine a kettle on the bile, a big orange ca-at pur-r-r-rin' awa by the fi-ire. And repudiation of the vision comes not from the boy but from the girl: Ach awa' man, and doan't be da-aft!

'These middle scenes have a throbbing interblend of comedy and tragedy. Howard Connell is the funniest stage-drunk since Arthur Sinclair's Paycock. And I should think there has been nothing quite like the violent true-Glasgow dialect heard on the London stage ever before. It is delivered with gusto by the brilliant Glasgow Unity Players. It made first-night ears quiver, eyes pop and boiled shirts wilt. And anyone who imagines this dialect to be overdone should be told that, on the contrary, it has been considerably toned down for London consumption.

'Robert Mitchell's production is worthy of his matter. He is imaginative with his lighting and his noises off, and suggests a whole world elsewhere with his static stair-head objects – a pram (for human felicity in the most overcrowded life), a bicycle (for the rare prospect of freedom and clean air).'

But *The Times* wrote a patronising notice saying: 'It has been interesting to have this view of the work of the Glasgow Unity Theatre. Their accomplishment is not always equal to their ambition, but two or three performances are promising – Miss Betty Henderson's (more than promising) as the unattractive lady, Miss Marjorie Thompson's as the humorous old lady who has seen better days and intends to see them again and Mr. Russell Hunter's as the newsboy. Every one is inclined to shout, perhaps for fear of not being heard in a large theatre.'

Whilst *The Observer*, after giving a good account of the play, could not resist a snobbish Southern English comment: 'English ears – indeed any ears unused to the havoc that Glasgow makes of decent Scottish speech – will find some of it difficult, but none of it is dull.'

The audience response was good but the word got around that the dialect was difficult to understand and it certainly required a little more attention on the part of the audience than the West End was accustomed to give. The result was that business did not keep up and the play had to be taken off at the end of seven weeks.

During our run at the Garrick we met Anthony Hawtrey, a well known actor and director, who ran the Embassy Theatre, Swiss Cottage. Hawtrey was always on the look out for good new plays, some of which he hoped to transfer to the West End. *No Room at the Inn* had started in this way. Tony Hawtrey liked our production and invited us to do a season of plays at the Embassy. So in the spring and summer of 1948, we presented there a season consisting of a revival of *The Gorbals Story*, our other Scottish plays, *Men Should Weep*, *Starched Aprons* and *The Laird O' Torwatletie* and added a production of *Juno and the Paycock*, after which we toured *The Gorbals Story* in England and Scotland. But now, impressed by our London showing, the Howard and Wyndham circuit was open to us and we played in the number one theatres where we had never played before.

This production of *Juno and the Paycock* brought me in touch for the first time with one of the neglected giants of contemporary theatre. It was an unfortunate start to our relationship, because O'Casey didn't want to confirm the permission his agents had given us to do the play and, in the the end, quite unfairly, made us pay a very high royalty. However, this production led to our meeting and Eileen and I became firm friends of the O'Caseys, visiting them from time to time at their house in Devon. Later, after Sean died, I continued to be in contact with his family - with his daughter Siobhan, who became an actress and also an antique dealer, with Breon, who became a brilliant jeweller and with Eileen O'Casey, who wrote so gracefully several books of memoirs of her years with Sean. Apart from his first three great plays, *Juno and The Paycock*, *The Plough and the Stars* and *The Shadow of a Gunman*, O'Casey has remained a neglected playwright in this country. On the occasion of the centenary of his birth, I tried to arrange for productions of some of his later plays but only succeeded in arranging splendid productions of *Juno* and *The Shadow of a Gunman*, both produced by the Royal Shakespeare Company. The Court produced *Cock A Doodle Dandy* in 1959, probably his best late play, but it was not a success, and has not been revived.

Before reaching the Garrick we had run up a considerable debt, mostly owed to printers. This weighed heavily upon us and we were only paying it off very slowly. Following *The Laird O' Torwatletie* at the Embassy, which was even more difficult for the English to follow than *The Gorbals Story*, since it was in a kind of pastiche of eighteenth-century Scots, we returned to Scotland playing the Howard and Wyndham's Glasgow theatres, the Royal and the Kings, to enormous audiences. But alas, Scottish law allows creditors to take all a company's share of the box office takings (less only that needed to pay the salaries,) with the result that, although our debts were reduced, our day-to-day cashflow problems remained.

And whilst we toured, we were preparing a new production to present at the end of the 1949 Edinburgh Festival. This was *The Flowers O'Edinburgh*, another play by Robert McLellan, author of *The Laird O' Torwatletie*, a comedy set in 18th-century Edinburgh concerning the Scots gentry's dilemma in deciding whether to speak English or Scots. It was not ideally suited to the company's talents and was not a success. Touring was resumed – mainly with *The Gorbals Story* – but on the one hand the company was becoming dissatisfied with this life and on the other hand individual members were getting offers of work elsewhere. During all this time the members of the company had been receiving a top salary of £10 per week plus a touring allowance: it was increasingly more difficult for them to make ends meet.

Nonetheless we pressed on with another new production mounted by the full-time company and directed as usual by Bob Mitchell: *The Lambs of God* by Benedict Scott. Set in the town of Dromnouil in Central Scotland in the 1930's, it was a sensitive and often poetic treatment of homosexuality. It was seen and liked by Jack Hylton and, with the title changed to *This Walking Shadow* and Freda Jackson joining the Glasgow cast in an important role, it was presented at the Playhouse Theatre in the West End on 29th June 1949. But it was not a financial success and came off after a short run.

Through an understanding between the Jewish Institute Players and Glasgow Unity, there had been a tradition of doing Jewish/American progressive plays, such as *Awake and Sing* by Clifford Odets and *Morning Star* by Sylvia Regan. Now, between productions of plays with the full-time company, we began to put on professional performances of some of these Jewish plays in London. The Embassy was an excellent base for this and our first such production was *Morning Star* under a new title *The Golden Door*. For this we assembled a fine cast of Jewish actors, including Alfie Bass from London Unity, and Meier Tzelniker from the Yiddish Theatre in the East End in his first English-speaking part. I introduced Meier to Bob Mitchell, having seen him play Shylock at the Yiddish Theatre and now, for the first time, I began to take more of a share in the artistic decisions of the company. The play was directed by Bob Mitchell and designed by two of our regular Glasgow Unity designers, Helen Biggar and Eli Montlake. Helen had also designed for London Unity.

This play, set on the East side of New York between the years 1910 and 1931, was a Jewish family saga inspired by Odets' early plays, in the same way that our Glasgow Unity Scottish slum plays had been inspired by O'Casey. It opened at the Embassy on 21st September 1949 and ran for a record 16 weeks.

After this the original Glasgow Unity company all took part in the film of *The Gorbals Story*. It was basically a film of the play, shot with little imagination, and did little justice to the original. It was an opportunity lost, its only virtue from the point of view of Glasgow Unity being that it provided a little money for the organisation and the members of the company. Bob did not direct the film and bore no responsibility for its failure.

The Gentle People by Irwin Shaw, another play originally produced by the American Group Theatre, was our next production. Meier Tzelniker and Alfie Bass were back with us again, acting the two old friends who are the centre of the play. Playing with us as the Jewish daughter was the brilliant black actress, Hilda Simms, who had been the star of *Anna Lucasta*. I thought she was fine in the part but I remember some people being worried by a black woman playing a Jewess. However, this was not an early example of colour-blind casting, since Hilda Simms was a very pale skinned black woman and it required very little imagination on the part of the audience to accept her as Jewish. It was a fine play, well done, and appreciated by the audience, but did not do sufficient business to make a transfer to the West End possible.

I was then able to set up a season of three Jewish plays at the Saville Theatre, London under the auspices of Bernard Delfont and Ben Kanter, and with their financial guarantee. The first play was *Spring Song* by Bella and Samuel Spewack, who had written *Boy Meets Girl*, already staged by the London Unity professional company. The second play was *The King of the Schnorrers* by the famous Jewish writer Israel Zangwill and the third play was Clifford Odets' *Awake and Sing*. The company was assembled with the deliberate intention that as many as possible could play in all three plays; some played in two and some in one. *Spring Song* opened on 4th September 1950 and ran for four weeks. It was the most popular play of the three, being another Jewish family play set on the East side of New York, similar in feeling to *The Golden Door*. *The King of the Schnorrers* was a play set in London's Jewry towards the end of the

18th century. It had a large cast and was really beyond the resources of our company and our director. Ernest Milton gave a remarkable performance but that didn't save it, for apart from our own deficiencies, it was not the kind of play that our audience wanted from us. They wanted realistic plays dealing with the problems of contemporary life. *The King of the Schnorrers* was a sort of Jewish *School for Scandal*. It was expensive and only ran three weeks. Then *Awake and Sing* opened, the finest play in the group. It is probably Clifford Odets' best play, but the audience preferred the more sentimental *Spring Song*.

Glasgow Unity was nearing its end. Still weighed down by its debts, with the company more and more difficult to keep together, tours of the *The Gorbals Story* continued in Scotland with part-timers joining available full-timers to make up the cast. In May 1951 at the Embassy Theatre we presented an extremely interesting New York Jewish play by H.S. Kraft. It was called Café Crown and it was set in the real café next to the stage door of the Yiddish Theatre on the East side of New York. It had a warm reception and a respectable run at the Embassy, i.e., three weeks and that was that. We followed it with a production of Ibsen's *Ghosts*. This was a play that had been produced by the part-timers in Glasgow, but our production really had nothing to do with Glasgow Unity beyond the fact that Bob directed it and I was the General Manager. We had a strong cast: Beatrix Lehmann, President of Equity and a long-time supporter of London Unity as Mrs. Alving, John Ruddock as Jacob Engstrand, Frederick Valk, a friend of Unity's and of its magazine, *New Theatre*, as Pastor Manders, Douglas Montgomery, a star American actor, as Oswald and the leading Irish actress of the day, Siobhan McKenna, as Regina. I had seen Siobhan in *Fading Mansions* and urged Bob to let me try to get her for our production. He was quite happy about this but it was very difficult to persuade her. She didn't know anything about us or the quality of our work. I have never thought of myself as being particularly good at persuading people to do something, however, I was determined to have Siobhan in our play, and eventually I was successful. We remained good friends and worked together again several times in the future. We had hoped that *Ghosts* would be the sort of success that might transfer and make some money for Glasgow Unity. Alas, it was not to be. Ibsen was not box office then, even with the strong cast we had assembled, and we quickly had to bring in *Arms and the Man* to the Embassy. Although this was billed as being presented by Glasgow Unity, it had nothing at all to do with us, and was not even directed by Bob Mitchell. It must have been brought in to fulfil our contract with the theatre.

Robert Mitchell and I decided to part company after the production of *Ghosts*. Up to that time we had still hoped to keep Glasgow Unity going and to be able to return to Scotland and work with our company there. Now, without a subsidy and without a theatre, and with debts on the one hand and the company more and more dispersed, we realised that it was hopeless, at any rate for the time being. Meanwhile, many members of Glasgow Unity did not understand the situation and criticised us for not returning to Glasgow. I, for my part, did not feel that there was a place for me any longer in Glasgow Unity. Instead I wanted to find a way of working in the theatre in London. I thought Bob should return to Scotland and continue to work in Glasgow Unity if he could, or elsewhere in the theatre in Scotland if he could not. Bob, however, saw himself as an important director who could work as a freelance any-where in England. I did not want to be tied to him on that basis, so we went our separate ways, although from time to time over the next few years we came together to collaborate on particular productions at the Embassy.

Ghosts was produced in June 1951. Three years earlier I had been given the job I had applied for whilst waiting to be demobbed, that of Editor of the *New Theatre* magazine. This magazine had been re-launched by Unity Theatre in April 1946 with Elkan Allan as its editor. After two issues, Ted Willis had taken over as editor, and from that time for the next two years he and Alec Bernstein had between them edited the magazine very successfully. It became the leading theatre magazine of its time. Unity Theatre had transferred its ownership to an independent, non-profit distributing Company, the directors of which were Alec Bernstein, Patricia Burke, Peter Copley, Beatrix Lehmann, Peter Ustinov and Ted Willis. Most of the leading theatre personalities of the day wrote for it: in one issue, for example, we find articles written by J.B.Priestley, Michael Redgrave, Tyrone Guthrie, Peter Brook, Clifford Odets and George Devine; whilst in the same issue Paul Rotha, Jill Craigie and Ralph Bond discussed the future of documentary film. However, by November 1948, Alec Bernstein, under the name of Alexander Baron, had written his first novel, *From the City, From the Plough,* probably the finest novel about the ordinary infantryman to come out of World War II. Alec gave up full-time work on the magazine to concentrate on his writing.

Ted Willis' career as a writer had also begun to take off and his play, *No Trees in the Street,* directed by Basil Dean and starring Beatrix Lehmann, had opened at the St.James' Theatre in the West End in July. Ted had therefore asked me if I could combine my work for Glasgow Unity with editing the magazine, and, since most of my work at that time was involved in arranging tours or seasons for Glasgow Unity, many of them in London, I agreed. I did so at a difficult time. Just after the war it was easy to sell any well illustrated magazine, but by 1948 this was no longer the case. The economic problems of the country and the cold war changed the whole situation, and it was now a struggle to keep the magazine afloat, even though it continued to have the same high standard of contributors and the same support from the profession. For instance, in our April 1949 issue, which was centred on the American Theatre, Paul Robeson discussed the social background with Alexander Baron, Arthur Miller wrote on 'The American Scene', Helen Hayes wrote on 'Thirty Years of the Theatre Guild' and Rosamund Gilder reported on The Broadway Season. John Gielgud, Frederick Valk and Alec Guiness wrote short pieces in reply to Brecht's article in the previous issue. Arthur Miller wrote on 'Tragedy and the Common Man' and Hugh MacDiarmid on 'O'Casey's Farewell to Ireland'.

New Theatre not only provided a forum in which theatre artists could discuss theory and practice, it also advanced a constructive policy for the theatre of the day. But it did not last. The issue dated July 1949 carried an editorial which said 'After a three year battle against under-capitalisation, rising costs and shrinking income from advertisements, we are forced to make an unwelcome retreat.' At that time we hoped to continue as a quarterly, but we were never able to do this. Since the death of *New Theatre,* there have been other magazines that have attempted to do the same job, in particular *Encore,* which came out in the fifties and sixties. Nothing like it exists today, though with the new printing technology available I should have thought it possible. Is there no one around waiting to have a go?

I had come back to London with *The Gorbals Story* in February 1948 and returned to my flat in South Hill Park Gardens, where Eileen and I began our life-long partnership.

I must take up the thread of my story where I left it off in July 1951, after Bob and I had agreed to go our separate ways. For the year from 1st July 1951 to July 10th 1952, I worked on a rather unsatisfactory basis for Tony Hawtrey at the Embassy. Tony was an extraordinary man. A talented actor and director, he lived like a lord without any visible means of supporting such a life style. Indeed his life see-sawed between going to the races in his Bentley and dodging the bailiffs, who were always about to occupy the Embassy. Having lived all my adult life with a father who was on the verge of bankruptcy, and working for London Unity, Glasgow Unity and the *New Theatre*, all of which were rather in the same position, I felt quite at home at the Embassy. Even when we had put on our season of Jewish plays at the Saville Theatre, guaranteed by Bernard Delfont, I found myself in the same situation, sitting for hours in Bernard's office waiting for the money that was due to us and which I urgently needed but which Bernard clearly had not got himself. Bernard, like all these people, like my father, like Hawtrey, was so charming that he got away with murder. Tony Hawtrey ran the Embassy using various non-profit distributing companies, so that he did not have to pay entertainment tax. However, doing it this way meant that he could not simply treat the box office takings as his own, but it was difficult to get him to understand this. It was his habit to go into the box office, grab hold of any takings that were available and go racing with them. It was always his intention to replace any deficiency when the time came, and on balance he was probably subsidising the theatre himself more than it was subsidising him. But it was not possible to know for certain. I found it very difficult to accept Tony's way of working. I also suffered personally from it, because I could never rely upon receiving whatever it was had been arranged between us, which in any case was not very much. I'm not sure how I got through that year financially but I do know that at the end of it, when Eileen and I decided to get married, we were absolutely broke and had to borrow £50 from Ted Willis to enable us to go on our honeymoon to the South of France.

(*Above left*) My paternal grandfather

(*Above right*) My father

(*Below*) My mother with my sister Natalie, my brother Paul and myself c. 1925

(*Above left*) Myself on leave from the army, 1942

(*Centre*) Myself and Eileen, 1953

(*Below*) Ted Willis as a young man with his Labour
League of Youth badge c. 1937

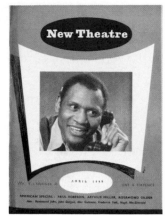

(*Above left*) Robert Mitchell

(*Above right*) Cover for *New Theatre* April, 1941 featuring Paul Robeson

(*Below*) *Women of Twilight* Rene Ray (l) Miriam Karlin (r)

(*Below right*) Cover for *Smoke* No. 1, September 1941

(*Opposite page, above*) Wolf Mankowitz and me, 1959

(*Centre*) John Craxton's front cloth for *The World of Sholem Aleichem*

(*Below left*) Original programme cover for *Mother Courage*

(*Below right*) Orson Welles in *Moby Dick*

(*This page, above*) *The Party* Elsa Lanchester, Charles Laughton and Joyce Redman

(*Below*) *Look Back in Anger* with Kenneth Haigh and Mary Ure

(*This page, above*) *A Taste of Honey* Murray Melvin and Frances Cuka

(*Below*) *The Long and the Short and the Tall* Kenji Takaki, Peter O'Toole and Alfred Lynch

(*Opposite page, above*) *Rhinoceros* Laurence Olivier and Duncan Macrae

(*Below*) *The Hostage, (facing camera left to right*) Yootha Joyce, Eileen Kennally, Howard Goorney, (kneeling) Celia Sulkeld

(*Above*) **Albert** Finney as *Billy Liar*

(*Below*) Promoting *Billy Liar*

During the year, my task was to find plays suitable for production at the Embassy. I found a few, the most interesting and successful being *Women of Twilight*, a play about a home for unmarried mothers, run by a monstrous woman who exploited them. This play was written by a young woman, Sylvia Rayman, who worked in a milk bar in Swiss Cottage near the Embassy, which is where I found her. The rights she had already sold or leased to a well known actress, Jean Shepherd, who ran a small repertory theatre somewhere in South London. Jean was reluctant to let us have the rights, but eventually I was able to make a deal with her. Tony was enthusiastic and decided to direct the play himself. He got a strong cast, all women, most of whom had worked at the Embassy before, either for him or for Glasgow Unity. The play opened on 15th October 1951 and it went down well with critics and public alike. We made a deal with Jack Hylton and he transferred the play to the Vaudeville on 7th November. It was then revived the following year and, again under Jack Hylton's banner, was presented on 18th June 1952 at the Victoria Palace, with Freda Jackson now playing the leading role and some other small changes in the cast.

On 27th December 1951 we put on *The Merchant of Yonkers* by Thornton Wilder. It was excellently directed by André Van Gyseghem, well cast with Robert Edison, Martin Miller, Sophie Stewart, Alfie Bass, Jessie Evans, Peter Baylis and Nigel Hawthorne, and got completely panned by the critics. Some years later under the new title, *The Match Maker*, it was a smash hit in the West End and an even bigger hit as the musical *Hello Dolly!*. I suppose our timing must have been wrong but I couldn't understand the critics' reaction, blind and foolish though I already knew them to be.

One day Sam Wanamaker, who had had an important success in London with Clifford Odets' *Winter Journey*, phoned me and said he'd seen a wonderful production in a basement in Manchester, which he and Michael Redgrave wanted to bring into the Embassy for a few weeks. This production was Theatre Workshop's *Uranium 235* by Ewan MacColl, directed by Joan Littlewood. Thus I met this extraordinary theatre group, many of whom became my friends in the years that followed. The play opened on 12th May 1952. I agreed with Sam about its quality and introduced Gerry Raffles, the manager of the company, to the owner of the Comedy Theatre in the West End, to which

Uranium 235 transferred. This was Theatre Workshop's first visit to the West End. At that time, they were a touring company without a home of their own.

A few weeks later when Eileen and I were married and returning from our honeymoon in the South of France I learned that the recently opened Royal Court Theatre Club was looking for an Artistic Director. The rest you know. I go back now to the time when, after serving as the English Stage Company's General Manager, I returned to producing plays in the West End with Wolf Mankowitz.

Part Four

The Long and the Short and the Tall

with Wolf Mankowitz in the West End

We were back to being West End producers again, but right back where we started from, having lost our original backers. On my leaving full-time work at the Royal Court, Wolf – who amongst his other activities was a literary adviser to Columbia Pictures – got me a part-time job with Columbia advising them on plays that might make good film material. I do not recall them ever taking my advice, but they paid me a small retainer which was useful. Whilst we were both working with Columbia and wondering about our next production, we found a play, *The Deserters*, by a young American writer, Thadeus Vane, for which Columbia agreed to put up all the capital in exchange for an option to buy the film rights. It is the only play that I have ever produced that I really regret doing.

We had an American director, Alan Schneider, who later became important as Beckett's director in New York. We had a very decent cast headed by Elizabeth Sellars. And yet the play, which was about an American deserter in World War II being hidden by some nuns, was totally clichéd without any of the qualities which both Wolf and I looked for in a play. Why did we do it? I think we were too anxious to get going again. Hunger for activity made us blind to the play's faults, though that does not explain why Schneider and Elizabeth Sellars both fell for it too. We took it on tour, realised we had laid a rotten egg and quietly dropped it off the end of the Pier after a week at the Theatre Royal,

Brighton. Some people thought we should have brought it into London but I am sure we were right to abandon it.

Thadeus Vane was a curious case. I read several other plays by him. Each was entirely different from the others. None was completely without talent. Sometimes I wondered if he was a ghost putting his name on other writers' scripts. I never heard of any of the other plays being produced.

So far this has been a tale of commercial failure, but now our luck started to change. Wolf had written the book for a musical, *Expresso Bongo*, about a pop singer and his manager. It was 1958, not long after the start of the careers of a new breed of working-class pop stars singing rock and roll. Monty Norman and David Heneker wrote the music and, with Julian More, the lyrics. It was a bigger show than we had produced before, a medium sized musical with a cast of about 25. Again we found a partner in Neil Crawford of Strand Productions to produce it with us and find half the required capital. Billy Chappell, who had worked with us on *Moby Dick* was signed to direct, and a fine cast was assembled led by Paul Scofield. We were using Wolf's office in Piccadilly Arcade as our headquarters, and I remember Paul coming into the office there and signing his contract very quickly, as if he didn't want to hesitate for fear of changing his mind. In fact, during the years that followed I found that if Paul did not say 'yes' almost immediately, he invariably said 'no'.

Paul played the pop star's agent, Jimmy Kenny the pop singer. Millicent Martin, in her first leading part in the West End, played Paul's girl friend. Other important parts were played by old friends from Unity days: Meier Tzelniker, Hilda Fennemore and George Tovey. Victor Spinetti and Susan Hampshire appeared for the first time in the West End, and Charles Gray and Hy Hazell were also there in important roles. We opened at the Saville Theatre on 23rd April 1958. The first half was a triumph, the second half a disappointment. I think Wolf and Billy Chappell, and probably the rest of us, had not been critical enough on the short tour. The musical, which had a tough, cynical flavour, not a little influenced by *The Threepenny Opera* and probably by such American musicals as *Guys and Dolls* and *Pal Joey*, had some good, sour songs, such as one that went 'Nothing is for nothing, nothing is for free, I'll look after you Jack, you look after me.' It played for nine months, almost breaking even, and was made into a film, though not by us, starring Laurence Harvey and Cliff Richard.

Then came our first commercial success. Renée Goddard, who had let me down with rather a bump in Berlin, was sharing a house in Hampstead with Philip Saville and his then-wife, Jane Arden. Jane had written a play which Renée persuaded her to show me. I thought it had some good writing and some good parts and was worth doing. Bob Fenn, of MCA, was agent for the play, and one day, after we had taken an option, a script was on Bob's desk when Charles Laughton came in to see him. Charles noticed the script, asked if he could read it, and I think to everyone's amazement, fell in love with it. He wanted to direct the play and appear in its leading part. The play was called *The Party* and concerned the homecoming of a father who had been in a mental hospital after having a breakdown, just before his daughter's birthday party. It had excellent parts for the daughter, played by Ann Lynn, and her boy friend, introducing the young Albert Finney to the West End stage. Charles and I had heard about this young actor, who was said to be doing great things at the Birmingham Rep and we went up to see him as Macbeth. In the play he was covered with whiskers, but when Charles and I went round to his dressing room after the performance and the whiskers came off, there was this marvellous young actor revealed to us. We both had no doubts, and when the play opened, Albert's big scene with Charles was the success of the evening. But that comes later.

There is no doubt that Charles over-estimated the play and the ability of its author. It needed work on it; this Charles realised but he could not get Jane to do what he wanted. Jane knew how much Charles respected her talent, and treated him as badly as the girl in the play treats her father, making him dance attendance on her. We went on a short tour before coming into London. Whilst we were in Manchester. Jackie Squire, a young member of our company, knowing of Laughton's great interest in painting, introduced him to the Manchester working-class painter, Alan Lowndes. Charles invited him to go up to his hotel and take some pictures with him, but the hotel thought Alan was a down-and-out and would not admit him. Later Charles bought quite a few of his paintings and introduced him to Sydney Bernstein and other friends, who also became patrons. Alan painted scenes of working-class life in Manchester and Salford, somewhat influenced by Lowry. Later he moved to St. Ives.

At the time of *The Party*, Charles' great enthusiasm was for the Post War School of Paris abstract painters, such as De Stael, Menessier and Soulages, and often in his dressing room as he waited to go on, he would talk to me about them and their work. I have not known any other actor in whose life painting played so important a part.

Charles Laughton, who was a very sensitive and sophisticated man could also be very childish. Going with him and Elsa Lanchester, who was also in the play, from Newcastle to Liverpool, we stopped on the way at a ruined Abbey, which was a tourist beauty spot. Whilst we were walking in the grounds, Charles complained that he could not go anywhere without being recognised. But after a while, when nobody took the slightest bit of notice of him, he began to pull faces and do all sorts of things to draw attention to himself. Charles was amazingly thin-skinned. He could be hurt more easily than anyone I have ever known and so he was not easy to work with, but on the whole we worked and got on well together. On a bad day Charles said that the only good thing about me was my wife. Just as he loved paintings, he enjoyed pottery, and Eileen as a potter started with a distinct advantage.

The Party opened at the New Theatre (now the Albery), at about the same time as Harold Pinter's first play *The Birthday Party*, opened at the Lyric Theatre, Hammersmith. Pinter had originally called his play *The Party*. He changed the name to avoid confusion with our play. At the time our *Party* received a moderately good welcome, whilst Pinter's *Birthday Party* was slated by the critics. Today *The Birthday Party* is considered to be a modern classic whilst *The Party* remains of interest only because of Laughton's and Finney's appearance in it. It ran for seven months, making us our first profit. Ken Tynan thought that Laughton had killed it in the same way that Steinbeck's Lennie killed the mouse. He did, however, add, 'Mr. Finney, playing Miss Lynn's boyfriend, shares the best scene of the evening with Mr. Laughton, who rises like a salmon to the occasion; few young actors have ever got a better performance out of their director.'

Charles continued to have faith in the play and I have a letter from him written in October 1958, when the run was almost over, showing that he was still hoping that Jane would re-write so that he could do it in New York. She never did, nor could she. On the whole I am sure that writers refuse to re-write because they cannot, not because they are unwilling. Sometimes they cannot because they have said all they have to say, or because time has gone by and the subject cannot be revived in their imagination, and sometimes it is because the nature of the work is such that the re-writing requested is not organic, does not belong to it, and the one who wants the re-writing has not understood the nature of the original work. Jane could not, rather than would not, make the changes Charles asked for.

After the run of The Party, Charles made a film, Spartacus, and then went to Stratford-upon-Avon to play Bottom in Midsummer Night's Dream and Lear. Albert Finney went with him. There was a great bond between these two actors, and it was at Charles' suggestion according to Elsa that Glen Byam Shaw engaged Albert for the Stratford season, where he scored a considerable success.

Charles was an admirer of Brecht and had written to New Theatre magazine in May 1949 saying 'I am very happy to hear of your great interest in Bertolt Brecht, who is in my view the most important living theatrical figure'. And he offered to demonstrate Brecht's ideas to 'any group you could get together' on his next visit to London. Unfortunately, by the time he came, the magazine had been defunct for nine years and I had forgotten his offer. Laughton had translated Galileo with Brecht in 1947 and played the part in Los Angeles and New York in a production directed by Brecht and Joe Losey. Brecht and his circle admired Charles greatly and it is an enormous pity that his performance in Galileo was never seen in London. Despite our production of The Threepenny Opera and the English Stage Company's Good Woman of Setzuan and the 1956 visit of the Berliner Ensemble to London and Paris, which influenced so many of our theatre workers, London was not yet ready to put on major Brecht productions. Only the R.S.C. and the National have the necessary means, and neither of these companies had yet been formed.

Following the disaster of Joan Littlewood's production of Mother Courage, my relationship with Joan Littlewood and Gerry Raffles was not close. I found it difficult to forgive them for the way they had treated Karl Weber, Brecht's assistant, and for their failure to discuss with us both their problems and proposals regarding the production. However, all this was forgotten and forgiven when in May 1958 I went down to the Theatre Royal, Stratford, East London, and saw Joan's production of Shelagh Delaney's play. A Taste of Honey. This play made a wonderfully fresh and original impact on the audience. It tells the story of Jo, a young girl, her mother Helen, described as a semi-whore, Peter the mother's lover, Jo's lover, a young Negro who deserts her and Geoffrey, a young homosexual who looks after Jo when she becomes pregnant. All these characters have been created by the author without an ounce of sentimentality. They are funny, alive and kicking from start to finish, both in their conception and in their realisation in Joan's production. It has been said that a certain amount of the play was created in production. I do not know how much of the original was in the final script and I do not think it matters. Author, director and cast had worked together to create a joyful evening from a story that in other hands might have been tragic. The author was a 19-year-old working-class girl from Salford. I went into the New Theatre the next day full of this great evening, and bumping into Donald Albery on the steps of the theatre which he owned, I told him about it and said how much I would like to bring it into the West End. That led to him going to see it and proposing that we presented it together in the West End, which is what we did.

In 1959 Wolf and I presented four productions in the West End, all of them at Albery theatres. Three of these were directed by Joan Littlewood and started at her theatre in East London. The first, *A Taste of Honey*, opened at Wyndham's Theatre, later moved to the Criterion and had a run of over a year. The second was the one that I consider to be the best Joan ever did, Brendan Behan's *The Hostage*. Again this was a loosely constructed play, which was changed and added to in rehearsals. It is about a young Cockney soldier, held as a hostage in a Dublin lodging-house for an I.R.A. man who is to be hanged in Belfast. The soldier is accidentally shot in a raid on the house by Civic Guards. It is full of comedy, ballads, satirical songs and dancing, and when he is killed at the end of the play he gets up and sings:

The bells of hell go ting-a-ling-a-ling
For you but not for me,
O death where is thy sting-a-ling-a-ling,
Or grave thy victory.

It was an enormous success with the public and critics. Harold Hobson wrote in *The Sunday Times*, 'What I do know is that it made on me the impression of a masterpiece . . . a masterpiece should have magnanimity, and Mr. Behan's portrait of this young English soldier is magnanimous indeed. Above all it should have life, and should have it more abundantly. Life is what *The Hostage* is rich in; it shouts, sings, thunders and stamps with life . . . The Irish, the southern Irish and the I.R.A. Irish have found in Mr. Behan a dramatist in the line of O'Casey. They should treasure him and be proud of him.'

Joan's third production was *Make Me An Offer*, by Wolf Mankowitz, based on his novel of the same name, music and lyrics by Monty Norman and David Heneker. This production introduced some new actors to Joan, in particular Sheila Hancock, Wally Patch, Victor Spinetti and Roy Kinnear. These four she particularly liked and they remained her friends for many years. Also in the cast were Daniel Massey, who played the lead, Meier and Anna Tzelniker and – when Meier became ill – Martin Miller. Wolf did not get on well with Joan, nor she with him. He did not like having his script changed by the actors; Joan always enjoyed improvisation and felt that changes helped to keep the work fresh. So there was constant friction between them. Despite this, the show was a success and transferred into the New Theatre for a profitable run.

Sometime in 1958, my old friend Harvey Unna from the Progressive Players (previously North West London Unity), who had directed several plays that Eileen had designed, told me about a new play by a new author, Willis Hall. It was originally called *The Disciplines of War* or *Boys It's All Hell*, and was presented by Oxford University students in Oxford, and at the 1958 Edinburgh Festival. Later it was produced at the Nottingham Playhouse by the Repertory Theatre there. Harvey, who had now become a literary agent, gave me a copy. The play dealt with a small group of British soldiers on patrol in the Malayan jungle during the Japanese advance on Singapore in early 1942. I thought it was exceptionally well written and observed, and Wolf and I went up to see it in Nottingham. We took an option on the play and I asked George Devine if he would like to do it with us at the Court, to begin with. He agreed, and Lindsay Anderson, who had previously only directed one play on a Sunday night, was invited to direct it. He began by casting it brilliantly. Albert Finney, upon whose services I had an option after *The Party*, and who had played in a Willis Hall radio play, was given the leading part of Bamforth, the cockney 'bolshy' soldier. Pat McGoohan, who had been Starbuck in *Moby Dick* was asked to play Sgt. Mitchem, but for some complicated reason, which I have now forgotten, refused the part, and Robert Shaw was cast, his first leading role in London. Other actors who later became well known were Ronald Fraser, Alfred Lynch and Bryan Pringle. The cast was completed by Edward Judd, David Andrews and the Japanese actor, Kenji Takaki. I mention them all because this was one of the finest all-round casts ever assembled for one of my productions, and shows on what a high level Lindsay began his career in the theatre. Alan Tagg, who had designed the set for *Look Back in Anger* and many other Court productions, was our designer. Then shortly before rehearsals were due to begin we were struck a terrible blow. Albert Finney became ill, was wrongly diagnosed by the theatre doctor of that time, and late in the day was found to have peritonitis. He could not play.

A couple of weeks earlier, John Osborne and I had gone to Bristol to see a relatively new actor in a production of *Look Back* at the Bristol Old Vic. I shall always remember that journey, because on the train on the way to Bristol I had said to John, 'Now that *The Entertainer* production can be looked back on calmly, the whole thing having been a great success, is there anything at all you wish you had changed?' and he had said simply 'No.' Peter O'Toole was the actor playing Jimmy Porter, and we were both impressed. So when Albert fell ill and had to withdraw from the cast of Willis Hall's play, I thought of Peter. Fortunately he was free and immediately accepted the part of Bamforth. Peter at the Bristol Old Vic, and Albert at the Birmingham Rep, were the two foremost actors of their generation, and the best examples of the new non-U breed of actors that the new times and plays were demanding.

Finding a new title for a play when it already has one is always difficult, but none of us liked either of the earlier titles and eventually Lindsay came up with *The Long and The Short and The Tall*, which we all thought was much better. The play opened in early January 1959, played for an unusually long run of three months at the Court and transferred for another three months to the New Theatre. It brought a small profit to the producers and fame to Willis Hall, a Yorkshireman who was living in Nottingham before the success of his play brought him to London.

Hitherto, he had gone to an office to work on his scripts, mostly I think for T.V. or radio. The success of his new play changed his life, as happened with so many of the Royal Court's young lions.

Lindsay directed the play impeccably, despite his lack of experience, but he had an uneasy relationship with Peter O'Toole, a hard-drinking wild man, one of the lads. Lindsay was decidedly not one of the lads. A puritanical perfectionist, in the course of his career he formed close relationships with some actors, but not with the cast of The Long and the Short.

Ken Tynan wrote 'Mr. Hall's play is not only boisterous, exuberant and accurate; it is also beautifully written. Moreover, it is performed in what, for the London theatre, is a new style of acting . . . with his actors I could find no fault, and in the case of Mr. O'Toole . . . I sensed a technical authority that may, given discipline and purpose, presage greatness. The play lacked stars and it had a down beat (that is anti-war) ending in which the patrol was decimated. These facts may explain why, despite enthusiastic notices, it ran in the West End for only three months. It will, anyway, be remembered as a portent.'

It was in fact exactly the kind of play that Wolf and I and the English Stage Company had wanted to present, directed and performed in an exemplary way.

1959 was a good year for us. Two productions that we initiated and two productions brought in from Theatre Workshop, all successful artistically and financially, and all socially and theatrically progressive. At the Evening Standard Drama Awards for 1959, our two companies won all the awards except one: Best play: The Long and The Short and The Tall; Best Musical: Make Me An Offer; Most Promising Playwright: John Arden for Serjeant Musgrave's Dance and Arnold Wesker for Roots, both presented at the Royal Court; Best Performance by an Actor: Eric Porter in Rosmersholm presented at the Court and in the West End by the English Stage Company. Awards of this kind are not to be taken too seriously but, as Tynan might have said, it was a portent.

The three productions directed by Joan Littlewood that we transferred to the West End were the last I worked on with Joan. There were a number of reasons for this. I had the opportunity to transfer Fings Aint What They Used To Be with Donald Albery, but, because I did not feel it

was as good a piece of work as her earlier productions decided –
wrongly I now think – not to. Another reason was that Joan herself was
very ambivalent about the transfers, complaining that they broke up her
Company. However, it was her own and Gerry Raffles' decision, and they
probably could not have survived at the Theatre Royal without the added
income transfers brought them. They were never given a satisfactory
subsidy by the Arts Council, who tend to base their scale of subsidies on
where the theatre is situated, rather than on the talent of the artists
involved. Thus the Bristol Old Vic would always get a bigger subsidy
than Theatre Royal Stratford, even if an idiot was running Bristol and a
uniquely talented woman like Joan running Stratford East. That is why
an artist like Peter Brook had to go and work in France in order to get
the support necessary to run his company. Britain does not treasure its
best artists as France does, let alone considering them to be national
treasures as does Japan. Joan was scandalously neglected and her company allowed to disintegrate. When will we learn to cherish genius rather
than buildings?

Sometime during 1959 I read a review by Ken Tynan of an amateur
production of a play entitled *The Lily White Boys* by Harry Cookson,
which concerned three Teddy Boys, who from being petty criminals
graduate to becoming successful in society through exploiting 'the
legitimate racket'. I read a script and thought that with lyrics and music
added it could make a good piece of satirical theatre. I asked Lindsay to
direct and we invited the poet Christopher Logue to write the lyrics and
Tony Kinsay and Bill Le Sage, jazz musicians who had worked with
Logue before, to compose the music. Harry Cookson and his agent,
Peggy Ramsay, were happy to co-operate. When, however, the addition
of the lyrics made certain changes in the text necessary, Cookson became
upset and, though he did not stop the work going forward, did not help
it or co-operate. He did not like the fact that Christopher's lyrics and the
changes made in the script made the work sharper and less sentimental.
Albert Finney, now recovered, agreed to play the leading part, Georgia
Brown, Shirley Ann Field and Ann Lynn played the girls. Sean Kenny,
now a leading set designer, who had worked on *The Hostage*, designed
the set. Wolf and I agreed to produce the piece jointly with the English
Stage Company for a run at the Royal Court after a try-out week at the

Theatre Royal Brighton. Opinions about it were mixed. *The Times* in a leading article on 'The New Musical' wrote: ' . . . those responsible for *The Lily White Boys* make a powerfully conceived plea for the intellectually derisive, socially aware and politically alive musical comedy.' Jack Lambert, however, in his round-up of 'Plays in Performance' in *Drama* wrote, 'Mr. Harry Cookson's book for *The Lily White Boys*, is a great deal better than Mr. Logue's lyrics: but both could learn a lot from Gilbert . . . *The Lily White Boys* in its derivative and slightly shop-soiled way makes a pleasant evening in the theatre, though the music is dull.' Thank you Mr. Lambert.

It ran for six weeks at the Royal Court and played to goodish houses, 68 percent of seats being sold, but we didn't consider this successful enough to enable us to transfer it. I thought it was an excellent show, the nearest thing to a Brechtian piece of theatre created at that time in London. One of the boys became a successful businessman, a second became a corrupt trade union leader and the third a policeman. Each in his successful 'legitimate' role was shown as being more immoral than he had been as a petty crook. The women had similar exemplary careers.

I was discussing with Orson Welles our next collaboration when we opened in Brighton. He came down with me to see *The Lily White Boys*. He wasn't very impressed, but the only constructive criticism I can remember him making was that he thought the steps in Sean Kenny's set were too high (it consisted of three levels, one above the other, up which the aspiring Lily White Boys had to climb). However, they seemed to work alright. Orson and I were together again because I was planning a production of Ionesco's play *Rhinoceros*.

Eileen and I, on a short visit to Paris with Cecil Tennant and his wife, took them to see Jean Louis Barrault's production of Ionesco's play. Jean played the lead, the only man who stands out against the rest of the conformist population who turn into rhinoceroses. I thought the part might be suitable for Laurence Olivier and hoped Cecil, who was Olivier's agent and manager, might agree with me. He did, and so having obtained an option on the play through Peggy Ramsay, we approached Olivier with the idea. He accepted on condition that we first produced it at the Royal Court, where, after the success of *The Entertainer* he felt most secure. I proposed that we should ask Orson to direct the play and Zero Mostel to play the part of Hugo, the first man we see turn into a rhino.

Olivier agreed and George Devine was delighted to have the play produced at the Court. Orson agreed and Zero, whom I had met after seeing him play Bloom in *Ulysses in Nighttown*, accepted the part. I was sure he would be wonderful in it, the only actor I could think of who would be able to transform himself into a rhino on stage. Everything was thus going well when Zero was knocked down by a bus in New York and so badly injured that he had to withdraw from the cast. He played the part later in New York with great success. Unfortunately our replacement, Duncan Macrae, although the leading Scottish actor of the time, was not physically right. Orson, who I suppose could see himself in the part, never really found a way of getting Duncan to do it. We had an excellent cast for all the other parts, including Joan Plowright as Daisy, the girl-friend of Berenger (played by Olivier). It was, incidentally, during this run, that the news of their relationship broke in the press.

There were problems during rehearsal. Although Olivier had presented Orson as Othello at the St. James Theatre some years previously and had agreed immediately to the idea of him directing the play, there was not much in common between the two, and Olivier found Orson's rehearsal methods irksome. Orson wanted to work in great detail on some scenes, such as the first scene in the café, where the rhinos are seen charging down the street and the people are 'deliberating whether or not the rhinoceros which passed by just now was the same one that passed by earlier or whether it was another.' There is a contrapuntal form of dialogue in this scene, which Orson orchestrated very exactly and painstakingly and which was one of the best scenes in the eventual production. He went back to drilling the cast endlessly in this and one or two scenes that particularly interested him, whilst other scenes, which did not interest him, he directed in a rather perfunctory way. This method of directing prevented the cast from doing uninterrupted run-throughs of the play, which Olivier felt were needed. On top of this, Orson's booming voice in a rather small rehearsal room, made Larry propose that Orson should leave them alone for a few days to run through the scenes by themselves. A most unusual request which Orson, not unnaturally, was rather reluctant to agree to but did, on the understanding that nothing in the production would be changed. Despite this rift, they were all back together after a few days, but Orson as usual was not really ready by the first night and during the opening performance was using a walkie-talkie set to give last minute instructions – very nerve wracking for everyone. At the curtain fall I had no idea as to whether it was a success or not. Parts of it seemed brilliantly directed, other parts might have been directed by anyone. Olivier's part was that of a Chaplinesque little man, who nevertheless heroically stands out against the rhinos. Larry played it well but ordinary little men are not what he was best at. Duncan Macrae, as I have said, was a good actor but physically not right for the part. Nevertheless, there were sensational scenes. Orson as usual had done everything himself, including the sets and the sound, and during the last act the stage seemed alive with the beasts. Next day the newspapers were all raves and we were a tremendous success, packing out the Court for the six weeks we ran there and transferring to the Strand for a further eight weeks, also a sell-out. Ionesco was very upset when the run ended, thinking that we should have replaced Larry, who had only agreed to play the short season, but we were sure this would not have worked. Joan Plowright had left the cast at the end of the run at the Court and had been replaced by Maggie Smith. Both she and Larry were pestered by the press and, if for no other reason, this would have made a longer run with Olivier impossible. However, as I have said this was not one of his great roles, and after fourteen weeks he had had enough of it. We and Ionesco were lucky to get him for the play, which I think was worth doing but was not one of Ionesco's best. *The Chairs* was a much more original work. Ionesco's short plays are the ones for which he will be remembered, rather than his full-length plays. After our production of *Rhinoceros* I only met Ionesco once more, that was in New York during the run of the play there. I just happened to be in New York on some other business when I met the author in the street outside the Algonquin Hotel on a rainy afternoon, looking like the saddest man in the world. Although Zero Mostel was playing the role he should have played for us, Ionesco was not happy about the production, nor with his New York producer, nor with New York. Despite his displeasure at the play not running longer in London, I think we both felt we were on the same wavelength, friends in an alien city. Ionesco had a face like a potato and the sad soul of a clown. He spoke no English and I spoke very little French, so we did not get to know each other well, even though I was involved in three productions of his plays.

During the period that followed our production of *Expresso Bongo*, Wolf Mankowitz had been very busy with his own work and had not been very much involved in the work of our production company, except in so far as he was consulted upon and approved the main decisions taken. He was of course actively involved on a day to day basis with *Make Me An Offer*, since he was the author of the book. After *Rhinoceros*, however, we undertook a production which Wolf initiated and in which he became fully involved. This was a revue entitled *The Art of Living*, based on the work of the American columnist Art Buchwald, with sketches by Julian More, and lyrics by Monty Norman, David Heneker and Julian More, and music composed by Norman and Heneker. Additional sketches were written by Johnny Speight. It was devised and directed by Laurier Lister and presented by our Company jointly with Donald Albery. The idea had come from Wolf and during the preparation of the show he seemed for the first time to want to take on the role of active producer. This was not according to our arrangement, although I should probably have let him get on with it, since it was much more his kind of show than mine, but I couldn't take him seriously as a producer. I felt he was playing a part in a Hollywood film when he started to direct operations from the stalls at an audition. Anyway, we quarrelled and decided to each go his own way after *The Art of Living*. I do not think it was because of this rift in our relationship that the show failed. It had a good cast headed by the American, Hiram Sherman, and included Edward Woodward and Graham Stark. It opened in August 1960. The following May, *Beyond the Fringe* opened in London. *The Art of Living* was already out of date. That style of intimate revue, of which this was our second attempt following *The Punch Revue*, was no longer wanted, and in any case obviously we had not got the knack of making it successful. We had tried on both occasions to inject a little bit of extra quality into the format by basing our revues on good contemporary, witty writers, but despite taking on board expert directors in the shape of Vida Hope and Laurier Lister, neither show took off. *The Art of Living* was a better show than *The Punch Revue*, but the pudding did not really rise.

Wolf and I arranged our split, helped by Oscar Beuselinck, without too much difficulty. It was reported in the *Evening Standard* in such a way as to make it seem like my victory. This probably provoked Wolf into writing a short story also printed in the *Standard* containing a rather bitter caricature of me. However, although annoying at the time, yesterday's papers are soon forgotten. Wolf and I, although we did not work together again, were fairly soon back on friendly terms. He produced a couple of shows without success, but producing was not really his game and he gave it up soon afterwards. I think it is a pity that Wolf did not stick to his work as a writer but diversified his activities in so many directions because of the need to make money. He had, though, a certain restless energy and entrepreneurial ability which made him discontented with the lonely life of a writer. His early novels *Make Me an Offer* and *A Kid for Two Farthings* and his play *The Bespoke Overcoat* held out the promise of great things that never came, although the book of *Expresso Bongo* was a very good stab at a new direction for British musicals. Wolf wrote some interesting film scripts too, but he never stuck at one thing long enough, always running off after the next bright idea that struck his fertile brain. So although he had talent as a novelist, poet, scriptwriter, journalist, antique dealer and business man, he never stuck at anything. Perhaps he enjoyed this life of change and different challenges, but something was undoubtedly lost by it. Wolf is a warm, likeable man, who can often wrongly feel himself threatened, and when he feels this he can turn suddenly vicious. I have not seen much of him since the years we worked together and perhaps he is no longer so ready to see danger where it does not exist. I hope that is the case, for the sake of his own peace and happiness.

I formed a new company, Oscar Lewenstein Plays Ltd, and John Osborne and Tony Richardson plus two of my American angels, Donald Flamm and Doris Abrahams, agreed to take shares in it and became directors.

We were fortunately able to start off with a big success. Willis Hall and Keith Waterhouse had adapted Keith's novel *Billy Liar* for the stage, and Wolf and I had taken an option on this. When we split we asked them who they would like to produce the play and fortunately they decided to stay with me. I invited Lindsay Anderson to direct *Billy Liar* and everyone concerned agreed that Albert Finney should be Billy. The play was in one set designed by Alan Tagg and had a cast of eight. Mona Washbourne was Billy's mother and George Cooper, who had previously been in the Theatre Workshop Company and had played Tiger Brown in our *Threepenny Opera* production, was his father. The production was capitalised at £6,000 and opened at the Theatre Royal, Brighton. There was an unfortunate dress rehearsal, in the middle of which Willis and Keith, who had probably drunk too much, had a quarrel with Lindsay (with whom they were not temperamentally in harmony in any case). This quarrel at such a time had repercussions later on, which I think were unfortunate for us all. The play made no great impact on Brighton but we had been able to book the Cambridge Theatre for its London opening. The Cambridge was a larger theatre than we wanted but the only one then available, so we had decided to take it. It almost proved disastrous. *Billy Liar* had only so-so notices on opening and did poor business for its first two weeks. Had it continued at that level the theatre could and would have given us notice to end the run. Fortunately a late notice by Harold Hobson sent the business up over the 'break' figure and a couple of weeks later the opening of Woodfall's film *Saturday Night and Sunday Morning*, in which Albert Finney played the leading part, gave him some very useful publicity which helped still further. Then an extract from the play shown on television, filled the theatre to capacity. Though *Look Back in Anger* and *Billy Liar* were both helped enormously by having an extract shown on T.V., this did not always happen, and some plays were killed rather than cured by an extract being shown. So we had a great success on our hands, the greatest in financial terms that I had enjoyed. By playing in the Cambridge, we were doing much bigger business than would have been the case had we been in the sort of theatre we should have preferred. Some brief extracts from the notices will give an idea of the play's impact: 'Has the outward veneer of a riotous farce and the inner heart of a significant comedy: Its hero is like some 20-year-old 20th-century North Country Walter Mitty', Milton Shulman in the *Evening Standard*. 'Is very funny and its implications are deep', Harold Hobson, *The Sunday Times*. Albert made a great popular success in the central part. After the play had run to packed houses for nine months, we released him so that he could play the name part in John Osborne's *Luther*, and Tom Courtenay took over as Billy. Although Tom gave a splendid performance, it had not got the bravura quality of Albert's and the business, though continuing to be profitable, was half of what it had been. With Tom, the play ran for a further nine months. By this time I was working closely with Tony Richardson in Woodfall Films and we wanted to make a film of *Billy Liar* with Lindsay directing and Albert playing the leading part, which seemed to be the obvious way to go. We made an offer for the film rights and Tony, John and I went to Acapulco for the film festival where *The Entertainer* was showing, leaving the authors to consider it. Whilst we were away they sold the film rights to Joe Janni for John Schlesinger to direct with Tom Courtenay playing Billy. They did this because they did not want Lindsay to direct the film. The result was a film which was not a real success, which I am convinced it would have been, had our team made it.

My next important theatre venture was a season of three French avant garde plays, the rights of which I had acquired, and which my company presented at the Royal Court with the English Stage Company. We opened with *Jacques* by Ionesco which was in fact a double bill of *Jacques* and *The Future is in Eggs* which is a play with the same characters as *Jacques* three years later on. R.D.Smith, who had directed the first play at the Hampstead Theatre Club and was an old friend of mine from my Communist Party days, again directed, and we had an excellent cast, but no stars, and the play was not a success though very funny.

The second play of the season was Sartre's *Altona* directed by the American, John Berry, who had brought the play to my attention. John had been a member of Orson Welles's Mercury Theatre Company in New York and was a victim of the McCarthy repression in America. Sean Kenny designed the set, and we had a strong cast: Claire Bloom, Basil Sydney, Kenneth Haigh and Diane Cilento.

In a programme note to the Paris production of the play, Sartre described it thus: 'A family of big German industrialists the von Gerlachs live near Hamburg in an ugly old mansion in the middle of a park. When the curtain rises the father, who has only six months to live, calls together his daughter Leni, his younger son Werner and Werner's wife Johanna in order to inform them of his latest wishes. Johanna guesses that, after the father's death, her husband will be sacrificed as always to Franz, the elder son. The latter, who has been officially reported dead, has locked himself up since his return from the front in a hunting lodge, and refuses to see anyone except his younger sister Leni. In order to save Werner, Johanna determines to investigate the mystery of Franz's seclusion. In doing so, she unwittingly serves her father-in-law's ends. Old von Gerlach makes use of her in order to obtain the interview with Franz which the latter has refused him for 13 years. The play ends with a double suicide after the father has at last succeeded in seeing Franz again.'

In this play, Sartre expresses himself on a great many important topics – the political use and effects of torture, the affluent state of Western Europe, the inherent weakness of Capitalism, and above all the nature of the desire for possession. It provided a long and difficult evening in the theatre but was successful, and we were able to transfer it for a limited run in the West End after packing the Royal Court.

The third, last, and in my opinion, best play in our season was *The Blacks* by Genet. This play, described as *A Clown Show* by the author, was directed by Roger Blin who had directed it in Paris and had early in the life of the English Stage Company brought the French production of Beckett's *Endgame* to the Court. It was again designed by André Acquart and looked absolutely wonderful. In the fifties and sixties there were few opportunities for black actors to act in good plays with decent parts for them. The Court from quite early on had been in the forefront of those trying to change this situation and had presented several plays by black writers, but it was hard to find an experienced black cast to cope with the difficult language of Genet's play, and in fact we did not succeed in this. The cast looked wonderfully right. They came from the West Indies, all parts of Africa, and one actress was from India, but the audience found their accents difficult to understand. When someone told Genet this, he said, 'make it even more incomprehensible'. The play was not a success but I can still see clearly in my mind's eye Rashidi Onikoyi dangerous as Mr. Archibald Absalom Wellington; Bloke Modisane obsequious as Douf, and most clearly of all I remember Felicia Okoli as Miss Stephanie Virtue Secret-Rose. I can still hear that beautiful Nigerian woman speaking, 'softly as in a state of somnambulism' as the stage direction says, 'I am the lily-white Queen of the West. Only centuries of breeding could achieve such a miracle.' Despite its almost complete failure with the critics and the public this is one of the productions I look back upon with most pleasure.

In 1958 Tony Richardson, having directed *Look Back in Anger* successfully both in London and New York, directed his first feature film based on this play. He formed a film Company with John Osborne and Harry Salzman, a Canadian entrepreneur who later produced the James Bond films. They called it Woodfall, after the street in which John Osborne then lived. The following year Tony directed *The Entertainer* as a film for Woodfall, and in 1960 produced for Woodfall *Saturday Night and Sunday Morning* which Karel Reisz directed and in which Albert Finney played the starring role. Albert had already played a small part for Tony in the film of *The Entertainer*, following his appearance in *The Party*. Tony's next film project was to be *A Taste of Honey*, but before this was set up, Harry Salzman and Woodfall parted company and Tony asked me to help him in the preparation of this film which he proposed to direct and produce himself. Up to this point Woodfall's choice of subjects – and actors – for its films was running in parallel with the activities of the English Stage Company and my own Company, and, now that we were sharing offices in Curzon Street to which we had moved during the run of *Billy Liar*, the connection became even closer. I remember well having dinner with Tony one night at the Escargot Restaurant in Greek Street, when we decided for the first time to shoot *Taste of Honey* entirely on location. Tony's earlier films had been made in a studio, as was the invariable way in England in those days. In deciding to make *A Taste of Honey* on location, Tony was influenced by the way in which the directors of the French new wave were making their films. We also thought it would save money, as well as giving the film a more authentic look. Tony asked me to join him and John as a director of Woodfall, but at the time I thought that I should continue to concentrate on theatre. I also was not sure that I should enjoy working on films as much. So for the time being I just gave Tony a hand with casting and any other matters on which he thought my advice and help might be useful, and did not take a credit on *A Taste of Honey* or his next film *The Loneliness of the Long Distance Runner*, in which Tom Courtenay, following his performance in our production of *Billy Liar*, played the lead. Tony Richardson was now more and more involved in film making. In 1960 he directed *Sanctuary* in Hollywood, in 1961 *A Taste of Honey*, the film of the play which he had previously directed on Broadway, and in 1962 *The Loneliness of the Long Distance Runner*.

I went over to New York to be present at the Broadway opening of *A Taste of Honey*, in which Joan Plowright played the young girl and Angela

Lansbury her mother. It was produced by David Merrick and I remember shortly before the first night, he wanted to cut the small jazz group that was part of the production, but Tony resisted and won the day. After the opening we had the usual New York experience. There was a party at Sardi's. When the notice for the *New York Times* came out and was found to be unfavourable, everyone melted away. In New York it is not safe to be seen to be in contact with failure. Nevertheless, all the other notices were good and the play had a successful run there, even though I did not think the New York production was anything like as original and unsentimental as Joan Littlewood's production. However, that would almost certainly not have worked on Broadway.

Part Five

The Ghandi of Threadneedle Street

or the knack of surviving despite doing my own thing

In 1961, between his productions of *Honey* and *Loneliness*, Tony Richardson returned to the Royal Court Theatre to direct John Osborne's new play, *Luther*. This proved to be a highpoint for all of us. It was directed by Tony Richardson at the top of his form, and was designed most beautifully by Jocelyn Herbert. It was presented by the English Stage Company in partnership with my company which had released Albert Finney from *Billy Liar* so that he could play the leading part of *Luther*. It was cast with some of the Royal Court's finest actors, including George Devine, Peter Bull, John Moffatt, Julian Glover and James Cairncross, and in other important parts were Bill Owen, Peter Duguid, Dan Meaden and Charles Kay. The music was composed and arranged by John Addison. The play opened at the Theatre Royal, Nottingham on June 26th 1961 where, according to John Osborne, I was downcast because it got a poor notice in *The Guardian*. I have no memory of this and it seems as unlikely as many of John's other memories, since we never paid much attention to provincial reviews. At any rate, the production moved to Paris and the International Theatre Season at the Sarah Bernhardt Theatre, where Albert won the award as Best Actor for his performance and everyone was in good spirits. Many of the English critics came over to Paris and reviewed the play before it came into the Royal Court a few weeks later. Ken Tynan in *The Observer* called it 'the most eloquent piece of dramatic writing to have dignified our theatre since *Look Back in Anger*'. In the *Sunday Telegraph* Alan Brien wrote: '*Luther* is full of argument and invective. Scene after scene comes alive when ideas are thrown from hand to hand like grenades.' It packed the Court before transferring to the Phoenix Theatre in the West End for a long run.

I had reached this point in my memoirs when I read John Osborne's second volume of autobiography, *Almost a Gentleman*. In his play, *Luther*, after Luther has left the stage at the end of his meeting with Cardinal Cajitan, the Cardinal says 'that man hates himself . . . he could only love others.' When I read the play I had thought this was a fair summing up of John himself but I wondered then and I wonder now, if a man who hates himself can love others. John's autobiography certainly bears out the first part of the statement. It leaves the second part still an open question. Certainly it suggests that such a man finds it easier to hate than to love. I think it is a terribly sad book, for it covers with spleen a most exciting and exhilarating period in the history of the theatre and the cinema in which John himself played a major part, which at the time he appeared to enjoy, both as regards the work and the companionship of his colleagues. But it now seems that, apart from George Devine for whom he has consistently maintained his love and admiration, and Tony Richardson for whom his love and admiration have wavered, he has not many good words to spare for the rest of his colleagues of those days, or for most of the women who loved him and whom presumably he loved. Thus he was married to Jill Bennett for nine years, during which she played and inspired many parts in his plays, and yet he has nothing good to say of her. I knew Jill over a period of about 20 years and was aware of her love and concern for John, and I find it impossible to believe that the woman I knew could have justified this filthy onslaught. She was cast constantly in leading parts by John and his directors, yet John can quote with approval a remark he says Tony Richardson made that Jill was 'the worst actress in the world'. Tony Richardson often said things he didn't really believe just for effect or a misguided joke. John knows this perfectly well, but why then quote him in an obvious instance of that folly, when John obviously could not have believed it at the time? John has nothing good to say about Oscar Beuselinck, his solicitor for something like 30 years, who was his close friend and must have served him well, otherwise he would not have retained him. I was a friend of John's for about 20 years, and with the English Stage Company produced five of his plays. I thought we were good friends but from his book you would not have suspected it. The truth is that this auto-biography is a work of fiction based on some reality, but altered to suit the author's present feelings. As such it is a good read, for John still writes with an energy and brilliance that defies comparison. But do not be misled by that word 'autobiography' – it is a clear violation of the Trades Description Act.

1962 was a busy year for me. Not only did I work as Associate Producer on *Tom Jones*, which was my first experience of working right the way through the production of a film, but I also produced several shows at the Arts Theatre, in partnership with Michael Codron, and several at the Theatre Royal, Stratford East, in partnership with Michael White. None of these shows was successful commercially. The best was *The Secret of the World* by Ted Allan, whose earlier play *The Ghost Writers* – about Hollywood during the McCarthy period – Wolf and I had produced at the Arts Theatre in a production directed by Bernard Braden early on in our partnership. Ted's new play was directed by John Berry, who had directed Sartre's *Altona*, and the two leading parts were played by Berry and Miriam Karlin. It dealt with the reaction of a Canadian Jewish Com-munist Trade Union leader and his family to the speech by Khrushchev revealing Stalin's crimes. It was a very powerful play on an important contemporary theme not tackled by any other writer. Ted Allan wrote a passionate attempt at a major tragedy. The 'kosher butchers', as Bernard Levin and Robert Muller, the critics of the *Daily Mail* and *Daily Express* were known, praised the play highly. Robert Muller in the *Daily Mail* wrote: 'A play at last! Into a dismal season, Mr Allan's powerful new drama – finely written, moving and dynamic – exploded last night like a shower of fireworks . . . Sam Alexander's world begins to crash one day in 1956, when Khruschev denounces Stalin in his speech to the 20th Soviet Congress. And brilliantly Mr. Allan pinpoints his hero's dilemma. If the speech is no fake, then everything he has believed in, everything he has worked for, is a lie, a cruel, horrible mockery of his idealism . . . The play's highly intelligent, and indeed irrefutable political content is delicately balanced with the private struggles of Sam's family: the conflicts between generations, between husband and wife, between ideologies. Particularly persuasive are the quiet moments between Sam and his wife, as they become gradually separated and turn into enemies.

'The play is directed with passion by John Berry, who also gives an unforgettable performance as Sam Alexander, the most detailed, gripping and compelling work I have seen lavished on a modern play for at least a year.'

Bernard Levin in the *Daily Express* agrees with Muller and adds: 'We are also seeing some acting. As the vanishing hero, Mr. John Berry (though he needs more discipline in his acting) is superb in his bravura, his mingled love and despair, his desperate search for the truth he left behind him.

'As his wife, Miss Miriam Karlin can play the first three-quarters of the play – ostensibly her usual wisecracking Jewish mother – on roller-skates, and this she does: this is not acting, it is very clever existing.

'But her last scene demands that she get off her easy ride and fight her way into a deeper, harder style. And Miss Karlin rises to the occasion.

'Trotsky was wrong,' says Sam Alexander, 'but we didn't need to split his head open for it. That is the terrible question that his mind cannot answer, and from a mind's failure Mr. Allan has fashioned a play that shall do any man's heart good to hear him roar.

'Let him roar again! Let him roar again!'

Harold Hobson in *The Sunday Times*, whilst being more critical of some aspects of the play wrote: 'In a Lilliputian theatrical season of shoddy revue and trivial comedy, Ted Allan's *The Secret of the World* (Theatre Royal, Stratford E.) towers uncertainly like a maimed giant.

'This is a play that in achievement falls far short of its author's ambition, which flames with an Attic anger against destiny, and a defiant but despairing scorn of the powers that control the universe. Mr. Allan at present has not the mastery of the fiery words that are needed to make his rage incandescent . . .

'Nevertheless, Mr. Allan has taken to himself a tremendous theme, and he has grasped the dimensions of its meaning in terms of the human and the superhuman. In spite of one character who is only the enfeebled ghost of Shotover, it is an exciting thing in the theatre to come once again upon the old Greek rebellion against fate, and to contemplate in awe and wonder the repeated and pitiful, the shattering yet not entirely disheartening fall of man.'

But it was not a success with the public. Although it was doing quite well at Stratford East, we did not feel it had the makings of a West End success and regretfully terminated its run after Stratford. Ted Allan went on re-writing the play, sending me a revised version almost every year, without improving it. A pity. It probably needed Ted's passion and knowledge of the subject and a writer of Arthur Miller's stature to bring it off.

The other productions I was associated with at the Arts and Stratford had not this scale or ambition, though *The Scatterin'*, an Irish play with songs by James McKenna directed by Alan Simpson, which we did at Stratford, and *End of Day*, a Samuel Beckett anthology by Jack McGowran at the Arts, were well worth doing. At the Comedy Theatre in the West End I produced two plays by women with big leading roles for actresses. The first was *My Place* by Elaine Dundy, Kenneth Tynan's wife. It was directed by John Dexter and starred Diane Cilento. It concerned a modern young actress and her circle. The second was *Play with a Tiger* by the novelist Doris Lessing. It was directed by Ted Kotcheff and starred Siobhan McKenna and concerned the life and loves of a modern woman. The plays were harbingers of the women's movement and for the first time on the stage presented a true picture of independent women in love in England in 1962. Neither play did well, though Doris Lessing's, which was based in part on some sections of her *Golden Notebook*, was highly praised by Graham Greene and other discerning critics. For instance, 'Written with lacerating passion and truth', Robert Muller in the *Daily Mail*, 'The most troublingly poetic play in London', Harold Hobson in *The Sunday Times*, 'Ought to be seen by anyone interested in contemporary living', T.C. Worsley in the *Financial Times*. It might have done better a few years later. Doris Lessing was not then so widely recognised as an outstanding novelist, and the 'new woman' was resented rather than welcomed. And certainly neither of these plays had the power and theatrical force that had compelled Jimmy Porter's survival.

My Place was the first production I had worked on with John Dexter and I was surprised to find how efficiently and speedily he knocked the production into shape and then disappointed that, after having done this, he could not deepen or improve it. I worked with John again a few years later and formed the opinion that he was a brilliant stage director but that his skills were superficial. Organising exciting stage action, rather than revealing character, was his speciality.

Our one successful commercial production that year was *Semi Detached* by David Turner. This was another play brought to my attention by Harvey Unna, who persuaded me to go and see it at the Coventry Repertory Theatre, where it was having a successful run. It was an attempt at a modern Jonsonian comedy, dealing with the machinations of a Midlands Insurance district supervisor, Fred Midway.

Fred's philosophy is summed up in his advice to his son 'You've got to lie, scrounge, and deceive with the rest of us, but never put yourself in a position where anyone can accuse you of it.' Leonard Rossiter played Fred in Coventry and the play was a great success there. I decided to produce it in London and asked Tony Richardson to direct it. He accepted and we both agreed that Laurence Olivier should be asked to play Fred. Olivier liked the project and accepted the part and we cast all the other parts very strongly: Mona Washbourne playing Fred's wife Hilda, James Bolam his son, Eileen Atkins his daughter. John Thaw, Patsy Rowlands, Kenneth Fortescue, Joan Young and Newton Blick made up the rest of the cast. The set was designed by Loudon Sainthill. It should have been a triumph, but Olivier never found the way to play his part. Everyone else, Tony, Joan Plowright and I, all thought that he could play the part of a brilliant con-man, a sort of Mosca of the Midlands, standing on his head, but he insisted first on playing it in an unbelievable Midlands accent, and then on having a make-up which made him look so seedy that no one would have bought a used car from him, let alone an insurance policy. All this attempt at a Midlands reality inhibited him from playing the main line of the part, which was a quick thinking, fascinating rogue and although, being Olivier, there were excellent things in his performance, when it opened at the Saville Theatre in London on 5th December 1962, the play did not get enthusiastic notices, many critics finding the attack on this Midlands trickster snobbish. However, because it was Olivier, we had a good advance and a profitable run, during which Larry moaned and groaned at his hard life (he was preparing for the opening of the National Theatre at this time) and longed for the run to end. Olivier's Company and Donald Albery were my partners in this venture, and Larry had to stay in for the run of the play. Night after night when I went in to see him he exercised his ability to make one feel very sorry for 'poor old Larry'. Many people thought we should have brought Leonard Rossiter and the Coventry production into the West End. I did not agree, I knew that what seemed good in Coventry would not have worked in the West End. When the play opened in New York, the point was proved. Whilst the play was on tour, prior to the West End, a deal was made with a New York producer for it to be presented there. When the time came, Larry of course was not available and would certainly not have wanted to do it there, so the New York producer decided to take the Coventry production over. It was a total disaster: Leonard Rossiter's performance seemed a pale shadow after Olivier's.

Olivier's difficulties in finding a way to play the leading parts in *Rhinoceros* and *Semi Detached*, both lower middle-class characters, reminds me that he had the ability or quality of appearing quite ordinary when he was not acting. You could pass him in the street and not notice him. I was once waiting in a train on Brighton station when a middle-aged man, puffing and blowing, almost fell into the carriage. It took me several minutes to realise that it was Olivier and that he was not acting. Strangely enough he found it very difficult to play a very ordinary man on stage.

I ended 1962 with two unsuccessful productions of plays by Keith Waterhouse and Willis Hall. Following the production of *Billy Liar* we had produced another play by Keith and Willis in the West End: *Celebration*. This time we did bring down the original cast and production from the Nottingham Playhouse, directed by Val May. The play dealt with two large working class families in the north of England who are faced simultaneously with two of the biggest events of their lives – a wedding and a funeral.

Robert Muller, critic of the *Daily Mail*, thought it 'An enjoyable and immensely likeable entertainment. Certainly most of our comic writers could take lessons from Waterhouse and Hall in making their characters live. They achieve their effects by the most careful documentation; their comedy is distilled not from similar plays of the past, but from life.'

The *Evening Standard* agreed: 'A boisterous essay in comic realism, executed with lethal accuracy of observation and limitless high spirits.' Of course, it was unfashionable, had no stars and could not find an audience in the West End theatre of that time. I brought this play down from Nottingham in its original production because I admired the play, the direction, and the cast, and could see no way of improving or strengthening it. I was aware, and so were my backers, that we were taking a chance but, having done so well with *Billy Liar* and *The Long and the Short and the Tall*, we wanted to continue to produce the work of these authors. And anyway, you never know, miracles do sometimes happen.

The whole question of transferring productions from one type of theatre to another is an interesting one. I have transferred plays from provincial repertory theatres to the West End, from small London theatres such as the Theatre Royal, Stratford East, the Royal Court and the Hampstead Theatre to the West End and from off Broadway to the West End. In general I preferred to bring in the original cast and production, because in most cases I did not think I could improve upon it. Sometimes these transfers were successful, quite often not, for even when they got excellent notices on first being presented, there was no guarantee that they would be well received on their transfer; quite often it was difficult to get another full set of notices if the play transferred fairly soon to the West End, so that the main source of unpaid publicity was lost. There are absolutely no rules, but if you see a play outside the West End that you think is splendid and you want to give it a longer life, sometimes of course it works but many are the plays hailed in Hampstead only to be shot down on Shaftesbury Avenue. The audience have paid much less to see the play in the theatre where it started, the critics have a different standard by which they judge plays in the West End or out of it, and a play seen in a very small auditorium is a quite different experience from seeing it in a larger house.

We tried again at the end of 1962, bringing a new comedy by Hall and Waterhouse, *All Things Bright and Beautiful*, starring Peggy Mount into the Phoenix. Again good notices from, amongst others, *The Times*, *Evening Standard* and *Daily Express*, but again the West End audience did not want to know. The last production of work by Keith and Willis with which I was associated was a double bill *Squat Betty* and *The Sponge Room*. This was presented at the Royal Court, directed by John Dexter with a cast of Jill Bennett, George Cole and Robert Stephens. A disaster. Later Keith and Willis wrote some successful plays and a musical for the West End. I was not involved but I do not think it's sour grapes that makes me think they were not a patch on their early North country plays.

One day late in 1962, I had an unexpected visit from Bill Gaskill and Peter O'Toole. They told me they wanted to do a production of Brecht's first play *Baal*, which had never been done in this country before. Would I be interested in producing it? I only had a vague memory of the play, which I had never seen but had read some years before, but catching their enthusiasm and knowing that with O'Toole it was necessary to strike while the iron was hot, I said I'd be happy to do it with them. Peter's company agreed to put up part of the capital required and I hoped that Peter's participation would enable us to make a success of a difficult play by a commercially unpopular author. *Lawrence of Arabia* had not yet been released but O'Toole was already a name to be reckoned with. It was while we were working on this production that Peter dubbed me the Ghandi of Threadneedle Street.

Baal was written in 1918 when Brecht was 20 years old. The plot is summarised in John Willett's book *The Theatre of Bertolt Brecht*: 'Baal, a poet and singer, drunk, lazy, selfish and ruthless, seduces (amongst others) a disciple's 17-year-old mistress, who drowns herself. He mixes with tramps and drivers, and sings in a cheap night club. With his friend, the composer Ekart, he wanders through the country drinking and fighting. Sophie, pregnant by him, follows them and likewise drowns herself. Baal seduces Ekart's mistress, then kills him. Hunted by the police and deserted by the woodcutters he dies alone in a forest hut. A contemporary German setting, against a background chiefly of darkness, wind and rain.'

This very young, poetic play was beautifully designed by Jocelyn Herbert mainly using a series of slide projections onto the backcloth – still quite a new technique then. Harry Andrews played Ekart but never seemed to be at ease in the part. The whole production was a gallant attempt which didn't quite work. O'Toole was extremely nervous towards the end of rehearsals and wanted to postpone the opening for a day or two. It would not have helped, although perhaps two extra weeks of rehearsal might have done, if that had been planned from the beginning. It had a short run at the Phoenix Theatre but was the sort of enterprise that might now be undertaken by the National Theatre or the

Royal Shakespeare Company. Apart from O'Toole's Company, I had the support of Bernard Delfont who for a number of years around that time put up a large share of the capital I required for my productions, not because he wanted to make money but because he wanted to be involved in what he described as 'tony' productions. I could not have done many of them without him. Bernard Delfont was on the one hand very warm and friendly, on the other quite a shrewd business man, not too careful with the truth, never liking to say 'no' but never feeling bound by a 'yes'. One day I remember him saying, 'You can rely absolutely on anything Lew (Grade) says, but as for me you mustn't believe a word I say.' What could be more disarming?

That year, 1963, because I was working on *The Girl with Green Eyes*, I only produced one other stage play, *Luv* by Murray Schisgal. Murray was a New Yorker and his play a sort of Woody Allen before its time. It concerned three middle-aged New Yorkers each anxious to prove that he or she had had a harder childhood than the others. Ted Kotcheff directed it at the Arts with Fenella Fielding, Dick Emery and George A. Cooper. I thought it was wonderfully funny with the sort of Jewish New York humour I love in films such as *Annie Hall*, but the critics were not enthusiastic and the public did not respond.

In the autumn I was in New York for the opening there of *Tom Jones* and *Luther*. 'I know two Oscars,' said my young son Pete – in 1963 he was seven years old – 'but who is the other one?' He had heard Eileen speaking about three Oscars that had been awarded to Tony Richardson, John Osborne and John Addison for their work on the film, *Tom Jones*. The two Oscars he knew were me and my solicitor Oscar Beuselinck. That year we had *Luther* running on Broadway at the same time that *Tom Jones* was opened in New York City. Tony Richardson had directed both, John Osborne written both, Albert Finney was the star of both. John Addison had composed the music for both, Jocelyn Herbert had designed both, George Devine, John Moffatt and Peter Bull were featured actors in both and I had been an Associate Producer of *Tom Jones* for Woodfall and the Co-Producer with the English Stage Company for *Luther*. Everything had come together to make the whole thing the sort of success story that New York loves. There were perhaps a couple of clouds no bigger than a man's hand. For one thing, Tony seemed for the first time not to welcome the advice or criticism of his colleagues: I noticed it and Jocelyn noticed it. For another, Albert showed a side of his character that we had not seen before. David Merrick, the American producer of *Luther*, had been difficult in some way with Albert's contract. Albert paid him out by insisting on leaving the production on the exact day his contract permitted him to leave, even though this was in the middle of a week. It probably served Merrick right, but it was a strange thing to do, since Albert had no urgent reason to leave on that day rather than play until the end of the week. Albert then went off for a long holiday, travelling round the world and taking his time about it. Another unusual thing for a young actor to do at that stage of his career. Albert has been going his own way in his own time ever since. Did this admirable quality prevent him from becoming the successor to Laurence Olivier as head of his profession? Difficult to know. Anyway the choice was his to make. As for Tony, I had not thought success would change him in any way. I thought he was too intelligent to take it seriously. It seemed to be more in character when he used his Oscar as a door stopper. His strength had always been in his ability to get a good team working with him and to get the best out of them. He had made people feel that their suggestions were welcome. I hoped this would not change, but feared it might.

But for the moment all was well. As previously arranged, Tony went straight on from the opening nights of *Tom Jones* and *Luther* to direct Brecht's *Arturo Ui* on Broadway for David Merrick. I stayed on in New York for the opening. Christopher Plummer played Ui in what was one of Tony Richardson's finest productions. However, business was not good, and Merrick was proposing to take it off. I felt that a fight should be made to save it, and other people shared that feeling. Merrick agreed that if Tony and I could raise the money to cover the weekly running costs, we could take it over and continue the run. I was going around New York seeing people with this aim in view when the news of Kennedy's assassination came through. It was like that day in 1939 when I was trying to raise funds for the support of anti-fascist young refugees, when war with Germany was declared. Obviously no one was interested in what I was trying to do. Kennedy was dead, *Arturo Ui*, a parable about the rise of Hitler, set amongst gangsters in an imaginary Chicago, came off, and I went down to see my new friend Carson McCullers in the country just outside New York. I arrived at her door, rang the bell, and

Carson in her nightdress came to open it and said 'They've shot Oswald.' Then we watched the replay on T.V. That fine production of *Arturo Ui* did not stand a chance against such competition.

Whilst I was in New York that year, 1963, I saw a production at the Living Theatre of *The Brig* by Kenneth Brown. I had not liked their most famous production, *The Connection*, which Michael White had brought to the West End, but I found *The Brig* to be a compelling and brilliantly executed piece of theatre. It was directed by Judith Malina and designed by Julian Beck, the two founders of the Living Theatre. When I heard that, after surviving since 1951, their theatre was being taken away from them because of a failure to pay certain taxes, I asked them if they would like to bring their production to London for a short season. They were very happy to do this because it was their intention anyway to transfer their activities to Europe. I got in touch with an American producer, Arthur Lewis, who had been connected with the musical *How to Succeed in Business Without Really Trying*, which I had at one time hoped to be involved in presenting in London. He agreed to co-present *The Brig* with me at the Mermaid Theatre, which Bernard Miles made available for a four week season.

The Brig is both a formal and intensely realistic picture of life in an American military prison. It opened at the Mermaid Theatre on 2 September 1964. Its impact on an audience was overwhelming as these short extracts from the notices show: 'A drill, a fist in the guts, a hangover, a nightmare', (*The Sunday Telegraph*). 'Shattering', (*Daily Express*). 'Devastating', (*New York Times*). 'Horrifying, inescapable, and brilliant', (*Daily Mail*). It was all too much for the London audience of those days, and, although it had a reasonable four week run at the Mermaid, there was no possibility of giving it an extended run in the West End. The Living Theatre Company went off to Europe to prepare their productions for a tour there. They then began the nomadic life which was to bring them, after visiting many countries, back to the Roundhouse in London's Camden Town, when I had the privilege of presenting one of the most amazing seasons in a theatre that London has seen. But that was not until 1969. Before that Julian and Judith returned to New York to serve a jail sentence on federal tax charges.

In 1964 the Royal Court Theatre closed for some work to be done. George Devine had hoped to make a major reconstruction of the theatre, but in the event not enough money was available and only some improvements to the stalls bar, the seating and the decorations could be afforded. Whilst the Court was closed, it was decided to present a season of three plays in the West End, all to be directed by Tony Richardson and all to star Vanessa Redgrave. The three plays were to be Chekhov's *The Seagull*, Brecht's *St Joan of the Stockyards* and a new play by Michael Hastings, *The World's Baby*. My Company with Bernard Delfont and Tennents agreed to co-present the season with the English Stage Company.

A fine company of actors was assembled for *The Seagull*, which opened the season. Vanessa played Nina, Peggy Ashcroft Arkardina, Peter Finch Trigorin and George Devine was Dorn, giving perhaps the best performance of his career. All were splendid. The production had great notices and played to packed houses. When George as Dorn said, 'I don't know, maybe I don't understand anything, maybe I've gone off my head, but I did like that play. There is something in it. When that child was holding forth about loneliness, and later when the devil's red eyes appeared, I was so moved my hands were shaking. It was fresh, unaffected . . . Ah, I think he's coming along now. I feel like telling him a lot of nice things about it', it might have been George speaking back at the Royal Court. And he looked so handsome. It was a wonderful start to the Company's West End season. Alas, towards the end of the run and shortly after the start of rehearsals for *St Joan of the Stockyards*, Vanessa became pregnant and her doctor told her she should stop working. What were we to do? The play had a large cast. It was difficult and unlikely to be a success without a big star; only Vanessa's presence in the Company had made us select it. We were saved from total defeat by the fact that Siobhan McKenna, the Irish actress, had played the part in a production I had arranged in Dublin the year before, and she very gallantly agreed to take over at very short notice. The young directors at the Royal Court all offered to help and, in the short time we had, each one took particular scenes and worked on them. Some critics thought that this caused stylistic disunity in the production; I don't think it did, but was a fine example of all hands to the pumps in time of need, and a very Brechtian way of working after all. Despite all these difficulties I thought it was an excellent production of a wonderful play. Probably Siobhan was rather too romantic, more Joan of Arc than St. Joan of the Stockyards, and she didn't have Vanessa's drawing power. The play was a Marxist parable. Writing after seeing a German production, Kenneth Tynan described it thus: 'Brecht's piece is a bitter attempt to illustrate the interdependence of capitalism and religion, or – to put it more precisely – of profiteering and charity. As a portrait of Chicago, the play is less than convincing, but as a satire on the relationship between those who take and those who give, its pungency is tremendous.' I am sure that it was this pungency rather than any stylistic weakness which got up the critics' noses. They hated it, but for me the production by Tony Richardson, with Jocelyn Herbert's fine decor, was one of the most enjoyable I have ever had a hand in. To have the most openly Marxist of all Brecht's plays being performed at the Queen's Theatre in the very heart of the West End was a joy I shall not forget. What an heroic piece it is. Poetic and heroic, it could not find an audience and had to be withdrawn after a few weeks. Perhaps with Vanessa it might have worked. Our third play, *The World's Baby*, was dropped from the repertoire and the season closed. A sad fate for the English Stage Company's first attempt to mount a season in a larger theatre. George and I both made various attempts to do this, but they had never got beyond the planning stage. George had a scheme to do something at the Chelsea Palace, which fizzled out. I had worked on a plan with Laurence Olivier, George and Granada to turn the Met in the Edgware Road into a popular theatre, but that collapsed when it was decided to drive a road through the old theatre. Later, when I was Artistic Director of the Royal Court in the seventies, I had hopes of taking over the Old Vic, but they came to nothing. So the Queen's Theatre Season represents the only time when the English Stage Company actually presented a season of plays in a large theatre.

In 1963 I saw at the Arts Theatre Club an evening of short plays by Charles Wood under the title *Cockade*. Here was a very interesting new writer. Charles had been brought up in a theatrical family and had later served in the regular army. These two backgrounds obsessed him, and most of his future work was concerned with one or other or both of them. I got to know him well and produced three plays by him in the next few years, all jointly with the English Stage Company. The first was *Meals on Wheels*, directed at the Court by none other than John Osborne, who refers to it in his autobiography as a 'bizarre comic extravaganza of such inventiveness that nobody understands it.' 'I don't understand it either,' he adds. But we all set out to try and make it work. It was exactly the kind of play the English Stage Company was formed to produce, and Charles Wood exactly the kind of author it was formed to encourage. Of course the critics did not like it and it failed at the box office, but Charles went on to write three more plays that were presented at the Court.

Dingo was set in the Second World War in North Africa; it was refused a licence by the Lord Chamberlain and had to be presented under Club conditions. That meant that only members of the English Stage Society could buy tickets. The play subsequently formed the kernel of Richard Lester's film, *How I Won the War*, the script of which Charles Wood also wrote. *Dingo* was not a financial success of course, but an unforgettable experience for those who saw it.

The third play was *Fill the Stage With Happy Hours* about life backstage in a Weekly Repertory Theatre. It reminded me of my days at the Embassy Theatre with the Hawtreys. The Embassy of course was not a weekly rep, but it shared the same semi-public back stage life, particularly with its rows between the husband and wife, going on under the eyes of the few loyal members of the public who supported the theatre. At about this time Michael White was preparing to present the American Open Theatre at the Vaudeville Theatre, when the Lord Chamberlain refused them a licence. The Court arranged with Michael to turn itself again into a club theatre and have the Open Theatre do their season there, with Charles Wood's play taking its place at the Vaudeville. Bill Gaskill directed and Harry H. Corbett and Sheila Hancock played the leading parts. It was not quite strong enough and just too quirky for the West End, with the result that it had much the same limited run of a few weeks that it would have had at the Court. In addition to producing these three plays, I started Charles on a very successful career as a screenwriter, commissioning him to write his first screenplay for *The Knack*, which I produced and Richard Lester directed. Charles went on to write a number of films for Lester, including *The Bed Sitting Room*, which I produced. Charles Wood also wrote the final script for Tony Richardson's film, *The Charge of the Light Brigade*. This in turn led to his first real success in the theatre, *Veterans*, which was staged at the Court in 1972 and was inspired by his experiences working on that fine film.

It was in the mid sixties that I got to know Joe Orton. Woodfall Films, with whom I was then working, had decided to make a programme of three short films, each selected and directed by a different director. In the beginning these were to be Tony Richardson, Karel Reisz and Lindsay Anderson. Eventually Karel dropped out when he found the subject he had selected needed full length treatment. Lindsay decided he wanted to make a film with Richard Harris that would be a kind of modern Bacchae set in a Holiday Camp. I suggested that Joe Orton, whose early plays I knew, might be commissioned to write it and so arranged to have lunch with his agent, Peggy Ramsay, at L'Escargot to discuss it. At the lunch Peggy told me about Joe's second full-length play, *Loot*, which had had a disastrous tour and folded without coming into London. I asked to read the script: it was one of the funniest plays I'd ever read. I was sure that the production and/or the casting of Kenneth Williams as the Police Inspector Truscott must have been the cause of its failure and decided that I would like to produce the play from scratch. First I asked Michael Codron, who had been the original producer, if he would like to do it with me 50-50, but he would only do this if the new production took over the losses of the first one. I could see no reason why we should do this, since we should not be using any of its elements. Indeed I had not even seen it. As I was about to produce the film of *The Girl with Green Eyes* in Ireland at that time, I felt I had to have a partner and I asked Michael White to do *Loot* with me, which he gladly agreed to do. We arranged with the London offshoot of the Edinburgh Traverse Theatre, who were presenting a season of plays at the Jeanetta Cochrane Theatre in Kingsway, to produce the play there first, with the idea that Michael and I would subsequently move it to the West End. Charles Marowitz, the London Traverse's director at that time, agreed to direct. There were immediate conflicts between Charles and me over casting. I wanted Michael Bates to play Truscott and Ann Lynn to play Fay. Charles was not happy with either, Michael Bates because Michael did not like improvising during rehearsal – Ann Lynn because – I can't remember why he didn't want her – but I was away in Ireland and had to leave the decisions to Michael White. Eventually it was agreed that Michael Bates should play the part and Ann Lynn not. I was upset about this but too deeply involved in the film to play a constructive part in solving the problem. Although Sheila Ballantine made a good shot at the part, I have always thought it should have been more strongly cast. I did not think Marowitz's production first-rate and certainly Joe did not either, but the play worked astonishingly well and had almost a complete set of rave notices. It ran for over a year at the Criterion Theatre in the West End, won the *Evening Standard* award as the best play of 1966 and was eventually made into a bad movie. It has been repeatedly revived over the years.

But back to the modern Bacchae. Orton duly wrote *The Erpingham Camp* using this idea, but by that time Lindsay had decided on something else for his part of the Woodfall Trilogy. Joe turned his screenplay first into a T.V. play which was produced in 1966, and later into one half of a theatre double-bill which was staged at the Court in 1967, directed by Peter Gill. I was not involved in that production but enjoyed it as a member of the audience, and some years later had the idea of turning it into a musical but did not pursue it. I still think it was a good idea.

Loot was not a fantastic success at the box office, but it had low running costs and it suited both the producers of the play and the theatre to let the run continue, even though business was not great. It finished its run with a small profit, made much larger by a brilliant sale of the film rights by Peggy Ramsay. Joe was dubbed 'the Oscar Wilde of the Welfare State' by Ronald Bryden, then critic of *The Observer*. True, but it was his crazy non-sense logic as particularly exemplified in many of the speeches of Truscott in *Loot* and almost every speech in *What the Butler Saw* that I found most appealing.

The third fine writer that I became associated with in those years was the Irishman, Brian Friel. His first play, *Philadephia, Here I Come*, was sent to me by his agent, Curtis Brown; it appealed to me strongly and I decided to produce it. I had another play that I was planning to do at the Dublin Festival in association with my old friends Hilton Edwards and Micheál MacLíammóir. This was a play that Hilton had sent me, but which he lost to another Irish producer, so, with Brian's agreement, I offered him the opportunity to produce *Philadelphia* in its place. The play opened at the Gaiety Theatre on 28th September 1964 as part of the Dublin Theatre Festival. Directed by Hilton Edwards, the leading parts were played by Maureen O' Sullivan, Patrick Bedford, Donal Donelly and Eamonn Kelly. It was received with enthusiasm by critics and public. Two notices must

suffice: 'Five minutes after the curtain went up on Brian Friel's
Philadelphia Here I Come it was clear that here at last was an authentic
voice . . . Mr. Friel examines with great delicacy and inexhaustible humour the circumstances and the kind of climate which made it inevitable
that an Irish youth must emigrate . . . (he) has produced the unmistak-
able sound of real people talking to each other and in this case living
through an important moment in their lives.' Peter Lennon in *The
Guardian*. 'The best drama is always rooted in the soil from which it
springs; and *Philadelphia Here I Come* is all Ireland.' Harold Hobson in
The Sunday Times. Despite this encouraging start, I did not think the play
stood a great chance of success in London. Again I had invited Michael
White to join me, and together we arranged instead for the play to be
presented in New York by David Merrick. *The New York Times* had a
critic at that time, by the name of Kaufmann, who had a habit of
attending a preview of the show he was going to review and writing his
notice from his experience of that performance. David Merrick suspected
that Mr. Kaufmann would not like our play and so he closed the theatre
on the night of the preview on the excuse that 'a rat had been found in
the theatre.' This got the play enormous publicity, Mr Kaufmann did not
like it, but all the other critics did, and we enjoyed a long and successful
run on Broadway followed by an equally successful tour. Apart from his
usual charming suggestion that the director should be sacked during the
pre-New York opening tour, David Merrick treated us and the Company
and everyone connected with the play well. I have never known him to
like a company of actors so much. I think it was quite the happiest
association we had with him.

After the end of the tour, and against my better judgement and, I
think, Michael's, but urged on by our investors and the fact that the
author also wanted his play to be seen in London, we brought the same
production and cast into the Lyric Theatre, where after a run of a few
weeks it died the death I had predicted for it The English West End
public at that time simply could not be persuaded to see Irish plays, even
an engaging one like *Philadelphia Here I Come*.

In July 1967, Hilton Edwards directed another piece by Friel, a
double-bill, entitled *Lovers*. He presented it in association with my Company at his own theatre, The Gate in Dublin, and afterwards, in somewhat the same way in which we had arranged to go to New York under

David Merrick's banner, the plays were presented by Helen Bonfils and Morton Gottlieb at the Lincoln Center, though on this occasion one important part was re-cast with an American star, Art Carney. The plays again enjoyed a success in New York. This time however, I did not present them in London, but leased the rights to a management then running the Fortune Theatre, and again London audiences failed to respond.

I was associated with Brian Friel in a number of productions in later years, but it was not until I had ceased to be active as a London producer that Brian himself broke through the resistance of London playgoers to Irish plays. *Dancing at Lughnasa* from the Abbey Theatre took London by storm in 1990, won awards as the best play of the year and moved on to conquer New York. It is a fine, moving, poetic play, Friel at his best. I wish I had still been around to produce it, but it shows that no matter how long you have to wait, if you plant and tend the right seeds, one day they will blossom. That's the kind of gardener I tried to be, no matter if sometimes the first fruits were not quite to the public's taste. In 1992 *Philadelphia Here I Come* was itself revived very successfully at the Kings Head Theatre but again it failed on transfer to the West End.

1968 was a year in which I worked closely with John Osborne. We had been friends since meeting in the early days of the English Stage Company. We had been partners in Woodfall Films but during the preparations for *The Charge of the Light Brigade*, for which John Osborne wrote the first draft script and which I was producing, both of us fell out with Tony Richardson, the director of the film, and each of us for our own reasons resigned from the project and from future Woodfall activities. From that time onwards, although a number of films were made in Woodfall's name, they were made by a new Woodfall company controlled by Tony. However, John and Tony were still both on the board of my theatre production company, and that year John wrote two plays, *Time Present* and *Hotel in Amsterdam*, which, because he had fallen out with the English Stage Company, he offered to me to produce. I thought that it would be wisest to start them off at the Royal Court and John agreed. Anthony Page, who since *Inadmissible Evidence* had directed all John's plays, was again asked and agreed to direct them. In both plays there was a principal character who never appeared. In *Time Present* it was a character who must have been inspired by memories of George Devine and also of Godfrey Tearle, a distinguished actor who had recently died. Tearle and Jill Bennett, who at the time of this production was John's wife, had had a close relationship which Jill later wrote about in her book, *Godfrey, A Special Time Remembered*. Another character, that of a young, politically involved but naive actress, played by Kika Markham, must have been suggested by Vanessa Redgrave's activities of that period. Jill herself played the principal role of Pamela, the daughter of the old actor, Orme, who is dying during the course of the play. *Time Present* was a great success at the Court, and we transferred it to the Duke of York's Theatre in St. Martin's Lane, bringing in to the Royal Court John's second play, *Hotel in Amsterdam*, with Paul Scofield playing the leading part of Laurie. In it a group of friends visit Amsterdam in an effort to escape for a little while from the unseen producer with whom they are all obsessed, and about whom they never stop talking. This did well at the Court too, and transferred to the New Theatre, also in St. Martin's Lane. Later that year we revived *Look Back in Anger* at the Court, with Victor Henry playing Jimmy Porter and Anthony Page directing, and we transferred this production to the Criterion Theatre, the first time *Look Back* had had a West End run. So John Osborne had three plays running in the West End, two of them side by side in St. Martin's Lane. I had by this time moved my office from Curzon Street to Goodwin's Court just off St. Martin's Lane and it was a great pleasure each time I stepped out of my office to see the whole of one side of Lower St. Martin's Lane occupied by John's plays. I particularly relished, in the great love scene in Act II, the way that Scofield would pick out the individual words and phrases and hold each one for a moment before going on to the next: 'Because ... to me ... you have always been the most dashing . . . .romantic . . . friendly . . . playful . . . impetuous . . . larky . . . fearful . . . detached . . . constant . . . woman I have ever met . . . and I love you ... I don't know how else one says it ... one shouldn't ... and I've always thought you felt . . . perhaps the same about me.' Minor works in the Osborne cannon they may be, but these two plays were deeply felt and had an urgency and passion found nowhere else in English play writing of that time and seldom since. Jill Bennett won the *Evening Standard* award for the best performance by an actress for her performance in *Time Present*, while *Hotel in Amsterdam* won the *Evening Standard* award for Best Play of 1968.

The only other theatre production I was involved with in 1968 was *Spitting Image*, a play by Colin Spencer which I saw first at the Hampstead Theatre Club and I decided to move to the West End. A funny and charming fantasy about two gay men who live together and one of whom becomes pregnant; on its opening night at the Duke of York's it was booed by the Gallery First Nighters, who found it shocking. It should have warned me of what to expect when we did Joe Orton's next play, but it didn't. In earlier days the Gallery First Nighters had been on the whole a progressive group, but the changes in attitude that the sixties brought had left them behind.

While *Loot* was still running at the Criterion Theatre, Joe Orton gave me a copy of *What the Butler Saw*, his new play. I thought it was the best thing he had done and immediately offered to produce it. As he reports in his diary, Joe finished typing the play on 16 July 1967. He notes: 'I added very little on this version.' This implies that what he was typing was already a revised version. Some people have suggested that the play remained unfinished at his death, but I am sure it was ready for rehearsal when he died and would not have been much revised during the rehearsal process had he lived, nor do I think it required revision. In the same entry in his diary Joe also wrote, 'Great relief to have finished *The Butler*. I can now give my mind full rein for the historical farce set on the eve of Edward VII's coronation in 1902 and called (at the moment) *Prick Up Your Ears*.' This was the title originally suggested by his lover and companion, Kenneth Halliwell, for Joe's film script, which was eventually called *Up Against It*. Joe thought *Prick Up Your Ears* 'too good a title for a film'. It was, of course, eventually used by John Lahr for the title of his Orton biography and for the film based on that book, so it was not wasted.

Joe told me about his projected Edward VII play and I did not ask for details because I was sure he would give me a script as soon as it was finished. I had the impression that he had the whole outline worked out in his mind, but at the time of his death no script was found. In July Joe and Kenneth came down to stay with me and my family in our house in Brighton for a weekend to discuss *What the Butler Saw*. A bizarre account is given in his diary from which I gathered that, fortunately for us, he considered my two sons sexually unattractive and that he failed to get a cup of tea at bedtime when he and Kenneth needed one. It wasn't our

habit to offer guests a cup of tea before they retired but I had hoped that
our relationship was sufficiently informal for him to have asked for one if
he wanted it. His whole account shows either that his diaries are a work
of fiction intended more for publication than as a record of the truth or
that one can be quite wrong about one's friends' reactions. Or both. John
Osborne's autobiography and Joe Orton's diary, what should I make of
them?

Discussing the casting of *Butler*, both Joe and I agreed to go for Arthur
Lowe as Prentice. Various names were discussed for Dr. Rance. These
included Ralph Richardson, who Joe had seen and admired in the T.V.
series *Blandings Castle* and Alistair Sim. In his diary Joe says he thought
Ralph 'a good ten years too old.' Sim was in fact slightly older than
Richardson. But of course we never thought this discussion was to be the
last we'd have on the subject. Joe had insisted that he did not want me to
produce the play with Michael White, who, following our association on
Loot, I should have automatically invited in with me. In May 1967,
according to a note in the published edition of his Diaries, Joe had written to Peggy Ramsay saying: 'Really though, I think its a miracle [*Loot*
has] run so long. We can't grumble at its falling off. The great middle
brow public never took it to their hearts. Which brings me neatly to
Broadway. I curse Michael White from the bottom of my pitiless soul for
getting some sucker to agree to on-Broadway. It will flop in a fortnight. I
was looking forward to the Establishment or the Cherry Lane . . . ' Joe's
fears proved absolutely justified. The Broadway production was a disaster, but the decision to go on-Broadway was jointly made by me and by
Michael. Whether Off-Broadway would have been better no one can say.

For instance, of the American production of *What the Butler Saw*,
which was produced off-Broadway, John Lahr writes: 'Orton destroyed
the boulevard safety of farce only to have the Americans restore it in a
campy, sloppy off-Broadway production which the critics characterised
as enchanting, sunny, disarming and friendly. Typically the American
commercial theatre had devoured Orton without digesting him. The
production was a commercial success and an artistic disaster.'

It was, therefore, quite unreasonable of Joe to quarrel with Michael on
this account after working with him apparently happily throughout the
run of *Loot*. I was absolutely unable to get Joe to change his mind, so we
discussed the idea of enlisting Binkie Beaumont of Tennents, who had

expressed interest previously in producing a play by Joe. Through Binkie we thought we'd have a good chance of getting the sort of cast we required, and the sort of first class West End theatre we thought would suit the play. I suggested we should try for the Theatre Royal, Haymarket, traditionally the most aristocratic theatre in London. Joe agreed that it would be a joke in itself to do the play there. We also wanted to have a Tennent type of naturalistic, plush set. We discussed the Lord Chamberlain and worried about what changes he would demand, but of course in the event the Lord Chamberlain's role as an official censor had been abolished before the play was produced.

At the same time as we were talking about *What the Butler Saw*, we were also involved together in setting up Joe's film *Up Against It*, which he had been commissioned to write by the Beatles, who had decided against it after he had written and submitted the first draft. I liked the script. Joe made some small changes, chiefly re-writing it for three boys instead of four, and I offered it to Dick Lester to direct. I thought that of all the directors I knew, Dick was the one most likely to respond to Joe's work. In his diary, Joe says 'Oscar told me that Dick Lester had more or less turned down the film.' I cannot think where this came from, because, in fact, after considering it, Dick said he did want to do it. It's true that he had not said this by the time Joe and I spent that weekend together, but early in August, I told Joe that Dick was interested and wanted to meet him to discuss the next steps. We arranged lunch on August 10th at Twickenham Studios, where Dick had his offices. I went down to Twickenham earlier in the morning and sent my car back with Derek Taylor, my chauffeur, to collect Joe at his flat and bring him down to Twickenham. When Derek rang the bell at the flat he got no answer, so phoned me to ask what he should do. I was very surprised because Joe was not forgetful about appointments and was certainly not likely to be about this one. I told Derek to go back and try again. When he went back, on again getting no reply, he looked through the letter box and saw a naked body lying in the room apparently asleep. Derek phoned me again. I was worried that perhaps Joe had been taking drugs. I suggested that Derek should call Peggy Ramsay and ask for her advice. She said 'Call the police.' As I waited at Twickenham, I became increasingly apprehensive. I did wonder if Joe had committed suicide, but thought it very unlikely. He seemed much too pleased with himself. Finally Derek phoned and told me that the police had come and found that Joe had been murdered by his room-mate, who had then taken an overdose and killed himself. I was astonished. I hadn't known how violent Joe's relationship with Kenneth had sometimes been.

I gave the news to Dick and spent the remainder of the day in a daze of disbelief. The whole thing seemed so unreal, more like a scene from one of Joe's plays. I went to his funeral at Golder's Green Crematorium. Harold Pinter and Donald Pleasance read poems, and the Beatles' 'A Day in the Life' was played on a tape recorder as the coffin was brought in. The 'service' was arranged by Peter Willes, Head of Drama for Yorkshire T.V. and a friend and strong supporter of Joe's. Peter Willes had had very little sympathy or liking for Kenneth Halliwell, and, in fact, at a dinner party shortly before the fatal night had, I was told, brutally insulted Kenneth saying to him 'You, you're nothing, absolutely nothing.' For a man with so little self assurance as Kenneth, this must have been devastating . . .

When Lester and I returned to the question of what we should do about the film of *Up Against It*, we decided to try to find another writer who could work on the project and make the changes that Dick had wanted to discuss with Orton. We tried several writers but none were successful in achieving what Dick wanted. So we had to abandon the project. United Artists had agreed to put up the money for the Orton film and Dick and I were able to pursuade them to back another black comedy that we had both of us wanted to film. This was *The Bed Sitting Room*, a play by Spike Milligan and John Antrobus. We now got down to working on this. Our old friend Charles Wood wrote the script and Ralph Richardson played the title role, which gave me the opportunity to ask him to play in *What the Butler Saw*.

Binkie Beaumont agreed to co-produce the play. And now, for the first and last time, I had a serious artistic disagreement with Peggy Ramsay. She did not like the idea of Arthur Lowe for Prentice. Neither did Binkie. Both of them completely underrated this splendid actor. So instead of Arthur, Stanley Baxter was cast. A good comedian but wrong in the same way that Kenneth Williams had been wrong for Truscott in *Loot*. To direct the play, Binkie suggested Robert Chetwyn, mainly known for West End comedies. I, who did not know much about his work, agreed. Wrongly, as it turned out.

The play went on a short tour to Cambridge and Brighton before opening at the Queen's Theatre, Shaftesbury Avenue. The owner of the Haymarket Theatre could not be persuaded to take it, even though, in the absence of the Lord Chamberlain, the references to Churchill's prick had been toned down at the instigation of Ralph Richardson. But the Queen's was almost as good. In Cambridge the play had gone down quite well, though Ralph had had some difficulties with his lines, but in Brighton some members of the audience were outraged that an actor such as Sir Ralph Richardson should lend his support to such a play. This upset Ralph very much and he replied personally to every protesting letter. He may have been a little old and slow moving for the part, but he brought a quality to the mad Inspector Rance the like of which will never be seen again. I do not think casting him was a mistake.

On the first night in the West End all went well until the Second Act, when that same group of Gallery First Nighters who had booed *Spitting Image*, decided to interrupt the performance. This they did by cat calling and heckling all through the last scene. This was made worse by the fact that in this scene, where the script calls for metal grilles to fall over each of the doors, we had a metal grid, like the front of a cage, which was lowered between stage and auditorium and effectively cut off the actors from the audience. I should have realised on tour that this was a not a good idea, for it made playing comedy much more difficult. That, plus the interruptions, made the last part of the play a complete disaster.

As John Lahr, Orton's biographer, wrote; 'Critics mistook the flaws in the production for limitations in the script, and Orton's best work became the most grossly misunderstood and under-rated.'

Only Frank Marcus in the *Sunday Telegraph* appreciated Orton's achievement. Under the headline 'A CLASSIC IS BORN', he wrote: '*What the Butler Saw* will live to be accepted as a comedy classic of English literature.' Not until 1975, when I was the Artistic Director of the Royal Court Theatre, was I able to make amends. I then arranged a season of Orton's three full-length plays in the course of which Lindsay Anderson directed a fine revival of *What the Butler Saw* and, as Lahr said, 'the play's reputation was firmly established.'

I knew Joe Orton for less than two years and although I saw Joe and Kenneth Haliwell quite often in the course of our work during that time, I never visited their flat and I cannot say that I got to know either of them well. Joe and I had very little in common except our enthusiasm for his plays. I found him charming and easy to work with and had no idea of the anger and anguish that are revealed in his diaries and in Lahr's splendid biography.

Part Six

The Living Theatre

epic theatre at the Roundhouse

The Roundhouse, Camden Town, was the scene of my second controversial venture that year. Reviled by conventional theatre-goers, applauded by the new alternative fringe audience, this was the first London visit of the Living Theatre since their years in Europe, following the Mermaid production of *The Brig*. Whilst in Europe, they created four new productions, *Mysteries and Smaller Pieces*, and *Paradise Now*, both devised by the Company, *Frankenstein*, based on Mary Shelley's novel, and *Antigone* by Brecht. The first of these had no script, though there was a set sequence of scenes.

Mysteries was introduced in the programme by two statements, the first by Artaud, the second by Julian Beck, which ran: ' . . . we aren't in New York because financial horror destroyed us there . . . this special performance is a public enactment of ritual games which are part of our work . . . If our work should succeed at any moment it is because we on the stage will reflect every man in the street; that is, we will have achieved Artaud's vision of the actor "being like victims burnt at the stake, signalling through the flames".'

There was no set; the action took place on a bare stage except for the use of four boxes in the second act. There were no costumes, each actor wore whatever he happened to have on before the show. There were few words. The first scene started with an actor standing at attention, facing the front, centre stage. He held this position for six minutes during which no word was spoken. Then nine other actors entered and performed a mime from the field-day clean up from the *Brig*. Then a fugue was chanted of all the words that appear on a U.S. dollar bill. The clean-up continued, a Commander screamed out a long gibberish order to which the cast replied with a roaring 'Yes, Sir.' Blackout. The last scene, and the most powerful, represented The Plague or a similar catastrophe.

The programme described it thus: 'The entire company silhouetted as they move about in a confused, trance-like state, some standing, heads bent, some sitting and clutching at their bodies, other writhing and moaning on the floor. A scream; a body thuds to the stage; others fall on top of him. Everyone is crawling over and under everyone else, violent assaults occur, bodies roll off the stage into the audience, the actors, gasping, blubbering, sputtering and wailing. Immense and uncontrollable paroxysms. Expiring with grimaces and shudders, the actors stagger, crawl and wiggle up the aisles, tears and saliva dribbling from their faces; they grasp the arms of seats on the aisles and double over at the feet of the people in the seats. Some run screaming out to the foyer, stepping on the others, to die out there. Death rattles and rigor mortis. Half an hour after the scene starts, the entire cast is dead. In the silence, six actors rise and, zombie-like, straighten the contorted limbs and torsos of the corpses, first putting the shoes of the dead onstage in rows, then carrying the stiff bodies onstage. The first ten bodies are put side by side, head to feet, in a neat row, and the rest are placed on top of them, in two smaller rows, forming a pyramidal body-pile. The carriers then step back and stand in a semi-circle, gravely observing the bodies.'

The effect was overwhelming.

But *Frankenstein* was the best of the four. It was visually brilliant, the set consisting of a huge scaffolding divided up into boxes, in which the individual scenes were performed. At one point the actors swarmed up on the scaffolding, their bodies backlit in silhouette, to form a twenty foot high monster swaying on the structure with two blazing red eyes in its head.

Antigone was a fairly conventional production of the play. I thought it the worst of their four productions and showed up the actors' weaknesses.

Paradise Now was amazing in quite a different sense. About a third was improvised.

Ronald Bryden wrote in *The Observer*:

'ROUSING THE AUDIENCE

'At one point during the uncategorisable event at the Roundhouse which the Living Theatre calls *Paradise Now*, its actors retreat to a green pool of light where they lean wearily back to back, breathing deeply and shouldering each other like sleepy horses. Slowly, their breath coming in hisses, they start eddying round the stage. The motion and sound are those of an embryonic hurricane.

'Their churning grows faster. Heads toss, green arms flail like wind-whipped palms or breakers. Deeper sounds, groans of a labouring volcano, erupt from the maelstrom of bodies. From the boiling, spinning knot, actors fly off headlong up the aisles, once more to hector, plead and argue incoherently with the audience. The revolution is a wheel spinning off living energy, they cry. Make it real! Do it now! Begin!

'That image of the evening's intention distils most of the best and worst, the bathos and superb power, of which the Living Theatre are capable. No company I've ever seen can contrive, when it wills, more compressed theatricality. None is more prone to centrifugal scattering of energy and talent in diffuse, time-wasting incoherence. But, as the image conveys cunningly, both are parts of one process. The Livers' faults are the other face of their virtues.

'*Paradise Now* makes no pretence to be a play in the usual sense. It is an exercise in audience-rousing: alternately a ceremony and under-graduate bull-session, balletic ritual and shouting match at Speakers' Corner. It recalls some nineteenth-century revival meeting on the Missis-sippi frontier: smatterings of liturgy punctuating raucous, corny huckster hysteria in an attempt to preach up a storm, wrestle, entrance and gal-vanise all-comers into instant salvation. But the religion is revolutionary anarchism: worship of the individual, his unhidden body and its senses and their total freedom.

'In other words, theatre as primitive, literal magic. The thing that bothers and enrages people about Julian Beck's and Judith Malina's travelling commune, I suspect, is that they are genuine symbolists. You can buy a handsome dossier at the Roundhouse on their recent Yale visit, in which senior New York critics and student activists alike foam at their pretension, artiness and naivety. But they believe that a symbol contains the reality it images; that a rite releases the power of the emotion it figures forth in metaphor. So that, to revolutionaries, they are ivory tower aesthetes, playing arty games with minority audiences and pretending this can change the world. Their talk is of demolishing States and prisons, but on stage their rebellion goes no further than stripping to jockstraps – even their nudity has to be symbolised. Preaching revolution, their only voice is mimed stage agression, the occasional fist, dusty foot or bawling mouth thrust in the face of startled aisle-sitters.

'Meanwhile to aesthetes, their art is hopelessly compromised by their insistence on 'making it real'. Each play is slowed by long, brooding pauses in which the cast work themselves and, they hope, the audience into the mood for the next bit of action. Control, intensity, are sacrificed while they thread the aisles, echoing the play's message to us, face to face in their own persons. *Paradise Now* is the end of the line. Having provoked us with yelled slogans, soothed us with pats and blessings (Holy hand! Holy ear!), they turn over the evening to us for long inert stretches in which people sit, mill and argue desultorily, like children at a party with no organised games.

'I hope I'm as much revolutionary as aesthete, but I minded the attempts at reality as much as I liked their artifice. You can't make a profession of watching plays without believing in them in the deepest sense: rehearsals of life. In their rituals, it seems to me, the Livers genuinely achieve what they preach: the sharpening of experience, the full exploitation of time, the initiation of revolution where all revolutions begin – in mind and feeling.

'Yet I can see that the intensity of those rituals comes from their conviction that they are not merely playing. I can see their need to believe that they are not just entertaining a mass of passive onlookers – The revolution will not come, intones Steven Ben Israel, an actor with the head of an angelic Blakeian lion, until people become people, not chairs. The whole power of the group is their magnificent ensemble training, a unity inseparable from the force of belief which holds them together, a ragged caravanserai travelling from country to country in their three battered Volkswagen vans, sharing each evening's take.'

The director and critic, Charles Marowitz concluded an open letter to the Becks in *Plays and Players* by saying: 'There is no doubt in my mind that yours is the most fertilising and significant theatre company in the world. You spawned the Open Theatre and made La Mama possible. You have inspired the young everywhere you have gone, and even though irrational and contradictory, your work nourished the spirit of revolution.' On the other hand, many critics, such as Milton Shulman of the *Evening Standard*, Lambert of *The Sunday Times* and Nightingale, then of the *New Statesman* found the work of the Living Theatre 'boring' and 'stupid'.

Night after night, the Roundhouse was packed with a young audience, most of whom were probably not regular theatre-goers. The season was publicised mainly through the alternative press, in particular by Jim Haynes of the *International Times* and the Arts Lab. Also in the audience almost every night were directors from the Royal Court and other subsidised theatres, and many, including Peter Brook and Bill Gaskill, were influenced in their future work by what they saw. It was not just the work but the whole nature of the Company.

In his book *The Empty Space*, Peter Brook writes ' . . . this group, led by Julian Beck and Judith Malina, is special in every sense of the word. It is a nomad community. It moves across the world according to its own laws and often in contradiction to the laws of the country in which it happens to be. It provides a complete way of life for every one of its members, some thirty men and women who live and work together; they make love, produce children, act, invent plays, do physical and spiritual exercises, share and discuss everything that comes their way.'

I have often wondered if Peter Brook would have started his own group in Paris had it not been for the Living Theatre's example. The Living Theatre was without doubt one of the inspirations behind the whole fringe theatre movement in both Britain and the U.S.A. Maybe in Europe also. And all this they did without a regular subsidy of any kind.

The Roundhouse season was presented in conjunction with an American, Victor Herbert, whom I had met in Paris when I was producing Truffaut's film, *The Bride Wore Black*, with Jeanne Moreau. Victor allowed us to use his flat for one of our locations. We gave the Living Theatre a small guarantee against a percentage of the takings. The guarantee was just enough to cover their modest living costs. The season just covered our costs with a little bit over, which we were able to pass on to the Living Theatre. But they were not an easy group to work with. For instance the Becks asked us to arrange some inexpensive accommodation for the Company where they could stay when they arrived until they made other arrangements. We found a hostel in Paddington, cheap and central. We sent them over some flowers to greet them.

When they saw their accommodation, Steven Ben Israel, one of their leading actors, threw the flowers into the street. The hostel was clean and bare. I think they would have preferred cardboard boxes under Waterloo Bridge. Most of the cast had contacts in London, anyway, made when they were there with *The Brig* and soon moved out of the Hostel to cosy nests of their own choosing.

At the beginning of their *Book of the Living Theatre* they have this page:

A is for alice
N is for new
A is for another or also
R is for reefers rebirth and repose
C is for cock c is for cunt
H is for harvest
Y is for you

They were anarchists, mystics, into L.S.D. and the psychological theories of R.D. Laing, in fact they perfectly exemplified the spirit of the student movements of the sixties. I did not agree with their politics or their philosophy although I was sympathetic to their anarchic critique of both socialist and liberal capitalist societies and I admired their spirit, their fantastic dedication to their work and to their cause. Julian was a brilliant designer, an impressive actor and an amazing organiser and leader. I was more doubtful about Judith's abilities as an actress, but as a director and as an inspiration to the Company, she had fire, passion and imagination of a high order.

The Living Theatre season was the first production I had mounted at the Roundhouse. Built as a locomotive turning shed in 1846, the building had been taken over by Arnold Wesker's Centre 42 in 1967. Arnold wanted to make extensive alterations but had to abandon the project when he was unable to raise sufficient money to do so. It was then run as an Arts Centre by the Roundhouse Trust, the Administrator of which was George Hoskins, who had been brought in by Arnold at Harold Wilson's suggestion. Hoskins, without any adequate subsidy, kept the building open, making it the centre for pop concerts and many of the most interesting fringe and alternative activities of the time. The Roundhouse was almost

derelict and had been used as a store, when Wesker had the brilliant idea
of turning it into a performing space. For myself, I liked it as it was and
think it would have lost its unique quality if Wesker's plans had been put
into execution. He would have turned an amazing, strong, rough, circus-
like space into a conventional palace of culture. Fortunately it remained
in its unimproved state, the perfect setting for the Living Theatre.

Despite the excitement, 1969 was a bad year financially. *What the
Butler Saw* lost money and the Living Theatre Season did not make any.
In addition to that we had two other financial disasters that year. The
first was a small scale American rock musical, *Your Own Thing*, which
had had a long run off-Broadway and which my company, together with
Tennent's, brought over to the Comedy Theatre. The show was good but
came at the wrong time and it needed the kind of small informal theatre
it had played in off Broadway, and which we do not have. It made little
impact, ran a few weeks and died.

The other production was a new play by Ann Jellicoe, author of *The
Knack*, *The Sport of My Mad Mother*, and *Shelley*, all plays that had been
produced at the Royal Court. Ann had never had a commercial success
in the theatre and she and I hoped that her new play, *The Giveaway*,
would give her one. It was a quirky, light, fantastic farce about the
strange results of winning a breakfast cereal competition. We cast it
strongly with Rita Tushingham, Roy Hudd and Dandy Nichols playing
the leads. Richard Eyre, then an up and coming young director, directed
it. The play opened at the Lyceum Theatre, Edinburgh, with which
Richard was associated at the time. Edinburgh loved it and it had a very
successful three weeks. I had grave doubts about its viability for the
West End, but I was alone. Richard particularly, now the Director of the
Royal National Theatre, was much too satisfied with his production. I
found him very unself-critical and, as a result, not at all easy to work
with. Time changed him, but not rapidly enough to save *The Giveaway*,
which we brought into the Garrick Theatre and had to take off very
quickly. It was, I think, the most complete disaster I ever had in the
theatre, yet had it been presented at the Royal Court, its considerable
charm might well have made it a limited success there.

Perhaps because I was still recovering from these blows, for the first time
in many years I produced nothing in the theatre or in films in 1970. My

company's overheads were covered by profits coming in from the films *Tom Jones* and *The Knack*.

The Arts Council had set up an Enquiry into the Theatre in 1967, the report of which did not come out until 1970. I was an active member of this Enquiry on which sat many of the leading figures of the entertainment world of the day, including Hugh (Binkie) Beaumont, Lord Bernstein, Richard Findlater, Robin Fox, John Mortimer, Sir Max Rayne and Kenneth Tynan. One member I got to know for the first time was Michael Elliott, later the inspirer and founder of the Royal Exchange Theatre, Manchester. A fine director with both the face and the integrity of a classical puritan. I never worked with him on a production – on the whole our tastes were different – but very quickly we established a mutual respect and liking which survived the years. A sub-committee, of which I was an active member, was set up to work out the details of a new theatre investment fund. In the words of the Enquiry's Report: 'The business of this body was to augment the output, improve the distribution and raise the standard of productions by making loans to responsible managements seeking to present new plays of interest and revivals of quality and to tour them as widely as possible.' The fund continues to exist to the present time. The Enquiry issued a report of some 80 pages and made recommendations concerning all aspects of the commercial and subsidised theatre, both in London and the provinces, which it is impossible to summarise here. It was particularly concerned with the serious decline in the touring system and stressed the need for increased subsidy. It questioned how much the London theatre should dominate the theatre in Great Britain. I think it was a useful report, which had considerable influence in the years that followed.

Following The Theatre Enquiry, I was a member of a number of Arts Council Committees. The one I enjoyed the most was the New Activities Enquiry, followed by The New Activities Committee. These bodies were concerned with the Arts Council's support of the new fringe artistic activities which had burst forth in the sixties. The Enquiry was set up to look into the nature of these activities and report back to the Arts Council its recommendations as far as their subsidy in the future was concerned. The Committee was chaired by Michael Astor, formerly a Conservative M.P., the Vice-Chairman was Jack Lambert, then Literary Editor of *The Sunday Times*, and the rest of the Enquiry was composed partly of new activities practitioners themselves, such as Peter Stark of the Birmingham Arts Lab, Jenny Harris and Ruth Marks of the Brighton Combination, Ian Bruce and Maggie Penhorn, and partly of various arts and establishment figures, such as Professor James Joll, Sir Edward Boyle M.P., and the artist, John Craxton. Apart from various heated discussions at meetings, the members of the Enquiry were invited to visit various parts of the country and view the new activities for themselves. I shall never forget visits to fringe festivals at St. Ives in Cornwall and Hebden Bridge in Yorkshire. Some of the groups on view were really exciting and innovative, like Welfare State, run by John Fox, and the John Bull Puncture Repair Outfit. Others were less talented, but all were letting their hair down and having a good time. Many of the groups had been started by ex-students from Art Colleges with the result that the visual side was stronger than the literary. Astor and Lambert looked as if they wished they were at Glyndebourne. I, on the other hand enjoyed a lot of what we saw very much indeed: it was clear that it would lead on to even more exciting work, provided it was supported and encouraged – and subsidised.

Back in the Committee room these differences caused a rift. Michael Astor was preparing a report which I and many members of the Enquiry thought was not supportive enough of the work we were seeing. One day he said 'If you disagree, you'd better write a minority report.' With a number of the other members of the Enquiry, particularly Peter Stark, Jenny Harris and Griselda Grimond, helping me, we prepared a report which urged the Arts Council to give more support to New Activities, asking for a modest two and a half per cent of their budget to go for this purpose. When the report was debated, everyone on the Enquiry except Michael Astor and Jack Lambert supported it and so it went forward to the main board of the Arts Council and a New Activities Committee was set up to advise the Council on future support for such work. For some time I served on that Committee too. For years afterward, the New Activities Committee was the single most influential force in British Alternative Theatre.

I was also a member of the Drama Panel of the Arts Council from 1970 to 1975. The Arts Council was organised then, and I suppose still is, upon the basis of having a number of specialist panels, which advised the officers of the Arts Council on the disposal of the available subsidy and other matters concerning the particular art form in which they were interested. The personnel of these panels served by invitation of the Arts Council, on an unpaid basis, usually for a period of three years. Some came from the subsidised and some from the commercial sector and others – such as critics or academics, not directly working as artists or administrators in the field with which the panel was concerned – were also invited to serve. I enjoyed my work at the Arts Council, particularly during the time that Lord Goodman was Chairman. When he left something of the life of the organisation went out of it. Although certainly no radical, Lord Goodman was available to everyone and found time for everyone. He and Jennie Lee were responsible for the best things done by the Arts Council and in their time (Lord Goodman was the Chairman for seven years from 1965) it was a really progressive body.

On 4th August 1970, Neville Blond died. He had been the Chairman of the English Stage Company since its beginning and his support and drive made the enterprise possible. Robin Fox, a leading theatrical agent and I were elected Joint Chairmen; I chaired the Artistic Committee and Robin the Management Committee and each was the other's deputy on those two committees. Bill Gaskill was now the Artistic Director at the Royal Court and I worked closely with him under the new arrangement. We got on well and I can only remember one instance when the Committee had to over-rule him. This was when Charles Wood submitted his play *Veterans* for production at the Court. Bill liked it, recommended it for production to the Artistic Committee and then said he would direct it himself. Charles Wood did not agree with the idea of Bill directing, and Bill was going to turn the play down on this account. We could not allow this to happen, and the play went ahead with Ronald Eyre directing. John Gielgud played the leading part. The play, and John Gielgud's appearance in it, shocked Brighton when it played the Theatre Royal, and each time Bob Hoskins, who played an electrician, said 'Fuck' – and he said it a great many times – a seat went up. However, when it came into the Court it was a great success though sadly John Gielgud, still bruised from his experience at Brighton would not transfer in the play, and so Charles lost his best chance of a commercial success.

In October and November, Bill arranged a Festival of Fringe companies and performers at the Royal Court under the title *Come*

Together. The idea was to show the best of the experimental work being done at that time. There were about twenty productions presented in the Theatre Upstairs and on the main stage, which Bill extended out into the auditorium and had part of the audience sitting on the stage. The Court itself produced *AC/DC* by Heathcote Williams, *Christie in Love* by Howard Brenton and *Beckett 3*: a programme of three short plays, *Cascando*, *Come and Go* and *Play*. Groups participating included the Brighton Combination, Pip Simmons, The Alberts, The Theatre Machine, and Ken Campbell's Road Show. Two items I shall never forget: Stuart Brisley's *A Celebration for Due Process*, which concluded with him vomiting on to the stage from a height of twelve feet and Peter Dockley's *Foul-fowl*, a sequence involving chicken feathers, carpet foam and actors painted blue. Philip Roberts in his book, *The Royal Court*, gives a fuller account of this wonderful event. Perhaps it is as well that Neville died before it took place. It might have killed him.

I thought of Neville again not so long ago when I was going round an antiquarian bookshop in the Charing Cross Road on the look out for books by or about William Blake. On a shelf I noticed the two volume Nonesuch edition of the Poems of John Milton illustrated by Blake. Inside each was the book plate of Neville Blond. The plate itself was typical of Neville. It was large and had a picture of his country house surrounded by a sheaf of wheat. At the bottom of the field, coming down from the house, was what I took to be a picture of his prize bulls. Beneath this was an illustration of his C.M.G. medal flanked by leather bound books and at the bottom of the plate his name in large letters. What surprised me was his choice of books. Had I misjudged him, had he really spent some of his time reading the Roundhead poet and the anarchist-mystic Blake? Did this explain his support for the Royal Court's fights with the Lord Chamberlain and its championship of such writers as Arden and Bond? Or, shameful thought, had he bought them for the same reason that Mike Frankovitch, London Head of Columbia Pictures for whom I worked at one time, had asked me to get so many feet of books to fill his shelves? Anyway, I bought the books and have them still, an unusual memento of an old ruffian who battled so hard, so successfully and so inexplicably for the Royal Court.

In January 1971, the English Stage Company suffered another loss when Robin Fox died. Robin had been very close to Neville Blond and had provided something of a bridge between George Devine and Neville: Robin being equally loyal and friendly to both men. Throughout the years he and I had been the main advisers to the E.S.C. on theatrical business matters. Robin was a very successful theatrical agent for most of his working life. He was also from time to time a theatre producer in partnership with Robert Morley, and at one time, with Peter Ustinov. I do not think he was very successful as a producer, so his close connection with the E.S.C. made up in some way for his disappointments as a producer. When Robin died, I became the sole Chairman of the English Stage Company and found myself giving a great deal of my time to the Royal Court.

During 1971 I produced two plays jointly with the E.S.C. The first was an adaptation of Wedekind's *Lulu* by Peter Barnes which I had seen at Nottingham Playhouse at a time when the Court was looking for a production to come into the theatre. I suggested Lulu to Bill Gaskill. It was directed by Stuart Burge, with Julia Foster playing Lulu. Bill agreed and brought the play to the Court where it did very well and later transferred to the Apollo Theatre in Shaftesbury Avenue for a season.

The second play was *The Lovers of Viorne* by Marguerite Duras. Peggy Ashcroft was the murderess, a role played by Madeleine Renaud at the Court in 1969 in the original French text, *L'amante anglaise*. This was Peggy Ashcroft's first appearance at the Court since 1959 when she had played in *The Good Woman of Setzuan*.

Apart from my work at the Court that year, I also presented two plays at the Roundhouse in 1971. One was a production of *Rabelais*, described as a dramatic game in two parts, taken from the five books of François Rabelais, adapted and directed by Jean-Louis Barrault and translated by Robert Baldick. Barrault's original production, in a wrestling ring in Paris, he had brought over to the Old Vic for a short run in 1969, at Laurence Olivier's invitation. In Paris and at the Roundhouse the play was performed on a stage the shape of a cross, surrounded by audience on all sides. Thus the Roundhouse was the perfect place to perform it, whereas at the Old Vic they'd had to have a rostrum coming out from the centre of the stage into the stalls. The play had a large cast headed by Bernard Bresslaw, Gerald Harper and Joe Melia. Jean-Louis' French company had been trained by him – particularly in the use of mime – to a standard that could not be reached in four weeks' rehearsal by an English cast. Also, in Paris Jean-Louis had played a part himself, and several parts in London. He did not do this at the Roundhouse. so I can't say our production equalled the French one, but it was an enjoyable evening. It did not do well enough for us to transfer it, but in any case that would have been difficult because there was no other performing space in London where we could set up our stage in the same way. I had originally asked Joan Littlewood to prepare a version and direct it. She had been interested but did not go through with it in the end. A pity, because although it was interesting to work with Jean-Louis, he was attempting to re-create a French production, while Joan would have given us an English view of Rabelais. The Roundhouse once again proved itself to be the perfect place for such epic theatre. It is a thousand pities that it could not have been used consistently for such a purpose: in Paris it would have been.

My Company's last presentation for 1971, and as it proved, its last for some years, was Théâtre du Soleil's production of *1789*, the story of the first year of the French Revolution, written and performed collectively by the Company and directed by Ariane Mnouchkine. Again the Round-house was the only space in London that would have worked for this production, which needed a large space. Five rostra were set up as temporary stages, leaving most of the centre of the Roundhouse free for the audience to stand and watch the show – and move around as the focus of the action switched from stage to stage. This was the first time London experienced what became known as 'promenade productions', of which *The Mysteries* and *Lark Rise* at the National Theatre and *Road* at the Royal Court were later examples. The audience's excitement at *1789* was almost contagious. It was like being at Speakers' Corner, like going to a fair, your attention grabbed by competing side shows.

A description in our programme read: '*1789* is the story of the first year of the French Revolution played by fairground actors, travelling mimes and mountebanks using all the devices of the popular theatre to give the people's view of the Revolution. In one of the show's most riveting episodes, all goes quiet and we gradually hear whispers. Approchez, approchez, whispers an actor and we cluster round. With rising excitement, as if he'd just come panting from the event itself, he gives a blow by blow account of how he and his comrades took the

Bastille. All round the theatre actors are whispering their story to little groups of listeners, some tell their story in English, those who cannot, tell it in French and have it interpreted. The voices weave together, mount to a triumphant crescendo of victory, the lights blaze on and the whole place explodes into carnival, here and now we become the people of Paris celebrating *la fête de la Bastille*. Here we shy coconuts at images of the Bastille; over there miniscule David defeats gigantic Goliath; there's a wrestling match between Tyranny and the People, acrobatics, wheels of fortune, escapologists, pretty girls handing out tricolour sweets and nosegays. It was infectious, you never wanted it to end.'

With the help of a subsidy from the French Government we had brought the Company over for four weeks. Every performance was packed. Our only problem was to prevent George Hoskins, the Administrator of the Roundhouse, letting too many people in!

This was without question one of my favourites amongst all the productions with which I have been involved. It could not be said to be a 'good' play, but it was wonderful, radical, popular entertainment and dull would he be of soul who could pass by and not be thrilled by it.

Part Seven

I Become Artistic Director of the Royal Court

Fugard's African season and Orton's trilogy

During the run of John Osborne's *A Patriot for Me* at the Royal Court Theatre, George Devine, playing the part of Baron von Epp, the drag-queen hostess of the ball scene, had had a heart attack, followed eleven days later by a stroke which paralysed the left side of his body. This was in August 1965, whilst Tony Richardson and I were away in France filming *Mademoiselle*. George went home from hospital two months later. His speech had returned almost to normal but his left arm and leg remained paralysed, confining him to a wheel chair. He made gallant attempts to regain the use of his hand and started work on his autobiography for Faber and Faber. But it was a losing battle. On 20th January 1966 George died. I visited him during his last months. His brain was as sharp as ever, as was his interest in affairs at the Royal Court, where Bill Gaskill, released by Laurence Olivier from his duties at the National Theatre, had taken on the job of Artistic Director. Gaskill remained in this job for seven years. It was hard going, particularly because Bill wanted to have a permanent company at the theatre – as George had had at the beginning – and refused for a time to recognise that this was a financial impossibility. His choice of play and actors also neglected to take financial hard facts into consideration; there were constant battles between him and Neville Blond, our Chairman. Under Bill's regime, however, a number of very important new writers were discovered and/or encouraged, particularly Edward Bond, whose first play had been produced on a Sunday in George Devine's time, Howard Brenton, David Hare, Charles Wood and David Storey. Bill himself, however, apart from his productions of Edward Bond, mainly directed revivals. In 1969, Lindsay Anderson and Anthony Page agreed to return to the Court and share the artistic direction with Bill. Peter Gill was also engaged as an associate director and for the next three years the theatre was either under the artistic direction of Anthony and Lindsay or Bill and Peter. When it was the turn of Lindsay and Anthony, they very soon found it impossible to work together, or rather Lindsay found he could not work with Anthony. The usual outcome was that Anthony ran the theatre and Lindsay directed one or two plays – in fact, he directed a total of four plays, all by David Storey, all very successful. During these three years the pattern was that the Anderson/Page seasons made money and the Gaskill/Gill seasons lost money, which is not to say that the first was better than the second, but that it would have been impossible for the theatre to have continued without the Page/Anderson successes. On the other hand, Gaskill and Gill were more adventurous and without their seasons the Court would not have been performing its function of sponsoring new writing and new theatre.

The different attitudes and temperaments of the four directors caused strains. Bill found working with Lindsay and Anthony a constant tussle, and at the end of 1971 or the beginning of 1972 told the Council that when his contract ended in August 1972 he would not wish to renew it. Neither Lindsay nor Anthony wanted to take over, and I, who was involved as Chairman in all the discussions about the succession, offered to take over myself. It meant a drop in income and a loss of independence, but money was still coming in from *Tom Jones* and the film of *The Knack*, which I had produced, and I was getting fed up with the conditions in which commercial theatre had to work. More and more it was clear to me that the plays I really wanted to produce were more likely to suit the Royal Court than the West End. I proposed that I should become the Artistic Director and that Lindsay, Bill and Anthony should stay on as Associate Artistic Directors, committing themselves to directing not less than one play a year and giving advice on the general running of the theatre. Lindsay and Anthony accepted, Bill decided that he wanted, not unnaturally, to make a break with the theatre. I invited

(*Above left*) Peter O'Toole as *Baal*

(*Above right*) Albert Finney as *Luther*

(*Below*) Paul Scofield in *Hotel in Amsterdam*

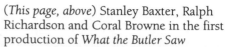

(*This page, above*) Stanley Baxter, Ralph Richardson and Coral Browne in the first production of *What the Butler Saw*

(*Centre left*) Lionel Stander and Siobhan McKenna in *St Joan of the Stockyards*

(*Centre right*) *The Living Book of the Living Theatre* - cover

(*Below*) Laurence Olivier and Mona Washbourne in *Semi-Detached*

(*Opposite page, above left*) Athol Fugard

(*Above right*) Brian Friel

(*Below*) Keith Waterhouse and Willis Hall

(*This page, above*) *Sizwe Bansi is Dead*
John Kani and Winston Ntshona

(*Below*) Michael Medwin and Betty
Marsden in the Royal Court
production of *What the Butler Saw*

(*Opposite page*) Page from The Tatler
on *The Girl with Green Eyes*
(originally to be called *Once Upon a
Summer*) Oscar Lewenstein, Edna
O'Brien, Lynn Redgrave, Rita
Tushingham and Peter Finch

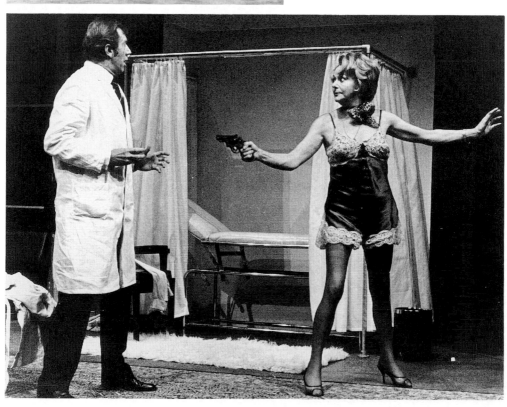

THE LONELY GIRL

A number of bright talents have been assembled for the Woodfall Films production of *Once Upon a Summer* based on Edna O'Brien's book *The Lonely Girl*. They include producer Oscar Lewenstein (*far left*), Miss O'Brien herself (*above left*) and Lynn Redgrave (*above*), youngest actress daughter of Sir Michael. Stars of the film (*below*) are Rita Tushingham and Peter Finch. Direction is by Desmond Davis and the picture is due for release in October

(*Above left*) *The Knack* with Rita
Tushingham, Ray Brooks and crew

(*Above right*) Myself, Tony Richardson
and John Osborne at Acapulco Film
Festival

(*Below*) *Tom Jones* day for night shooting
with Tony Richardson, Albert Finney
and crew

(*Above left*) *The Bride Wore Black:* myself and
Jeanne Moreau on location

(*Above right*) *Rita, Sue and Bob Too* with Siobhan
Finneran, George Costigan and Michelle Holmes

(*Below*) On location *Rita, Sue and Bob Too*: myself
Andrea Dunbar and Sandy Lieberson

(*Above right*) Myself, 1993

(*Below*) The family - clockwise from top left - Rosie, Pete, Ella, Sharon, Andie, Mark, Woody, Jack, self and Eileen

Albert Finney, a friend for many years, to be the third Associate. He accepted. I hoped that Bill and Peter Gill would return to the theatre from time to time to direct, and thus we should keep together the team that had been the backbone of the Court for the past seven years. When everything was all but arranged, Bill suddenly had second thoughts about leaving. He proposed that he should stay on as Artistic Director for a further period. But, as he admits in his book, it would not have worked, so the Council preferred to go ahead as agreed.

Although I had been associated with the Court for the past 16 years, the last three years as Chairman, and knew all the directors and other workers at the Royal Court, I had no idea just what taking on this job would mean in terms of stress, and how difficult I should find it to work in a more formal relationship with my colleagues there. Being the Chairman and trying to keep the peace between the various directors had not been easy, but compared to my new task it was a piece of cake.

When I took over as Artistic Director of the Court what did I hope to do? I was concerned to preserve all the strength of the past, and that was the main purpose in taking over. I wanted to continue our association with the four directors who had been working in the theatre in the immediate preceding period, and to continue our association with the leading playwrights we had worked with in the past: John Osborne, Edward Bond, David Storey, Christopher Hampton and Sam Beckett in particular. I made few changes in the staff but as time went on I was able to introduce into the Court several people I had worked with outside that theatre. For instance when Helen Montague resigned, having been the General Manager for most if not all Bill's Artistic Directorship, I brought in Anne Jenkins, whom I had met when working with Donald Albery, whose General Manager she was. I brought in Ann Jellicoe as Literary Manager, the first woman to be given this task. And when she eventually left, Donald Howarth, another old friend from earlier Royal Court times, took over.

Apart from continuing our work with past Royal Court writers, it was essential to find new ones and to make the main stage of the Court available to talented writers who had previously only had their plays produced in the Theatre Upstairs or on a Sunday Night. George Goetschius in his article on 'The Royal Court and its Social Context' printed in the brochure *Ten Years at the Royal Court 1956/66* asks: 'As a theatre of social concern, should it attempt to locate in contemporary society some group in need of a hearing and set about becoming its champion in the way in which it once became the champion of the needs of the new middle classes?' I did not consciously seek to do this but in fact over the next few years we did move towards a growing interest in plays by Irish, black and women writers, all of whom came from sections of society which had been under-represented and were beginning to demand to be heard.

First I had to look after a production of Arnold Wesker's *The Old Ones*, directed by John Dexter and arranged by Bill Gaskill before he left. I didn't care much for this play which centered on the lives of elderly Jewish people. Their different rooms were arranged on a revolve which I came to see as a kind of roulette wheel, with certain scenes which I disliked standing for the losing numbers. I hoped the wheel would not stop at these scenes when I came in to watch rehearsals. I don't think John Dexter was much more enthusiastic than I was. Bill must have scheduled the play at a moment when he just wanted to get things settled before he left. I cannot believe he really liked it. Perhaps loyalty to Arnold caused him to select it, but it is not loyalty but folly to put on a play you do not believe in because it is written by an old friend. Of course it is a question of degree. If you are not sure about a play by someone whose previous work you admire, then you should usually give the author the benefit of the doubt, but if you are certain that the play is not good and will do the author's reputation no good, then I think it's your duty, both to the author and the theatre, to reject it. This problem arose later with a play by David Storey, *Mother's Day*. I thought it was a poor piece of work. Lindsay, who had directed most of David's plays, agreed with me. I turned it down. My successors at the Court produced it. It pleased no one and I'm sure that it did the author a dis-service to stage it. I am told that this is the production over which David Storey punched Michael Billington. I'm all in favour of punching Michael Billington, but surely a better occasion could have been found.

Sometime before it was arranged that I should come to the Court as Artistic Director, I had met my old friend Brendan Behan on a visit to Dublin and had taken an option on his play *Richard's Cork Leg*. He had only written the first act and my option was to start with the delivery of the finished play. Alas, Brendan died before completing it, but Alan Simpson, a Dublin director whom I'd worked with several times, told me he had found notes left by Brendan from which he had cobbled up a second act and that he wanted to direct it in Dublin with the well-known Irish folk group, the Dubliners, playing the leading roles. I agreed that he could go ahead and arrange this. Noel Pearson, who was the Dubliners' current manager, arranged to produce it at the Abbey's Peacock Theatre and I passed over my rights in the play to the Royal Court, who invited the Abbey to bring their production over. And so it happened that a posthumous play by Brendan Behan was the first production presented under my Artistic Direction. It was, I thought, a good beginning.

Set largely in a graveyard, *Richard's Cork Leg* is a vintage collection of scenes, jokes and songs on the themes of love, religion, politics and death. In the words of *The Guardian*, it was 'a joyous celebration of life' and a wholly characteristic postscript to Behan's earlier work.

Next came *England's Ireland*, by a group of writers including Howard Brenton, David Edgar, David Hare and Snoo Wilson, produced for a Sunday Night. This collaborative play by a new generation of writers had been proposed for the Court by Bill Gaskill. It was an interesting experiment but I was very critical of the political views expressed. I did not feel then that the writers were serious political thinkers, nor was I impressed by many of their later political plays. This was probably due to the fact that I had spent my youth immersed in political activity and these writers seemed to me superficial, although totally sincere. I cannot now remember the individual plays of that collaboration, but only the general impression they made upon me. I suppose I should have been pleased that a group of young writers were concerned about so important a political question, which the theatre as a whole was inclined to ignore. *Eye Winker, Tom Tinker*, another Irish play by Tom MacIntyre, opened shortly afterwards in the Theatre Upstairs, and we presented a few weeks later *A Pagan Place* by Edna O'Brien, whose novel *The Girl with Green Eyes* I had produced as a film. It was directed on the main stage by Ronald Eyre, designed by Sean Kenny, with a very fine Irish cast including Dave Allen, Brenda Fricker and a young girl discovered at a Dublin school, Veronica Quilligan. In his review of this play for *The Sunday Times*, Harold Hobson called it 'A shining landscape of childhood's perilous happiness recollected in a troubled peace. If there is a

better play than this in London, then London must be extremely lucky. A wake in an Irish public house, a picnic by the sea, the revival of an old passion when a doctor calls on a middle-aged patient, a lesson by an eccentric schoolmistress, the conversation of a profligate priest with a young girl – Miss O'Brien makes of these apparently disconnected things a vision of life that is delicate and touching, illuminated by the light of a memory that is calmed but not assuaged.'

These Irish plays followed one another and occupied the Court from 19th September 1972 to the end of November. On 27th February 1973, I produced another Irish play, Brian Friel's *Freedom of the City*, about Bloody Sunday in Derry, on the main stage of the Royal Court directed by Albert Finney. Frank Marcus in the *Sunday Telegraph* wrote 'Mr. Friel's play is set in Londonderry in 1970. An unauthorised Civil Rights March has been dispersed with the help of C.S. gas and three demonstrators – two young men and a middle-aged mother of 11 children – take refuge in the Mayor's parlour in the Town Hall. Rumour inflates the trio to 40 armed rebels; they are besieged by tanks; and when they surrender in accordance with instructions issued from a loudhailer, hands held high above their heads, they are shot . . . Friel fleshes the awful, numbing casualty statistics which are becoming ciphers as familiar as the items pencilled in on some blood-stained laundry list and gives them breath and life'. Garry O'Connor in the *Financial Times* wrote, 'Brian Friel has, I think, written the best Northern Irish play so far to be presented since the present troubles began; it is also the least tainted by propaganda or the simplifications to which such a subject becomes prone, in the playwright's desire to treat an urgent and contemporary subject.' Despite these two notices, most of the critics came out against the play, displaying their chauvinism when faced with an honest criticism of the British army. The hostile reviews, combined with a spate of I.R.A. bomb scares, including several at the Court itself, meant that the play did poor business. The cast included Stephen Rea and I believe that it was from this collaboration between Stephen and Brian Friel that their splendid enterprise 'Field Day' came into being. When the bad notices came in I found myself singing the 'International' to Brian in an attempt to cheer him up. Brian had the last laugh, however. Following the success of *Dancing at Lughnasa*, he has the London critics grovelling at his feet, hailing him as 'the greatest living playwright'. The

London critics can usually recognise a good horse once he gets past the winning post.

On 22nd November 1972, Caryl Churchill's first full-length play *Owners* was presented in the Theatre Upstairs. Directed by Nicholas Wright, who at that time was the director of the Theatre Upstairs, this was an historic occasion, for Caryl was to become over the next twenty years one of the Court's most important playwrights.

Caryl Churchill was a feminist and socialist writer of obvious talent, yet I did not myself admire her plays as much as did many of my colleagues. She belonged to a group of writers, amongst them Howard Brenton, Howard Barker, David Hare, most of whom developed on the fringe in the sixties and later became associated with The Joint Stock Theatre, a touring theatre company formed by Bill Gaskill and Max Stafford-Clark. Whilst recognising the talent of these writers, I did not feel the same instinctive sympathy for their work as I did for that of the earlier Royal Court writers, finding their politics stuck uncomfortably onto their plays. However, Caryl was a woman and a playwright and there were not too many of them about. We all thought she should be encouraged and the best way to encourage an author is to produce his or in this case, her work. And so we arranged to present Caryl's next play, *Objections to Sex and Violence*, on the Royal Court's main stage. It opened there on 2nd January 1975. It was an interesting, original but somewhat tentative piece, which played its 27 performances to only 21 per cent of box office capacity, losing us about £9,500.

Caryl Churchill during my time was also appointed the Court's first woman resident playwright, and later more than repaid this early support for her work by writing such critical and box office successes as *Cloud Nine*, *Top Girls* and *Serious Money*, all of which were presented at the Court, directed by Max Stafford-Clark.

My own favourite of her plays is *Cloud Nine*. I find her *Serious Money* about the Stock Exchange, which was a great success, superficial and trendy.

To return to my first season, following *Richard's Cork Leg* and *A Pagan Place*, we had a new and extraordinary play by John Osborne to present in our main bill. This was *A Sense of Detachment*.

Michael Billington in *The Guardian* wrote, 'How to describe John Osborne's *A Sense of Detachment* at the Royal Court? A spiky, satirical, inconsequential collage? An attack on our own heartless, loveless, profiteering society in which language is corrupted daily? A moving threnody for a dying civilisation? The paradox of this (to me) pro-vocative, innovatory and exciting work is that it manages to be all these things, moving outward from purely theatrical satire to an eloquent examination of the world at large . . . sustainedly entertaining. It uses an apparently inconsequential form to defend timeless human values. It is full of Osborne's characteristic rancid eloquence. And it goads, provokes and agitates its audience as only a truly vital theatrical work can.'

The play shocked even some of the Court's usually unshockable audience. 'Oh, Lady Redgrave, how could you?', cried a member of that audience, throwing a shoe at Rachel Kempson in the course of one of the performances.

My wife, Eileen, was moved to tears by the play; I considered it to be one of Osborne's most original works. It played for its scheduled run of six weeks and then, because of its success, despite mixed notices, we ran it for a further five weeks late-night after the Beckett double-bill that followed it.

The Beckett programme, a revival of Krapp's Last Tape with Albert Finney and the first performance of Not I with Billie Whitelaw, both plays directed by Anthony Page and designed by Jocelyn Herbert, opened on 16th January. Beckett took an active part in the rehearsals but was not happy with Albert's performance, because, in his eyes, Patrick Magee had already given the definitive interpretation of Krapp, and he would have preferred the play to have been again presented with Pat. This was, of course, very unfair on Albert. Despite the fact that by then Beckett's early plays had become classics, Sam still felt very protective towards them. For instance a few years later when I was associated with the Roundhouse, Spike Milligan and Marty Feldman wanted to play Waiting for Godot. I thought they would give a very interesting inter-pretation of the play, but Sam would not give permission. Later he relented, but by that time it was too late, we could not get it together.

Billie Whitelaw in Not I delivers a monologue to a silent Auditor. Only her disembodied mouth is seen. To achieve this amazing effect Billie's head was held in a kind of vice so that the narrow beam of light would remain fixed on her mouth in an otherwise pitch black stage. The speech – forty minutes long – had to be delivered in a rapid monotone. Only an actor so dedicated to Beckett's work and with such technical mastery could have done it. It is not surprising that Billie was said to be Beckett's favourite actress.

Thanks to Beckett and the two actors, this extraordinary evening was a great success filling 97 per cent of the seats for its six week run. Without Albert I don't think it would have achieved this. It is interesting to note that, apart from a short season of *Oh! Les Beaux Jours*, imported from Paris, with Madelaine Renaud in 1971, Beckett had not been presented on the main stage of the Royal Court since *Waiting for Godot* at the end of 1964, when Anthony Page had staged a brilliant revival with Nicol Williamson, Paul Curran, Alfred Lynch and Jack MacGowran. It was a success, but not such a success as our double-bill.

Shortly after being appointed Artistic Director, I had had lunch with Christopher Hampton, during which I'd expressed my hope that the Court's writers would once again tackle the big social and moral questions of the day. I felt that, since George Devine's time, there had been a tendency for the focus of the plays to narrow. I was delighted to hear from Christopher that he was working on a play on the plight of the Brazilian Indians, juxtaposing the publicity surrounding the murder of one British diplomat with the anonymity surrounding the slaughter of hundreds of Brazilian Indians. This play was *Savages*. We invited Robert Kidd, who had staged Hampton's earlier plays, to direct it and I suggested Paul Scofield to play the English diplomat. As usual when he decides in favour, the answer came back quite quickly. Tom Conti, then a little known young actor, was cast in the part of the guerilla, Carlos. Michael Pennington and Geoffrey Palmer were other important members of a cast of 18. Jocelyn Herbert and Andrew Sanders designed the play, which after a promising six weeks run at the Court transferred for a West End run at the Comedy Theatre. Sheridan Morley wrote in *The Tatler*, 'It is my belief, in the light of 'Savages' . . . that Christopher Hampton is a major English playwright of a kind not seen since the arrival of Osborne . . . Having proved himself as a writer of comedy (*The Philanthropist*) and of tragedy (*Total Eclipse*) he has now come up with a tragi-comedy and a passionate, partisan, Shavian one at that. *Savages* concerns an ineffable English diplomat . . . called Alan West, though he could have been called Adam West considering that he stood for roughly the whole of western civilisation up against the Brazilian Indians whose cause, that of survival, is what Mr. Hampton is here fighting. Kidnapped by guerrillas and kept in a cell while his ransom is negotiated, West provides the backbone of a play which sets out to do nothing less than indict western man for his wholesale murder of a tribe few if any of us have heard of.'

Following *Savages*, came a play by another important Royal Court writer, Edward Bond's *The Sea*. For this play I was very happy to have Bill Gaskill returning to the Court to direct it, with Deirdre Clancy designing the production. Benedict Nightingale describes this play as 'a picture of a small Edwardian community filled with images and feelings of death, its main characters a tyrannical lady-of-the-manor, a tradesman turned paranoid by years of misuse, and two lovers representing a faint hope of a healthier future.' Bill assembled a strong cast led by Coral Browne, Ian Holm and Alan Webb. The scene on the cliff tops was outstanding: the way Bill choreographed the large cast on the small Court stage in that scene was Bill at his very best. The play enjoyed a moderately good run as far as size of audience was concerned; 65 per cent of the Court's capacity, making it Bond's most successful to date.

In August 1974 we presented another play by Edward Bond, *Bingo* directed by Jane Howell and John Dove, who had previously premiered it at Exeter with Bob Peck playing Shakespeare. Although I had thought that Bob Peck gave a decent performance, I did not think it would be strong enough to secure a large audience at the Royal Court. I was anxious to give Bond a real winner and persuaded him and a rather reluctant Jane Howell that we should ask John Gielgud to play the part. He accepted it and could not possibly have been more co-operative, begging to be given real direction and for the directors not to be in awe of him. Unfortunately, I do not think that Jane Howell and her co-director were able to establish an easy working relationship with their star, and the production, in my opinion, was nothing like as strong as Gaskill's *The Sea* had been. Despite this, the play with its strong cast (Arthur Lowe played a memorable Ben Jonson) did splendidly at the Court, playing to 97 per cent of seating capacity.

Benedict Nightingale wrote, 'How is it (we're to ask) that a man whom we worship for his humanity could bear to live in a society we know to have been so cruel? How can we, his descendants, bear to live in a society directly derived from it? . . . it's a fascinating play . . .'

Edward Bond was established as an author at the Royal Court at a time when I was not particularly active there. I admired his work but found him personally rather distant. Although I have known him for years, we have never had a close relationship. He was somehow always Bill Gaskill's author and I didn't feel that I contributed anything much, except for helping to get John Gielgud to play Shakespeare. Other than that, the plays went on exactly as they would have done in Bill Gaskill's time and I know Bond personally now no more than I knew him when we first met. There was a moment in the mid-seventies when we briefly joined forces in an effort to democratise the Royal Court's Council. We failed to do this and we have not met since. The play of Bond's which I find most exciting is his *Lear*, which I wish I could have revived in a strong production, with a real leading actor playing the central part. Richard Lester and I talked often about whether a film might be made from this play, but that is another project that remained a dream. There is something forbidding about Bond's work, which perhaps explains why such a creative and imaginative writer has not found a wider audience.

We had two financial disasters on the main stage towards the end of 1974 – *Runaway* by Peter Ransley played to only 18 per cent of box office capacity but 50 per cent of seating capacity, because we allowed the audience to pay whatever they liked for tickets when we saw how badly it would otherwise do. Ken Campbell's *The Great Caper*, directed by Nicholas Wright and starring Warren Mitchell, played to only 20 per cent of box office capacity, but it was an original and extraordinary play by a brilliant and unique artist, and our fault was not in producing it, but failing to find the audience it deserved. Ken Campbell went on to write many more amazing works for the theatre. I am proud that we can include him amongst the writers the Court helped on their way.

Meanwhile in the Theatre Upstairs an array of fringe activities was taking place, such as David Edgar's *State of Emergency*, Ken Campbell's *Roadshow*, Howard Brenton's and David Edgar's *A Fart for Europe*, The People Show 48, The Pip Simmons Theatre Group and Mike Leigh's improvised plays. In particular, we continued our association with the American playwright, Sam Shepard, by presenting his play *The Unseen Hand* in a production by Jim Sharman, an Australian director who was to work with us on a number of productions upstairs and downstairs during my term of office. Strangely enough, Jim, who had directed the London production of *Jesus Christ Superstar*, was introduced to the Court by Lindsay Anderson, a director I should not have thought would have been much in sympathy with Jim's work. But you never could tell with Lindsay.

One day Jim Sharman asked me to listen to a tape of some songs from a new musical, *The Rocky Horror Show*. I heard them and had no doubt it should be done. Jim wanted to do it in the Theatre Upstairs and Nicholas was enthusiastic too, at least he told me he was, though recently I was told that he remembers thinking it was awful. This is only an apparent contradiction. He was quite capable of thinking it was awful and reacting enthusiastically about it if he thought that was the appropriate and expected reaction, and the Theatre Upstairs was where Jim wanted to present it. He was not at all sure that it would work in a conventional theatre. Although it had a small cast of nine, it was an expensive show for the Theatre Upstairs and Michael White agreed to put up some money on condition that he would have the right to transfer it if it was a success. In that event the Court would have the right either to transfer it with him on a 50-50 basis, or if they did not want to take the risk, Michael could transfer the play himself, paying the Court 10 per cent of the profits and 1 per cent of the gross. I set these facts out here because there have been quite unfair rumours that the Court had a raw deal.

Richard O'Brien's musical had a perfect cast, most of whom transferred with the play and appeared in the movie. It consisted of Tim Curry, Julie Covington, Jonathan Adams, Christopher Malcolm, Little Nell, Richard O'Brien, Patricia Quinn, Paddy O'Hagan and Rayner Bourton, The sets were designed by Brian Thomson, and Sue Blane designed the costumes. Jim Sharman did a brilliant directing job. I can remember Jocelyn Herbert thinking it was like a Picasso when she first saw it. It was unique. And a complete sell-out. Michael White wanted to transfer it to the Chelsea Classic Cinema, where he thought that the Theatre Upstairs atmosphere could be retained in a larger house. The management committee of the Court decided it was too great a risk to take a half share in the venture and settled on the smaller interest, as previously agreed. As it turned out we were wrong, but with our slender resources we were not in a position to take risks, given that a considerable capital investment was required to convert the cinema, and later, yet another one as a semi-permanent home for the now-legendary show. I cannot blame the management committee for being cautious: everyone would have blamed them had the venture lost money. We had done our part and introduced a new and exciting work, which is what the Court was subsidised to do. We were not in a position to be theatre gamblers; this was an unusual venture which might well have been a commercial failure. Too many great successes at small theatres have been flops when transferred to the larger venues.

The George Devine award, named after the first director of the Royal Court, is given annually to up-and-coming artists, usually writers, in the theatre. In 1972 it was awarded jointly to two black playwrights, Mustapha Matura, a Trinidadian, and Michael Abbensetts, a writer born in Guyana, whom I later appointed as our first black writer in residence. In July 1973 his *Sweet Talk* was presented Upstairs in a production by Stephen Frears, later to become a well-known film director.

On 20th September one of the most important plays in my time as Artistic Director of the Royal Court, perhaps *the* most important play, was presented. This was *Sizwe Banze is Dead*, written by Athol Fugard and its two actors John Kani and Winston Ntshona. It came about in the following way. Donald Howarth, who had been one of the Court's earliest writers, had been working in South Africa, though against my advice, since I supported the A.N.C's request that British artists and sportsmen should not be seen to support the apartheid regime. Donald was as much opposed to this regime as I was but did not agree with my views on how to oppose it. While there he saw *Sizwe* at the Space Theatre in Cape Town and wrote to me about it. I had got to know Athol Fugard in 1971 when he directed and appeared in his play *Boesman and Lena* in the Theatre Upstairs. I had been very impressed with the play and had helped get it transferred to the Young Vic and in the course of this became friendly with Athol and his leading actress Yvonne Bryceland. After receiving Donald's letter, I got in touch with Athol and invited him to bring the play over and perform it at the Court. I asked him whether he would like to put it on Upstairs or downstairs. Athol is a very cautious man. He had presented his previous play Upstairs and decided he would feel safer putting on *Sizwe* in the same space. Nicholas

Wright was quite happy about this and accordingly I told Athol we would give him what he wanted and put the play on tour following its performances in the Theatre Upstairs, so that it could come into the Royal Court main house if its reception Upstairs seemed to make this a good idea, as I was sure it would. And that is precisely how it turned out. The play was an enormous, shattering experience; we sent it on tour and arranged for it to come back into the main house. But more of that later.

I have heard the Theatre Upstairs described in those days as the Glyndebourne of the Fringe. Not a bad description.

Whilst Bill Gaskill was Artistic Director he commissioned Howard Brenton to write a play for the Court. Brenton, who was very keen to break into what he thought of as the 'big' theatre, duly delivered his play *Magnificence*, in the hope that it would be presented on the main stage of the Court – his debut on a proscenium stage. I had followed his career with interest, considering him to be one of the most talented writers then working on the fringe. I remember talking to him about *Lay By*, a play which he had written with six other writers about the A6 murder, and which had been presented at the Court on a Sunday night in 1971. I had suggested that he might tackle a political theme. Later I wondered if I had been right to try to turn him in this direction, for I began to doubt if he had any kind of clear political vision. He was certainly an imaginative writer but I am inclined to think that the apolitical *Christie in Love* was his most successful play. Anyway, *Magnificence* was certainly an interesting attempt to write a political play that was also, to use the author's own words 'a kind of tragedy'. It shows the violent collision of two worlds – that of a group of radical protesters with that of a cabinet minister. It was Howard's first full-length play and, despite weaknesses, I thought it well worth doing. It was read by the other members of the Artistic Committee and, as far as I remember, although there was no great enthusiasm for it, no one opposed my proposal to present it for four weeks on the main stage – no one, that is, except Lindsay Anderson. But he not only opposed it, he went on opposing it, so that his views were known throughout the Court, and it began to be assumed that there was some question as to whether or not the play would be put on. In fact there was never any question about it. Although Lindsay thought it a feeble effort and did not like the way it was written or what it said,

I was sufficiently convinced of its merits to schedule it for production. And as I have said, none of the other members of our Artistic Committee opposed its production. There was a general feeling at the Court, in any case, that if we commissioned a work and it turned out to be at all possible, we owed it to the author to produce it. Max Stafford-Clark was chosen to direct the play, it was designed by William Dudley and lit by Andy Phillips. It was strongly cast with Michael Kitchen, Kenneth Cranham, Carole Hayman and Peter Postlethwaite playing the young radicals and Geoffrey Chater and Robert Eddison leading for the establishment. We had a system at that time of putting on certain plays for runs of four weeks, others for six weeks and some plays for eight weeks. Production costs for the four week runs had to be kept low but Howard's play did not suffer because of this, since the first few scenes were played in a single set and the remainder took place on a bare stage. During the work on the script prior to production, I had urged him to strengthen the arguments within the play against the views and actions of the principal character. The result, I'm sure, was to make the play more balanced and realistic. Nevertheless, it did not do good business, only 36 per cent of seating capacity and 26 per cent of box office, but it received some very good notices.

Billington in *The Guardian* wrote, 'It raises the kind of questions rarely debated on the modern English stage. At what point, if ever, does violence become a legitimate political tactic? To what extent is radical protest, without the support of the people, a form of self indulgence? How, if at all, does one puncture the discreet charm of the English bourgeosie?'

Irving Wardle in *The Times* wrote, 'It is scene for scene a wonderful piece of theatre; annexing whole new chunks of modern life and presenting them in a style at once truthful and magnified.'

Magnificence was followed in the main bill by the first of two plays by the Australian writer David Williamson. This was *The Removalists*, directed by Jim Sharman, his first production for us on the main stage. A comedy about police brutality, it was an efficient play, efficiently directed and acted. Not nearly so interesting a work as *Magnificence*, it nevertheless, although presented for four weeks under the same conditions, played to much better business: 53 per cent of seating capacity and 43 per cent of box office. David Williamson's second play, *Don's*

Party presented two years later in March 1975, was more interesting. Set during an increasingly drunken party of academics whilst the results of the Australian election were coming through, it was a funny, bawdy play, very well directed by Michael Blakemore. It was produced by the Court in association with Eddie Kulukundis. It played to about 55 per cent of seating capacity and 50 per cent of box office, not good enough to encourage the management to transfer it. It proved again how difficult it was to get a large audience at the Court in those days for an excellent play without a well known author or star.

David Storey had been an important writer at the Court ever since his first play *The Restoration of Arnold Middleton* had been presented there in 1967. Apart from this play, which had been staged by Robert Kidd, all David's plays, as well as the film based on his novel *This Sporting Life*, had been directed by Lindsay Anderson. Now David had offered us two new plays, *Cromwell* and *The Farm*, and I decided to present them, one following the other, after the run of *The Removalists*. I naturally offered them to Lindsay to direct, but he did not respond favourably to *Cromwell* which, unlike David's other plays, was written in verse. It is not about the historical Cromwell but considers Cromwellian themes. Set on a bare stage, the time and place are not specified but, since the first two actors we meet are Irish, we assume we are in Ireland at the time of Cromwell. For Lindsay this was all too vague and unspecific; not only did he not wish to direct the play but strongly advised David and the Royal Court not to present it. However, most of the members of the Artistic Committee and I liked the play and thought it was an interesting development for David. Anthony Page agreed to direct it and Jocelyn Herbert to design it. Albert Finney seemed to me to be perfect casting for the main part, Proctor, and was ready to do it. So we had a very strong set up until Anthony decided, for some reason that I have never understood, that he wanted Albert to play a different, and secondary role and persuaded Albert to do this. He cast Brian Cox, then a young, unknown actor, in the part of Proctor. Only after rehearsals started did Anthony realise he had made a mistake. He then asked Albert to revert to the part of Proctor, proposing that Brian should play the part he had cast Albert in. And now Albert's stubborn side came to the fore and, to teach Anthony a lesson, Albert refused to change parts though I am sure he would have been much happier playing Proctor. And so too would the author – and the audience. However, despite this foolish carry-on and an unenthusiastic press, the play did well, performing to 90 per cent of seating capacity and 83 per cent of box office capacity.

Anthony also displayed his capacity for dithering when casting another part in the play: he called back three actresses for audition time after time before making his final choice. Whether he had decided from the beginning to have Frances Tomelty I do not know, but I do remember that when he was casting Ted Whitehead's *Alpha Beta* and it was obvious to everyone in the theatre that he was going to have Rachel Roberts for the woman, he kept on auditioning for the part till it drove everyone mad.

Writing about the play in his book *Modern British Plays*, Benedict Nightingale says, 'The curious *Cromwell* is, at least in its latest stages, poetic and somewhat abstract, a secular *Pilgrim's Progress*, whose main character seeks a purpose first in military action, then in withdrawal from the social world, and, after his farm and child have been destroyed, moves onto a plane of spiritual aspiration whose actual character seems as indefinite to him and Storey as to us.'

Well worth doing for all that, I thought and still think.

Then followed *The Farm*, directed by Lindsay, designed by Hayden Griffin, with incidental music by Alan Price. The cast which was headed by Bernard Lee, whom I had last seen when he appeared in a Concert Party in Shanklin about forty years previously, also included two of Lindsay's favourite actors: Patricia Healey and Frank Grimes.

Writing of Storey's plays in his book, Benedict Nightingale has this to say, 'Storey's characters tend to be at odds with society, with those who should be nearest and dearest, and even with themselves. At worst, they are cut off from roots, families, satisfying work, fulfilling relationships, and the ability to comprehend and articulate what is wrong. Their hands are, so to speak, dissociated from their minds, their minds from their hearts, and both hearts and minds from their tongues . . . *The Farm* translates disharmony to a pastoral setting. The labourers are ignorant and passive, the farmer drunken and full of resentment at his gruelling work, at his barren daughters and (especially) at his son, an aspiring poet who has left home for the south. Even the farm is likely to be swept away by a six-lane highway, much as the art college of *Life Class* is to be replaced by an institute of engineering.'

The Farm worked well, but I found it less interesting than *Cromwell*. It received a friendly press and played to 69 per cent of box office capacity with 78 per cent seats sold. Because it had a small cast and was much less expensive than *Cromwell*, a West End management transferred it to the West End where it enjoyed a short run at the Mayfair Theatre.

The following year we did David's third play, *Life Class*. Directed by Lindsay and designed by Jocelyn Herbert, it had a strong cast headed by Alan Bates, and as usual Storey, plus Lindsay, plus a star, spelt success and it played for eight weeks at the Court to 96 per cent of seating capacity and 88 per cent of box office. It transferred to the West End for a good run.

Nightingale writes, 'This play specifically involves the collapse of creativity. The students seem mostly unruly and uninterested, and the teacher has come to believe that the only purpose left to the artist is to shape and savour the events around him. Accordingly, he precipitates and coldly observes an indecent assault on the class model, thus losing himself his job and prospects, as he has already lost his wife, his beliefs and his artistic reputation. There seems little hope for him . . . ' Nightingale ends his interesting article on David Storey by saying that he is 'exploring those concerns which have continued to preoccupy him throughout his career: why do we misuse, damage and scar ourselves and other people? Knowing his persistence and seriousness as an artist, one can safely prophesy that it . . . will lead to something new.'

David Storey is a big man, a handsome man and a very private man. His father had been a miner all his life, and I think David never felt comfortable with the middle-class life he was now living as a result of his success as a novelist and playwright. He lived round the corner from me in Hampstead during the time I was Artistic Director at the Court. I often saw him, we were on friendly terms, but I did not really get to know him. I wondered if anyone did. In a recent newspaper interview he said that he and Lindsay had absolutely nothing in common and that that was perhaps why their working partnership worked so well. I think he felt that only his father's work was real and that by becoming a writer he had in some way let him down, and let himself down. He saw himself principally as a novelist and said he wrote his plays when he could not for some reason get on with a novel. Fortunately for the Court and its audiences, these blocks seemed to occur quite frequently and David was one of the Court's most prolific writers from 1967 to 1975.

Peter Gill returned to the Court in the autumn of 1973 to direct a little known comedy by D.H. Lawrence, *The Merry-Go-Round*, which we opened at Brighton and then took to Brussels for a week for the Festival of Europe before bringing it into the Court. Peter Gill had had a great success a few years earlier when he had directed – and effectively reclaimed for the stage – three Lawrence plays at the Royal Court, but he was unable to repeat his earlier triumph with this play, which has to be recorded as an interesting failure.

Although the English Stage Company was principally concerned with new English playwriting, the Company had always tried to present interesting new work from other parts of the world. During the three years that I was Artistic Director, we presented on the main stage of the Royal Court four plays by Irish writers, three plays by South Africans, two by an Australian, one play by an American, one by a Trinidadian and one musical by a Japanese, performed by a Japanese company. All this is apart from a number of plays by non-English writers presented in the Theatre Upstairs.

I have already written about the Irish and Australian plays. The three South African plays were presented as *A South African Season* at the beginning of 1974. This consisted of *Sizwe Banzi is Dead* in the production earlier presented in the Theatre Upstairs, and *The Island*, both by Athol Fugard, John Kani and Winston Ntshona, and *Statements After An Arrest Under the Immorality Act*, by Athol Fugard. One day whilst walking back to the Royal Court with Athol from a rehearsal of *Sizwe*, prior to its production in the Theatre Upstairs, he told me about the two other plays. He had no scripts but a rather poor tape of a performance of *The Island* which he played to Albert Finney and me, and he could only give us an oral summary of *Statements*. Both *Sizwe Banzi* and *The Island* had a cast of the same two actors, John Kani and Winston Ntshona. *Statements* had a cast of three, led by Yvonne Bryceland, who was known to me from earlier Fugard plays. Based on what we knew of Athol's work and the work of his actors, we offered him the Season in the main theatre. The Season was a triumph, the critics were unanimous.

The Sunday Times sums up the general reaction. 'All three are an effective indictment of the inhumanity of authoritarian regimes through a compassionate, humorous examination of the everyday lives of totally credible people. There is no mention of the theory of apartheid . . . but you experience with unique vividness what it is like to have a black skin and live in South Africa; you taste the flavour of life. This is possibly the greatest service that the theatre can render.'

A South African Season was directed by Athol and designed by Douglas Heap. Ben Kingsley and Wilson Dunster joined Yvonne Bryceland in the cast of Statements. The Season ran from 2nd January 1974; 71 perform-ances were given, playing to 93 per cent of seating capacity and 82 per cent of box office capacity, and then Sizwe and The Island transferred to the West End and later to Broadway. Athol Fugard, who had had his passport taken away for a time by the South African government, but had continued to stand out courageously against the apartheid regime, now had his work acclaimed by the English speaking theatre world. He was a man, as he says himself, 'full of gross insecurities as a writer and director', now recognised for the first time as a playwright of world stature. We became close friends, and if there is one event for which I would like my period of Artistic Direction of the Royal Court to be remembered, it would be for 'A South African Season'.In this season the quality of the plays, direction and acting all reached the heights to which the Court aspired and a great success was achieved without the help of star names.

In the second half of 1974 we presented on our main stage, following A South African Season, some of the plays by non-English writers that I mentioned. The first was Sam Shepard's Tooth of Crime directed by Jim Sharman, designed by Brian Thomson, costumes by Sue Blane, musical direction by Richard Hartley, i.e, the same team that worked on The Rocky Horror Show, and the cast included three actors from that production. The set for this show was expensive by our standards and the production costs came to just over £12,000 against an average for that year of £7,700. However, Michael White, who had been our partner on The Rocky Horror Show, was again a partner on this one and shared the cost. Catherine Hughes, in her book, American Playwrights 1945-75 writes, 'Tooth of Crime is at times absolutely stunning in its verbal dexterity, its ability to employ language. There is no young American playwright who can touch Shepard in this,' Shepard went on in the years that followed to become a Pulitzer prize winner and the leading

American playwright of his day. Until our production of *Tooth of Crime*, Sam Shepard's work had been seen only in fringe productions. With this play he was at last given a production worthy of his stature. The play was not a financial success: Sam had to wait for this until he returned to the States, but I thought this pop *Golden Bough* was a brilliant and exhilarating evening in the theatre.

Play Mas by the Trinidadian writer Mustapha Matura was directed by Donald Howarth with sets by Douglas Heap and costumes by Peter Minshall, who had in the past designed many costumes for the Trinidad Carnival. The play was a good example of collaborative work. Mustapha, who had had earlier plays presented in The Theatre Upstairs, is a wonderful writer of colloquial Trinidadian dialogue and his first act, set in the Gokools' tailor shop in Port-of-Spain, was splendid. But he is not so strong on construction, and his second act, set three years later in the office of the Chief of Police during Carnival, did not work well in spite of the situation and colourful characters. Donald Howarth and I set to work with Mustapha and the second act was made to work much better, though never as strongly as the first. Donald cast the play well with some of the best West Indian actors living in London at the time, including Stefan Kalipha, as Ramjohn Gokool, Rudolph Walker as Samuel, later the Chief of Police, and Norman Beaton as Frank. The play was well liked, we made a special effort to attract a large black audience, the press was good and the play transferred for a run at the Phoenix Theatre in the West End. It also won for Mustapha the *Evening Standard* Award as Most Promising Playwright.

The third production in this group was *The City* described as 'A Motor Cycle Musical'. It was performed by the Tokyo Kid Brothers with book, lyrics and direction by Yutaka Higashi and music by Itsuro Shimoda. I first saw this group at the Oval in another musical, *The Moon is in the East, the Sun is in the West*, and arranged for them to play in the Theatre Upstairs in 1972. They were introduced to me by Ellen Stewart, the 'Mama' of the Café La Mama, first launching pad of so many American playwrights. She rang me from New York to urge me to see this group that she called 'The Tokyo La Mama'. In 1974, they took their new musical, *The City* to La Mama in New York and invited me to go and see it. Although it seemed unready, I was assured (and believed them) that they would get it together before coming to London, so I invited them to play a short season at the Court.

Yutaka Higashi, the writer and director, describes the Kid Brothers as 'a Japanese musical group of the post Hiroshima generation. We are the generation born after World War II when Japan was transformed by economic revival and American occupation policy. Honda motorcycles, Sony tape-recorders, Disney and Gary Cooper movies became our daily life. Hollywood, hamburger stands and rock'n'roll became more familiar to us than kabuki, tea ceremony or Zen.' He adds, 'The City is a drama of young people who grew up under the direct influence of another country's culture. These young people are Japanese yankees and motor cycle gangs. Their identities are questioned when a mixed-blood man shows up right in front of them. Born during the Korean War the mixed-blood man is an offspring of a Japanese woman and an American black G.I. . . . with his complex identity which surpasses westernised identities of these Japanese young people, he confronts the yankees.'

The Tokyo Kid Brothers worked with as much dedicated intensity as any group I have known, but this production was not a real success, probably mainly because the audience would have preferred a more 'Japanese' show such as their earlier one had seemed to be. The City was not the Japanese city of our imagination, but the Japanese/American city of reality. Nevertheless, it was an interesting production and Harold Hobson voted it the best musical of the year.

The Tokyo Kid Brothers were in many ways rather like the Living Theatre. They led the same kind of hard, nomadic life. Their political and philosophical views were not dissimilar. And naturally both groups had very little money. The English Stage Company were certainly not in a position to give them a generous deal and I believe they spent much of the money that should have gone on board and lodging for the members of the company on improving the production. The result was that free accommodation had to be found where possible, and Eileen and I had four of the Brothers, none of whom could speak more than a word or two of English, sleeping in sleeping bags on the floor of our table-tennis room.

I have often wondered what has happened to Higashi and the Tokyo Kid Brothers. I have heard nothing about them since they left London. A central image of The City was 'The Tomato Game'. The object of the game is to race, on a motor bike, at full speed towards a concrete wall and spin-turn to a stop at the last instant. The winner is the one who comes as close as possible to the wall without flattening himself against it, like a squashed tomato. With their passionate love of freedom I hope they have been able to continue their work fighting against a computer society where human beings exist only as numbers.

In the summer and autumn of 1974, Peter Hall's plans for the new National Theatre on the South Bank began to emerge and his demands for financial and other resources appeared to threaten the remainder of the subsidised theatre at a time of financial stringency. I discussed this matter with colleagues, the directors of various subsidised theatres, and drew up a letter to *The Times*, which they all signed. Apart from myself, the letter was signed by Lindsay Anderson (Associate Artistic Director of the Royal Court Theatre), Peter Cheeseman (Artistic Director of the Victoria Theatre, Stoke-on-Trent), Michael Croft (Director of the National Youth Theatre), Frank Dunlop (Director of the Young Vic), Michael Elliott (Joint Artistic Director of '69 Theatre Company, Manchester), Richard Eyre (Theatre Director of the Playhouse, Nottingham), Howard Gibbens (Director of the Bush Theatre), John Harrison (Director of Leeds Playhouse), Ewan Hooper (Director of Greenwich Theatre), Peter James (Artistic Director of The Crucible Theatre, Sheffield), Joan Littlewood (Artistic Director of the Theatre Royal, Stratford East), Charles Marowitz (Artistic Director of the Open Space Theatre), and Toby Robertson (Director of the Prospect Theatre Company). The letter, which appeared in *The Times* on 15th October 1974 offered general support to Hall and the National Theatre but went on to describe some of the serious dangers which might arise 'from the occupation by the National of so elaborate and prestigious a complex,' arguing that 'the National's name, and its huge initial ambitions, cannot exempt it from the same obligations to economize as the rest of us . . . Perhaps an even more important danger is the drain . . . on resources other than financial. For example, to staff the three auditoria, the National Theatre is said to be seeking 140 skilled technicians. It is doubtful whether there are many more than that number working in all the theatres of the country. From our own experience we can attest that the National has been busy for some time already, endeavouring to attract technicians with offers of salaries far in excess of anything these theatres can afford to pay. The implications of this are unhealthy.' Peter Hall reacted with intemperate fury to this letter. Meeting him by chance in the National Film Theatre the day the letter had appeared, he attacked me as if our letter had been motivated by some personal vendetta against him. Since I scarcely knew him and had never had any dealings with him, this was complete paranoia. Time proved that our warnings were only too necessary. We had had no problems with the National Theatre whilst it was directed by Laurence Olivier and, although Peter Hall obviously needed more resources for the South Bank, if he had handled the matter with the same sensitivity and generosity as Laurence Olivier had shown, he would not have had to face the united ranks of the rest of the subsidised theatre, who had no faith in his good intentions.

During my time as Artistic Director, the Court was basically organised in the same way as it had been from the beginning of the English Stage Company. There was a Council which had the ultimate responsibility, particularly for appointing the Artistic Director, obtaining the funds necessary, negotiating the Arts Council Grant, and making sure that the theatre operated within its means. The Council met about once every three months. The work of the theatre in between times was watched over by a Management Committee that met about once a fortnight and an Artistic Committee that met at irregular intervals to advise the Artistic Director. This Committee during my time as Artistic Director consisted of the three Associate Artistic Directors, who were Lindsay Anderson, Albert Finney and Anthony Page; the Literary Manager, for most of my time Ann Jellicoe and after her, Donald Howarth; the Resident Playwright, at first Howard Brenton, then Michael Abbensetts, then Caryl Churchill; the Director of the Theatre Upstairs, first Nicholas Wright, then Roger Croucher; and the casting director, who was Gillian Diamond when I first took over and then Patsy Pollock. Any Resident or Associate Directors we had working in the theatre at the time also automatically joined the Artistic Committee. In this respect, I particularly remember Max Stafford-Clark, Robert Fox, Anton Gill and William Alexander. In addition there were two invited members, Jocelyn Herbert and David Storey; and, for a time, Lois Sieff, as a member of the Council, chaired our meetings.

The meetings discussed the repertoire and any other artistic questions upon which I wanted to ask the Committee's advice or on which they wished to advise me. Meetings were quite stormy, the storms mostly blown up by Lindsay, who was dissatisfied with the way I was running the theatre and the way in which other people, mostly Anthony Page, were carrying out their obligations. Lindsay was a perfectionist, concerned about every detail of the work, particularly the publicity, photographs and programmes. Jocelyn Herbert was particularly concerned about standards back stage, an area where I was certainly weaker than previous Artistic Directors of the Court had been. Anthony himself, an iron butterfly, caused endless problems by the way he dithered over every decision he had to make, dithered, but generally got his way: and his way was usually apparent to his colleagues from the very beginning. On the whole, I found the meetings a great strain because, although the members of the Committee were all giving their time generously to the work, the particular atmosphere created – largely by Lindsay – had a nagging and combative rather than friendly and co-operative tone. Anthony Page said it was like a snake pit. And yet the snakes were all friends and despite, or perhaps because of the creative tensions, excellent work was being done.

The Management Committee was usually chaired by the Chairman of the English Stage Company. I resigned from this position when I took over as Artistic Director, and Greville Poke, who had been on the Council from the beginning as Honorary Secretary, became Chairman of the English Stage Company and so chaired the Management Committee. As Artistic Director I continued to attend these meetings, as did the General Manager, first Helen Montague, then Anne Jenkins. The accountant throughout my time there as Artistic Director was the excellent Jon Catty; we worked well together because, just as I was weaker on things back stage, I knew more about the business side than most Artistic Directors and played a major part in the decisions, good and bad, of the Management Committee. Other members of the Council attended the Management Committee from time to time when their expert advice could be of help to us. The Manager of the Theatre Upstairs and other members of the staff also came. During the period I am writing about the Management Committee meetings were comparatively peaceful. In the past it had sometimes been the other way round, the Council and Management meetings being stormy, the Artistic Committee peaceful.

The Council itself was something of a mixed bag. The President was George Harewood, the Chairman Greville Poke; these two and J.E. Blacksell, a Devon Headmaster, had been on the Council with me from the beginning and had been introduced by Ronald Duncan, as had Isadore Caplan, our solicitor. Dame Peggy Ashcroft, Jocelyn Herbert, John Osborne and Tony Richardson (who lived in California and never attended during this period) had come on because of their work with the Company. Neville Blond had brought in Norman Collins, Mrs. J. Edward Sieff and Mrs. Blond. I had invited onto the Council Michael Codron and Michael White, theatre producers, Alistair McAlpine and the solicitor John Montgomerie. Greville was not really a strong enough Chairman but in other ways the Council was well balanced.

Everyone who has been Artistic Director at the Royal Court knows that the theatre is small enough for the Director to have personal contact with everyone who works there, unlike the National Theatre, where at least in Peter Hall's day, many of the workers in the theatre had absolutely no contact with the Director. However, the very accessibility of the Artistic Director of the Court brings about another difficulty; to him is brought every small problem that arises in the building, and, even though he refers these to other departments, he is constantly being worried by detailed questions of administration when he should be considering and dealing with the major questions of theatre policy and keeping an eye on current productions. In my time all these problems were given added emphasis by the personality of Lindsay Anderson, who had no sense of proportion and wanted, like a small child, to have every matter with which he was concerned dealt with immediately without reference to anyone else's problems. One instance springs to mind. I was attending Ann Jellicoe's leaving party in the Theatre Upstairs, when Lindsay came along with some small problem. I said I would deal with it 'tomorrow'. I knew he would find this answer intolerable but I had no intention of leaving Ann and her party, and the matter was not urgent. Lindsay's reaction was like Rumpelstiltskin's when his name is discovered, but instead of stamping and making a hole in the floor Lindsay simply started to hit me. Fortunately I was rescued by the intervention of Mustapha Matura, and no harm was done except to our dignity, and that did not last. However, at one stage Lindsay became so infuriated by my

Artistic Directorship of the Court that he went so far as to initiate a scheme to have me sacked and to bring back Tony Richardson. Tony, however, was unwilling to return from California. And from Lindsay's point of view the idea was totally self destructive, as he knew well. Tony would not have put up with his tantrums for five minutes.

Why did I? It would have been perfectly easy to get him to resign, as everyone found out after I left. All one had to do was say no to a production he wanted to direct. When Nicholas Wright and Robert Kidd took over from me – they were largely his choice – he proposed to them that he should do *The Seagull*. When they said 'no' he left the Court, never to return.

I did not try to get rid of him because I thought, and still think, that for certain types of play he is a magnificent director, and that his work brought glory to the theatre. For this I was prepared to suffer for the sake of the English Stage Company. And there was another reason. Before taking over the Artistic Directorship of the Court, as I have already explained, I produced several plays which Lindsay directed and on which we had a perfectly good working relationship. But then, of course, as a rule, I was only doing one production at a time, and so could give Lindsay my undivided attention. Looking back, I now remember the one occasion when this was not the case. Lindsay was directing and producing *The White Bus*, a short film for Woodfall, on which I was the Executive Producer. But I was also producing with Tony Richardson the full-length film, *The Sailor from Gibraltar*, at the same time. Lindsay again became furious when I could not always be with his film.

The trouble was, that apart from admiring him as a director, I was fond of him, regarded him as a friend, and could not bring myself to admit just how destructive he could be. In fact, but for Lindsay, I do not think I should have wanted to leave the Court at the end of my three years' contract. There was even a moment, before the appointment of my successors, when Richard Eyre, then the Director of the Nottingham Playhouse, suggested to me that I should stay on and that he and I should run the Court together. A very tempting idea, but it came too late. By this time Lindsay had the bit between his teeth and was determined that I should go. But he would not take on the job himself.

Richard Findlater writes in his book 'When Oscar Lewenstein told the Council that he had decided to leave at the end of his three-year contract he also told them it seemed to him that, in spite of their past differences, Lindsay Anderson was the obvious choice as his successor, if the Council wished to continue with the current policy. The Council, wishing it, expressed a unanimous hope that Anderson would accept. He declined, however, because he felt that he was not the right man for the job at that time. It required considerable administrative ability which was not, he thought, his strong point.'

Lindsay strongly backed the joint application of Nicholas Wright and Robert Kidd, thinking no doubt that he could work with them more happily than he had been able to work with me. He made a mistake, both from his personal point of view and from the Court's, for within eighteen months of their appointment Robert Kidd had resigned and this automatically cancelled Nicholas Wright's appointment. Neither Lindsay nor Anthony Page have worked at the Court since I left, losing the base where so much of their best work had been done.

There was only one big upset on the Council during this period, but it led directly to my deciding that I did not wish to continue as Artistic Director when my three-year contract ended.

Early on in my time as Director I had put to the Council a plan whereby the English Stage Company would take over the Old Vic, then the home of Olivier's National Theatre.

In fact, there was an item in the programme for John Osborne's *A Sense of Detachment*, in December 1972, which reads: 'The Governors of the Old Vic have invited the E.S.C. to take a lease on their historic theatre when the National Theatre move out in 1974. This is an exciting prospect for the E.S.C. who have long wished to extend their work to a wider and more popular audience. There is no question of the E.S.C. abandoning the Royal Court, so the scheme needs extra subsidies from the Arts Council and other grant-giving bodies before it can be finally confirmed.'

Time went by and I drew up a scheme whereby Albert Finney and Paul Scofield would become the directors of our Old Vic arm while Lindsay took on the Directorship of the Royal Court. I would remain Artistic Director of the E.S.C. as a whole. The scheme envisaged not that the directors would work only in their own theatres, but that we would take a view on the plays we were going to produce and decide which was the best theatre to start them in, with the idea that some would start at the Royal Court and transfer to the Old Vic instead of to a West End theatre. But a year or so went by, the financial situation became more difficult, and the National Theatre's move was repeatedly postponed. I also did not realise how much the scheme was resented by Lindsay, who, as he subsequently made clear, had no wish or willingness to become Artistic Director of the Court or any other theatre. He was happy to criticise others, but, when it came to it, not willing to accept the kind of responsibility being Artistic Director involved. The Council was in any case becoming increasingly nervous about taking on another commit-ment, although it had endorsed the idea in 1972. In the event, urged on by the whole Artistic Committee, with the sole exceptions of Albert Finney and me, the Council turned the scheme down, without even seeing how far the Arts Council would go to support it. Even Greville Poke, who as Chairman had been in on all the negotiations with the Old Vic, did not say a word in defence of the project. In his book Richard Findlater comments: 'Oscar Lewenstein and Greville Poke were bitterly disappointed.' I certainly was, but Greville gave no sign of his disap-pointment. I felt let down on all sides.

It is probable, in the light of the financial situation, that the scheme would, in the end, not have got the subsidy it required. However, the Governors of the Old Vic had been willing to let us have their theatre at a very low rent, and the Arts Council had been kept abreast of the project and had not been discouraging. It would have been all of a piece with the dreams that George Devine had had about taking the Chelsea Palace, with the scheme by which Laurence Olivier and my Company were to have taken over the Metropolitan in the Edgware Road, with the English Stage Company's season at the Queen's Theatre and the plans that we had been discussing with the Hammersmith Council for a new theatre to be built there. I thought a project like this would give the E.S.C. new life and enable us to tackle some of the big plays, like those I had been producing at the Roundhouse. When the Council turned it down so lightly, only Elaine Blond recognised the blow it was to me. I realised that not only had I lost a scheme dear to my heart, but that I could not count on my artistic colleagues for any real support when it came to something that I wanted to do rather than something they wanted to do. I was finding the Court a big strain, probably because, in addition to everything else, I was beginning to suffer badly from arthritis.

So when I said I would go when my contract expired, I really meant it.

My contract as Artistic Director ended at the end of August 1975. I wanted to do something special and at the same time something that would help the Court's financial situation.

Don's Party was due to end its run on 12th April which left me a period of twenty weeks. I decided to present a Joe Orton Festival of his three-full length plays. During my three years, we had produced only one revival, D.H. Lawrence's *Merry-go-Round*, so I felt justified in reviving these three plays, which I hoped would establish Joe's reputation as a major playwright and in particular at last do justice to his last, and I thought, greatest play *What The Butler Saw*, the qualities of which few critics had recognised when it had been presented originally. My idea was that the three plays would be presented as a season, each directed by one of the Associate Artistic Directors, and if possible cast with a Company of actors, designed by the same designer, with even the posters designed by one person and the photographs taken by the same photographer. In the event, very few of these ideas were achieved. At first Anthony Page was to direct *Entertaining Mr. Sloane*; Albert Finney to direct *Loot* and Lindsay Anderson *Butler*. Anthony wasn't sure if he would be available. We waited for him as long as we could, then when he would not or could not commit himself, I asked Roger Croucher, the director of the Theatre Upstairs to step in and Roger accepted. Later Anthony said he could do it, but by that time it was too late. Albert and Lindsay, however, did go ahead but we soon found out that it would not be possible to have one company of actors playing in all three plays. Apart from the inherent difficulties of cross-casting, Michael White and Eddie Kulukundis were associated with us in financing and presenting the Season and wanted to be free to transfer each of the plays if it was successful. So, for many of the familiar reasons that had made it impossible in the past for the Court to have a permanent Company, not least the difficulty our directors had in agreeing on anything except a broadly humanist philosophy, the plays were not presented in true repertory, but one after the other, each for a run of six weeks or so. The set designers were all different, John Gunter for *Sloane*, Douglas Heap for *Loot* and Jocelyn Herbert for *Butler*. Even the programme covers and posters were not all designed by the same artist – Lindsay could not accept the designer who worked on the first two plays.

Entertaining Mr. Sloane was strongly cast. Malcolm McDowell played Sloane, Beryl Reid played Kath, his lascivious landlady, James Ottaway was Kemp, her father, and Ed, her brother was played by Ronald Fraser. Ronald Fraser had difficulties with his part and Malcolm McDowell and Beryl Reid felt they were not getting enough help from their director and asked Lindsay Anderson to take some rehearsals. Malcolm had appeared in several films directed by Lindsay and had complete confidence in him. Roger Croucher was not happy about this but it was necessary and successful.

The play did very well indeed at the Court, giving 41 performances and playing to over 90 per cent of capacity. It then transferred to the Duke of York's Theatre. *Loot*, although a moderate success for the Court, was a bit of a disappointment. I had hoped that Albert would have a triumph with what had been Joe's most popular play. In asking Albert to come on board as an Associate, I wanted to give him the opportunity to play parts and direct plays that would enhance his own career as well as helping the Court. Of my three associates, he was the one with whom I found it easiest to work. He was a great leader of a company who was always a good influence throughout the theatre. During these last months we had established an Emergency Fund to raise money to repair the roof of the Theatre. Albert organised money-raising shows on Sundays with such artists as George Melly, Nicol Williamson, Dave Allen, Alan Price, Cleo Laine and John Dankworth. He did much good work throughout my three years, but a real solid hit eluded him. I wanted Albert to cast Michael Bates, who had so brilliantly played Inspector Truscott in the original *Loot*, but Albert wanted to have a fresh actor in the part. Good though Phillip Stone was, he wasn't a born Truscott as Michael Bates had been. Jill Bennett as Fay was probably the strongest actress to play this part and the rest of the cast was good. But whereas it should have sold out, it only played to 73 per cent of seating capacity and 63 per cent of box office capacity. Good enough for the Royal Court, but not strong enough to transfer.

Lindsay's production of *What the Butler Saw* was, in my opinion, the triumph of the Season. The other two plays had already been recognised as successful works, *Butler* had not. Now with a company of good actors, no stars, the play shone forth as the comic masterpiece it undoubtedly is. The cast was: Michael Medwin as Dr. Prentice, Jane Carr as Geraldine

Barclay, Betty Marsden as Mrs. Prentice, Kevin Lloyd as Nicholas Beckett, Valentine Dyall as Dr. Rance and Brian Glover as Sergeant Match. Lindsay let controlled anarchy rip across the stage: the text of the play was played uncut and unaltered, exactly as the author had left it. It played to 83 per cent of seating capacity and 75 per cent of box office and it transferred to the Whitehall Theatre. But it had only a short run there proving that, without a star to sugar the pill, the West End was not yet ready to accept Orton, even in a great production of his finest play.

The Season did what it had set out to do, it established Joe Orton in his rightful place in the English theatre and in particular established the reputation of *What the Butler Saw*.

So my three years ended with an upbeat success and a show of unity in the Artistic Directorate. There was some satisfaction in that.

Part Eight

After Words

Exhausted by Anderson and arthritis when I left the Royal Court in 1975, I decided not to start up another theatrical production office but to take things more easily. My son Mark was now 22 and at Sussex University reading Social Anthropology in the School of African Studies. When he had left school he had gone to Tanzania with a video team led by Gary Belkin, to record life in the socialist Ujaama villages there. He returned to England to take up a place reading Mathematics at Warwick, but found he wasn't really interested. He wanted to do something relating to Africa and, advised by Kenneth Brecher, an anthropologist who had helped on *Savages*, Mark decided to move to anthropology. His brother Peter, who was 19, was spending a year working and travelling in Central and North America prior to going to university, so Eileen and I were living alone, with two houses, one in Hampstead and one in Hove, each with five or six bedrooms. We decided to sell our London house and move to Brighton, where Eileen had made herself a studio. She continued to make pots and to co-edit *Ceramic Review*, going to London one or two days each week for the purpose.

But my 'retirement' didn't last long. That same year at the Edinburgh Festival we saw a new play, *Dimetos*, written and directed by Athol Fugard. Though rather abstract, I thought it was interesting enough to be worth producing in London. I should have tried to make an arrangement with the Royal Court to present it there, but at the time I wanted to make a clean break and instead, in partnership with Eddie Kulukundis, decided to take it into the West End. We cast it very strongly, with Paul Scofield playing the Engineer, Dimetos, Yvonne Bryceland playing the part she had played in Edinburgh, Ben Kingsley and Celia Quick playing the other two parts. We opened at the Nottingham Playhouse and then came into the Comedy Theatre. Only Harold Hobson responded enthusiastically, saying that 'it was far and away the best offering at last year's Edinburgh Festival' and 'that it deals with a theme of extreme significance to us today.' He also said in the course of a long notice 'That *Waiting for Godot* triumphed over critical and popular disapproval is a good augury for what will eventually happen to Mr. Fugard's *Dimetos*'. Most critics just thought Athol had bitten off more than he could chew. It had a short run and after sixteen years I have seen no sign of Harold Hobson's augury being fulfilled.

Dimetos was presented in 1976. In 1977 I co-presented in the West End Mary O'Malley's play *Once a Catholic*, which had opened at the Royal Court, where it had been commissioned but not delivered whilst I was Artistic Director. The play was presented by Eddie Kulukundis, who invited me and two other producers to co-present it with him. His production company, Knightsbridge, was the active producer, and I did not play an important part in this production, for which Mary O'Malley shared the *Evening Standard* Most Promising Playwright Award in 1977. This play ran at Wyndhams for more than two years, the longest run of any play with which I was associated. In 1978 I co-produced with Eddie Kulukundis a play by Michael Hastings, *Gloo Joo*, about West Indians in London. This play, directed by Michael Rudman, ran for over 200 performances and won the *Evening Standard* Best Comedy Award for 1978.

I had also acquired the rights to six plays by Sean O'Casey with a view to arranging for their presentation in 1980 to celebrate the playwright's centenary. They were *Juno and the Paycock*, *The Shadow of a Gunman*, *Red Roses for Me*, *Purple Dust*, *Cock a Doodle Dandy* and *The Bishop's Bonfire*. I had hoped to present at least three of the plays, being a representative selection of his life's work, and at first considered forming a special company for the purpose, but later decided that one of the big national companies, either the Royal Shakespeare or the National Theatre, would be able to do the job better. Both wanted to present *Juno and the Paycock* and *The Shadow of a Gunman* but neither was interested in the later plays. I had discussions with their respective directors, Trevor Nunn and Peter Hall, and eventually decided to go with the Royal Shakespeare Company, because Trevor Nunn agreed to direct *Juno* himself with Judi Dench playing the lead at the Aldwych. The Royal Shakespeare also arranged for Michael Bogdanov to direct *Shadow of a Gunman* at the Other Place in Stratford. Both productions were excellent, the *Juno* a triumph with Judi Dench at her magnificent best in the leading part.

Felix Barker in the *Evening News* wrote, 'Has this great play ever had a more anguished or more relevant message? Not, I suggest since the original 1924 production. Has Sean O'Casey's tragi-comedy ever been better played than it was last night? Not in my experience, which covers half a dozen revivals spread over 30 or more years.'

I could not claim much credit for this triumph, except having had the good sense to accept Trevor's offer to do it. It was the last play in the West End for which I had a credit in the programme. I could not have chosen anything more representative of my theatrical ideals.

Peter Hall's Diaries, published in 1983, had a snide reference to this O'Casey season, together with a completely biased account of the incident concerning our letter to *The Times*. So much so that I had to have my solicitor write a letter insisting on changes, which were made in subsequent editions.

In 1980, a Bradford schoolgirl of 16 had her first play *The Arbor* produced as part of the Young Writers Festival at the Theatre Upstairs, and it was later moved to the Royal Court main stage. Andrea Dunbar's second play *Rita, Sue and Bob Too* was performed at the Royal Court on 14th October 1982 and won her the George Devine Award for that year. Donald Howarth, who was on the George Devine Committee, had read the play before it was performed and told me about it with great enthusiasm. I read it, thought it a wonderful piece of original work and decided to option it for a film. Five years later I made the film, co-producing it with an old friend Sandy Lieberson. Directed by Alan Clarke, it was shown at the Cannes Film Festival before opening in cinemas in the UK and later on Channel Four, which had been its main financier. It was well received by most of the press, only the Express newspapers denouncing it and attempting to stir up Andrea's neighbours on the Buttershaw Estate in Bradford, where it was shot and where Andrea lived. When the worried neighbours finally saw the offending film, they roared with laughter. Alan, Andrea and the actors, particularly Siobhan Finneran (Rita), Michelle Holmes (Sue) and George Costigan

(Bob), had brilliantly shown what life on a working-class estate in Thatcher's Britain was really like.

Philip French in *The Observer* wrote 'The happy giggling pair share him (Bob) as a lover, embarking on the affair in his red Rover in a nocturnal scene that has a shocking, non-prurient frankness unparalleled in our cinema, concluding with a sound effect (the thudding to the ground of a discarded condom) hitherto unrecorded in a British studio. This admirably acted comedy, the high spirits of which have been misinterpreted by some observers as callousness, celebrates the fortitude of Rita and Sue. The strength afforded by their friendship helps them survive in a desolate world of permanent unemployment that is destroying those around them and will eventually get them too.'

His words were prophetic in more ways than one: a few years later both Andrea and Alan were dead, one of a brain haemorrhage, the other of cancer. Andrea was still in her twenties; Alan was only in his fifties, one of the most brilliant directors of his time, whose career was mostly in television.

That to date is the end of my career in the theatre and films. These last two productions, *Juno* and *Rita, Sue and Bob Too*, represent rather clearly the kind of plays and films I had tried to present throughout my career. I tried to pursue a steady policy of presenting productions that criticise the status quo and show how the other half live. I have concentrated on contemporary shows, not because I myself do not enjoy the great plays of the past, but because I have felt the most useful contribution I could make was to support living authors and through them chronicle and comment upon our own times. How far I have succeeded in carrying out my self appointed role, this book will show.

My productions have been of work to which I personally responded. I have not presented plays that I thought would make money though they did not appeal to me. I do not think any successful producer can work in that way. I was lucky that, for at least some of the time, my taste was shared by the public and that the English Stage Company's subsidy enabled us to some extent to be ahead of public taste. Looking at the West End theatre today, it might seem that nothing has changed since I first began working in the theatre. But the Royal National Theatre, the Royal Shakespeare Theatre and the Royal Court did not exist then, nor did the subsidised regional theatres or the fringe, the best of which, such as the Théâtre de Complicité and Cheek by Jowl, continue despite the financial constraints. So perhaps something was done after all.

Eileen and I have spent quite a lot of our time in the last few years collecting pictures, pots and antiquarian books, I have made four or five visits to the United States lecturing on the theatre at various Universities and colleges. At one University, Louisiana State at Baton Rouge, where I went several times, they became so interested in the Royal Court Theatre that they organised a special conference on its work, to which they invited many of the artists who had worked at the Court. Sixteen went, plus various critics and academics from Britain and the U.S.A. Unfortunately, I was unable to go, having just had my second hip operation, but the discussion was recorded in a book, *Inside the Royal Court Theatre, 1956-1981 Artists Talk*, edited by Gresdna Doty and Billy Harbin, who had organised and initiated the whole event.

It is now 1993. Eileen is still editing *Ceramic Review*, Mark, the anthropologist, has become a systems analyst, Peter, after dropping out of university, has become a journalist on the World Service of the BBC, at present working in the African Service. Between them they have given us four grandchildren, Jack, Rosie, Woody and Ella. Better names than Silvion Oscar.

I am now seventy-seven years old. I do not suppose I shall produce any more plays or films, but you never know. Just recently I read a book that I thought would make a wonderful children's play . . .

I was born in 1917 the year of the Russian Revolution. It was the single most important event in my lifetime. Today people are writing off that great experiment as a total failure. Certainly it was a social experiment conducted under conditions that probably made success impossible. But perhaps in judging it we should be wise to remember Mao's reply when asked what he considered the results of the French Revolution to have been. He said 'It's too early to say.' I am still certain that only some form of socialism can give us the free, fair and peaceful society which we need if mankind and, indeed, our planet is to survive. And surely a species that can send men to the moon and produce Shakespeare and Tolstoy, Rembrandt and Leonardo, Beethoven and Mozart must be able to find a way of living together better than the present consumer-driven capitalist societies of the West. Despite the disappointments and failures, men and women will continue to search for something better – not Utopia, the search for that has brought enough misery, but something fairer and more free than the way we live now. To that search there will never be an end, but it will never be abandoned. To have been in the search party has made my life worth living.

Appendix I

*Plays presented or co-presented in London
by Oscar Lewenstein*

1955

The World of Sholom Aleichem at the Embassy Theatre, Swiss Cottage; dramatised by Arnold Perl; directed by Sam Wanamaker; front cloth designed by John Craxton; drawings by Ben Shahn; costume designs by Bernard Sarron; dances arranged by Tutte Lemkow; with John Barrard, Alfie Bass, Gerald Blake, Kitty Davis, Mark Dignam, Joan Drummond, Lou Jacobi, Miriam Karlin, David Kossoff, Tutte Lemkow, Minerva Pious, David Spenser, Jeremy Spenser and Meier Tzelniker.

Moby Dick at the Duke of York's Theatre; written and directed by Orson Welles, adapted from the novel by Herman Melville; associate producer William Chappell; music composed by Anthony Collins; stage decoration by Mary Owen; with John Boyd-Brent, Joseph Chelton, Jefferson Clifford, Harry Cordwell, John Gray, Gordon Jackson, Patrick McGoohan, Phillippe Perrotet, Wensley Pithey, Joan Plowright, David Saire, Peter Sallis, Orson Welles and Kenneth Williams.

The Punch Revue at the Duke of York's Theatre; devised and directed by Vida Hope; book compiled by Ronald Duncan; art direction by Joan and David de Bethel; musical direction by Geoffrey Wright; orchestrations by Phil Cardew; choreography by George Erskine-Jones; with Alfie Bass, Joyce Blair, James Browne, Paul Daneman, Andrew Downie, Annette Gibson, Malcolm Goddard, Rosaline Haddon, Binnie Hale, June Laverick, Wendy McClure, Denis Martin and John Palmer.

1956

The Threepenny Opera by Bertolt Brecht and Kurt Weill at the Royal Court, Aldwych and Comedy Theatres; English adaptation by Marc Blitzstein; directed by Sam Wanamaker; decor by Caspar Neher; musical direction by Berthold Goldschmidt; with Daphne Anderson, Victor Baring, Patricia Black, Georgia Brown, Donald Conlon, George A. Cooper, John Corbett, Renée Goddard, Aliki Hansen,

Charles Hill, Sylvia Langova, Lisa Lee, Ewan MacColl, Warren Mitchell, George Murcell, Bill Owen, Eric Pohlmann, Roland Randel, Maria Remusat, Charles Stanley and Una Victor.

1957

The Member of the Wedding by Carson McCullers at the Royal Court Theatre; directed by Tony Richardson; designed by Alan Tagg with costumes by Stephen Doncaster; with Ann Dickins, Vivienne Drummond, James Dyrenforth, John Hall, Neville Jacobson, Errol John, Geraldine McEwan, Orlando Martins, Garry Nesbitt, Dudy Nimmo, Richard Pasco, Bertice Reading, Anthony Richmond, Connie Smith, Greta Watson and Susan Westerby.

Nekrassov by Jean Paul Sartre at the Royal Court Theatre; translated by Sylvia and George Leeson; directed by George Devine; designed by Richard Negri; music by Thomas Eastwood; with Robert Aldous, Ronald Baker, Nicholas Brady, Marjorie Caldicott, Percy Cartwright, Harry H. Corbett, Margo Cunningham, Jane Downs, Felix Felton, Robert Helpmann, Kerry Jordan, Bernard Kay, Roddy McMillan, George Merritt, Martin Miller, Kendrick Owen, Milo Sperber, Anna Steele, James Villiers and John Wood.

1958

Expresso Bongo at the Saville Theatre; book by Wolf Mankowitz; music by David Heneker and Monty Norman; lyrics by Julian More, David Heneker and Monty Norman; directed by William Chappell; decor by Loudon Sainthill with costumes by Jocelyn Rickards; with Jan Arnold, Elizabeth Ashley, Frank Coda, Barry Cryer, Anne Donaghue, Nicholas Evans, Hilda Fenemore, Carol Ann Ford, Charles Gray, Trevor Griffiths, Rosaline Haddon, Susan Hampshire, Hy Hazell, James Kenney, Geoffrey L'Cise, Adrienne Marsh, Millicent Martin, Aubrey Morris, Ben O' Mahoney, Julie Musgrove, Paul Scofield, John Shackelle, Anna Sharkey, Victor Spinetti, Meier Tzelniker and George Tovey.

The Party by Jane Arden at the New Theatre; directed by Charles Laughton; setting by Reece Pemberton with costumes by Jocelyn Rickards; with Albert Finney, Charles Laughton, Elsa Lanchester, Ann Lynn, Joyce Redman and John Welsh.

1959

A Taste of Honey by Shelagh Delaney at Wyndham's and the Criterion Theatres; directed by Joan Littlewood; designed by John Bury; with Avis Bunnage, Frances Cuka, Nigel Davenport, Clifton Jones and Murray Melvin.

The Long and the Short and the Tall by Willis Hall at the Royal Court Theatre and the New Theatre; directed by Lindsay Anderson; designed by Alan Tagg; with David Andrews, Ronald Fraser, Edward Judd, Alfred Lynch, Bryan Pringle, Peter O'Toole, Robert Shaw and Kenji Takaki.

The Hostage by Brendan Behan at Wyndhams Theatre; directed by Joan Littlewood; designed by Sean Kenny; with Roy Barnett, Clive Barker, Ann Beach, James Booth, Stephen Cato, Glynn Edwards, Howard Goorney, Leila Greenwood, Yootha Joyce, Eileen Kenally, Alfred Lynch, Brian Murphy, Celia Salkeld and Dudley Sutton.

Make Me an Offer book by Wolf Mankowitz; lyrics and music by Monty Norman and David Heneker at the New Theatre; directed by Joan Littlewood; decor by Voytek; with Diana Coupland, Tom Fletcher, Howard Greene, Bernard Goldman, Sheila Hancock, Chuck Julian, Merelina Kendall, Roy Kinnear, Roberta Kirkwood, Frieda Knorr, Marjorie Lawrence, Martin Lawrence, Dilys Laye, Bernard Martin, Daniel Massey, Martin Miller, Wally Patch, Victor Spinetti, and Milton Sills.

1960

The Lily White Boys by Harry Cookson with songs by Christopher Logue and music by Tony Kinsey and Bill Le Sage at the Royal Court Theatre; directed by Lindsay Anderson; with Georgia Brown, Shirley Ann Field, Albert Finney, Willoughby Goddard, James Grout, Geoffrey Hibbert, Barbara Hicks, Monty Landis, Philip Locke, Ann Lynn and Ronnie Stevens.

Rhinoceros by Ionesco at the Royal Court and Strand Theatres; translated by Derek Prouse; directed and designed by Orson Welles; costumes by Stuart Stallard; with Philip Anthony, Michael Bates, Marjorie Caldicott, Monica Evans, Michael Gough, Gladys Henson, Hazel Hughes, Geoffrey Lumsden, Duncan Macrae, Miles Malleson, Laurence Olivier, Joan Plowright, Peter Sallis, Will Stampe and Henry Woolf. (Maggie Smith took over from Joan Plowright at the Strand).

The Art of Living based on the writings of Art Buchwald; music and lyrics by Monty Norman and David Heneker; lyrics and sketches by Julian More with additional sketches by Johnny Speight at the Criterion Theatre; devised and directed by Laurier Lister; decor by Voytek; with George Baron, Judy Bruce, Stella Claire, Barbara Evans, Craig Hunter, Jean Rayner, Carole Shelley, Hiram Sherman, Graham Stark and Edward Woodward.

Billy Liar by Keith Waterhouse and Willis Hall at the Cambridge Theatre; directed by Lindsay Anderson; designed by Alan Tagg; with Trevor Bannister, Ann Beach, Juliet Cooke, George A. Cooper, Albert Finney, Ethel Griffies, Jennifer Jayne and Mona Washbourne.

1961

Breakfast for One by James Doran at the Arts Theatre; directed by Silvio Narizzano; setting by Seamus Flannery; with Jill Bennett, Vivienne Drummond, Maurice Good, Jack Hedley and Mary Hinton.

Jacques by Ionesco at the Royal Court Theatre; translated by Donald Watson; directed by R.D.Smith; designed by Michael Young; with Madge Brindley, Zoe Caldwell, Selma Vaz Dias, Peter Duguid, Valerie Hanson, Denys Hawthorne, Mollie Maureen, George Merritt and John Moffatt.

Altona by Jean-Paul Sartre at the Royal Court and Saville Theatres; adapted by Justin O'Brien; directed by John Berry; designed by Sean Kenny; with Claire Bloom, Richard Butler, Diane Cilento, Julian Glover, Kenneth Haigh, Derek Newark, Nigel Stock and Basil Sydney.

The Blacks by Jean Genet at the Royal Court Theatre; translated by Bernard Frechtman; directed by Roger Blin; designed by André Acquart; music by Patrick Cowen; with Harry Baird, Brunetta Bernstein, Vida Deghanar, Rodney Douglas, Joan Hooley, Joseph Layode, Bloke Modisane, Neville Monroe, Felicia Okoli, Rashid Onikoyi, Lloyd Reckord, Neville Russell and Yolande.

Celebration by Keith Waterhouse and Willis Hall at the Duchess Theatre; directed by Val May; decor by Graham Barlow; with Donald Burton, Rowena Cooper, James Cossins, Colin George, Gabrielle Hamilton, Hilary Hardiman, Jeremy Kemp, Robert Lang, Gillian Martell, Carole Mowlam, Colette O'Neill, Morgan Sheppard, Virginia Stride, Antony Tuckey and Michael Williams.

Luther by John Osborne at the Royal Court and Phoenix Theatres; directed by Tony Richardson; designed by Jocelyn Herbert; music by John Addison; with Peter Bull, James Cairncross, Frank Davies, Stacey Davies, Peter Duguid, Murray Evans, Albert Finney. Derek Fuke, Julian Glover, Meryl Gourley, Roger Harbird, Carleton Hobbs, Charles Kay, John Kirk, Paul Large, Dan Meaden, John Moffatt, Bill Owen, Andrew Pearmain, David Read, Robert Robinson and Malcolm Taylor.

1962

My Place by Elaine Dundy at the Comedy Theatre; directed by John Dexter; designed by Voytek; with Diane Cilento, Annette Crosbie, Guy Deghy, Barry Foster, Betty Hare, Barbara Hicks, Tristram Jellinek, Mary Jones, Kate Lansbury, Janet Milner, Dandy Nichols, John Rees and Harry Towb.

Twists devised and written by Stephen Vinaver with music by Carl Davis at the Arts Theatre; directed by Stephen Vinaver; designed by Sally Jacobs; with Ann Beach, Fenella Fielding, Riggs O'Hara, Anton Rodgers and Michael Williams.

Play with a Tiger by Doris Lessing at the Comedy Theatre; directed by Ted Kotcheff; designed by Alan Tagg; with Anne Lawson, Siobhan McKenna, Maureen Pryor, Godfrey Quigley, William Russell and Alex Viespi.

The Secret of the World by Ted Allan at the Theatre Royal Stratford East; directed by John Berry; designed by John Bury; with John Berry, Bruce Boa, Raymond Carl, Pearl Celine, Gerry Duggan, Robert Gillespie, Graydon Gould, Miriam Karlin, Susan Marryott, Geraldine Moffat and Al Waxman.

The Scatterin' by James McKenna at Theatre Royal, Stratford East; directed by Alan Simpson; designed by John Ryan; with Billy Boyle, Eileen Colgan, Audrey Corr, Maurice Cowan, Donal Donnelly, Tony Doyle, Collette Dunne, Alex Farrell, Margaret Jenkins, Margaret Lyons, Wesley Murphy, Karin Petersen, Morgan Sheppard, Noel Sheridan, Susan Stanley and Malcolm Terris.

The Keep by Gwyn Thomas at the Piccadilly Theatre; directed by John Dexter; designed by Ken Calder; with Richard Davies, Windsor Davies, Jessie Evans, Tenniel Evans, David Garfield, Denys Graham, Mervyn Johns, Glyn Owen and Ken Wynne.

Fiorello at the Piccadilly Theatre; book by Jerome Weidman and George Abbott; music by Jerry Bock and lyrics by Sheldon Harnick; directed by Val May; designed by Graham Barlow with costumes by Alan Barrett and Audrey Price; with Bridget Armstrong, Bryan Blackburn, Marian Grimaldi, Peter Reeves, Nicolette Roeg and Derek Smith.

End of Day by Samuel Beckett at the Arts Theatre; directed by Donald McWhinnie; music by Miles Davis; with Jack McGowran.

Semi Detached by David Turner at the Saville Theatre; directed by Tony Richardson; designed by Loudon Sainthill; music by John Addison; with Eileen Atkins, Newton Blick, James Bolam, Kenneth Fortescue, Laurence Olivier, Patsy Rowlands, John Thaw, Mona Washbourne and Joan Young.

All Things Bright and Beautiful by Keith Waterhouse and Willis Hall at the Phoenix Theatre; directed by Val May; designed by Alan Barrett; with John Barrie, Juliet Cooke, Griffith Davies, Dermot Kelly, Eileen Kennally, Peggy Mount, Ken Parry, Brian Peck and Jack Smethurst.

The Sponge Room and *Squat Betty* by Keith Waterhouse and Willis Hall at the Royal Court Theatre; directed by John Dexter; designed by Ken Calder with Jill Bennett, George Cole and Robert Stephens.

3 at Nine an after dinner entertainment at The New Arts Theatre Club; directed by Eleanor Fazan; designed by Disley Jones with Roger Price and Annie Ross.

1963

Baal by Bertolt Brecht at the Phoenix Theatre; translated by Peter Tegel; directed by William Gaskill; designed by Jocelyn Herbert; music by Marc Wilkinson; with Harry Andrews, Terry Bale, Kate Binchy, Harold Goodwin, Gemma Jones, Bernard Kay, Marie Kean, Oliver Macgreevy, Trevor Martin, James Mellor, Mary Miller, Declan Mulholland, Arthur O'Sullivan, Peter O'Toole, Vivian Pickles, Tim Preece, Guinevere Roberts, Annette Robertson, Morgan Sheppard and Henry Woolf.

Luv by Murray Schisgel at the Arts Theatre; directed by Ted Kotcheff; designed by Timothy O'Brien; with George A. Cooper, Dick Emery and Fenella Fielding.

1964

The Brig by Kenneth Brown at the Mermaid Theatre; with the Living Theatre Company directed by Judith Malina; designed by Julian Beck.

The Poker Session by Hugh Leonard at the Globe Theatre; directed by Jim Fitzgerald; designed by William McCrow; with Pauline Delaney, Marius Goring, Joe Lynch, Peggy Marshall, Norman Rodway and Maureen Toal.

The Seagull by Chekhov at the Queens Theatre; directed by Tony Richardson; designed by Jocelyn Herbert; sounds and music selected by John Addison; with Peggy Ashcroft, Ann Beach, Kate Binchy, George Devine, Mark Dignam, Peter Finch, Derek Fuke, Reginald Gillam, Rachel Kempson, Philip Locke, Peter McEnery, Vanessa Redgrave, Paul Rogers and Malcolm Taylor.

St Joan of the Stockyards by Bertolt Brecht at the Queens Theatre; translated by Charlotte and A. L. Lloyd; directed by Tony Richardson; designed by Jocelyn Herbert; music by John Addison; with Brian Anderson, Robert Ayres, Bruce Boa, Patricia Connolly, Mark Dignam, Clive Endersby, Katie Fitzroy, Derek Fuke, Hal Galili, Dudley Hunte, Rachel Kempson, Siobhan McKenna, Michael Medwin, Roy Pattison, Denis Shaw, Nicholas Smith, Lionel Stander, Desmond Stokes, Malcolm Taylor, Dervis Ward and Thick Wilson.

1965

Meals on Wheels by Charles Wood at the Royal Court Theatre; directed by John Osborne; designed by Alan Tagg; costumes by Jocelyn Rickards; with Peter Collingwood, Liz Fraser, Caron Gardiner, Roy Kinnear, Lee Montague and Frank Thornton.

1966

Loot by Joe Orton at the Jeanetta Cochrane and Criterion Theatres; directed by Charles Marowitz; designed by Tony Carruthers; with Sheila Ballantine, Michael Bates, Kenneth Cranham, Gerry Duggan, David Redmond and Simon Ward.

1967

Philadelphia Here I Come! by Brian Friel at the Lyric Theatre; directed by Hilton Edwards; designed by Lloyd Burlingame; with Patrick Bedford, Chris Carrick, Larry Cross, Donal Donnelly, Patrick Duggan, James Dyrenforth, Robert Hewitt, Eamon Kelly, Alex McDonald, Anne Mulvey, Mairin D. O'Sullivan, Derry Power, Dominic Roche and Madge Ryan.

Fill the Stage with Happy Hours by Charles Wood at the Vaudeville Theatre; directed by William Gaskill; designed by Harry Waistnage; with Hylda Baker, Faith Brook, Harry H. Corbett, Helen Cotterill, Sheila Hancock, Stella Moray, John Trigger and Ken Wynne.

Dingo by Charles Wood at the Royal Court Theatre; directed by Geoffrey Reeves; designed by Charles Wood and Bernard Coulshaw; with Eric Allan, Robert Booth, Ian Collier, Gareth Forwood, Michael Francis, Neville Hughes, John Hussey, Mark Jones, Tom Kempinski, Leon Lissek, Barry Stanton and Henry Woolf.

1968

Time Present by John Osborne at the Royal Court and Duke of York's Theatres; directed by Anthony Page; designed by Tony Abbott and Donald Taylor; costumes by Ruth Myers; with Tom Adams, Jill Bennett, Katherine Blake, Geoffrey Frederick, Harry Landis, Kika Markham, Sarah Taunton and Valerie Taylor.

Hotel in Amsterdam by John Osborne at the Royal Court and New Theatres; directed by Anthony Page; designed by Tony Abbott and Donald Taylor; costumes by Ruth Myers; with Joss Ackland, David Burke, Claire Davidson, Isabel Dean, Susan Engel, Judy Parfitt, Paul Scofield, Geoffrey Wright and Derek Woodward.

Spitting Image by Colin Spencer at the Duke of York's Theatre; directed by James Roose-Evans; designed by Alan Tagg; with Lally Bowers, Barbara Bolton, Derek Fowlds, Julian Holloway, Michael Irving, Frank Middlemass, Di Seaney, Susan Williamson and Philip Woods.

Look Back in Anger (Revival) by John Osborne at the Royal Court and Criterion Theatres; directed by Anthony Page; designed by Tony Abbott and Donald

Taylor; costumes by Denise Heywood; with Jane Asher, Victor Henry, Edward Jewesbury, Caroline Mortimer and Martin Shaw.

1969

Your Own Thing by Hal Hester and Danny Apolinar; book by Donald Driver; music and lyrics by Hal Hester and Danny Apolinar at the Comedy Theatre; directed by Donald Driver; with Danny Apolinar, Les Carlson, Gary Files, Gerry Glasier, John Kuhner, Jenny Lee, Alan Martin, Leland Palmer and Marcia Rodd.

What the Butler Saw by Joe Orton at the Queens Theatre; directed by Robert Chetwyn; designed by Hutchinson Scott; with Stanley Baxter, Peter Bayliss, Coral Browne, Julia Foster, Howard Morse and Ralph Richardson.

The Giveaway by Ann Jellicoe at the Garrick Theatre; directed by Richard Eyre; designed by Colin Winslow; with Frank Abbott, John Barrard, Jane Bolton, Gawn Grainger, Michael Harvey, Roy Hudd, Dandy Nichols, Margaret Nolan, Stewart Preston, Rita Tushingham and Philip Woods.

The Living Theatre under the direction of Judith Malina and Julian Beck in a repertory of *Frankenstein*, *Mysteries*, *Paradise Now* and *Antigone* at the Round House.

1971

Lulu by Frank Wedekind adapted by Peter Barnes translated by Charlotte Beck at the Apollo Theatre; directed by Stuart Burge; designed by Patrick Robinson; costumes by Rosemary Vercoe; with Sheila Ballantine, Susan Brett, Michael Byrne, Julia Foster, Marilyn Fridjon, Jo Garrity, John Grillo, Paul Hennen, John Justin, Leonard Kavanagh, Chris Malcolm, Maggy Maxwell, Tom Owen, Edward Petherbridge, Francis Thomas, John Turner and Gordon Whiting.

Rabelais by Jean-Louis Barrault at the Round House; translated by Robert Baldick; directed by Jean-Louis Barrault; designed by Matias; music by Michael Polnareff; with Peter Armitage, Michael Attwell, Andrew Bradford, Bernard Bresslaw, Michael Cadman, Brian Coburn, Robert Gary, Constatin de Goguel, Gerald Harper, Bernard Horsfall, Steve James, Janie Kells, Max Latimer, Aletta Lohmeyer, Belinda Low, Rohan McCullough, Joe Melia, Alan Mitchell, Julie Neubert, Judith Paris, Diana Sawday, Rex Stallings, Ian Trigger, Bill Wallis, Jimmy Winston and Katya Wyeth.

The Lovers of Viorne by Marguerite Dumas at the Royal Court Theatre; translated by Barbara Bray; directed by Jonathan Hales; designed by John Napier; costumes by Nadine Baylis; with Peggy Ashcroft, Maurice Denham and Gordon Jackson.

1789 written and performed by Le Théâtre du Soleil at the Round House; directed by Ariane Mnouchkine; designed by Robert Moscoso; costumes by Françoise Tournafond and Christine Candries.

1976

Dimetos by Athol Fugard at the Comedy Theatre; directed by the author; designed by Douglas Heap; with Yvonne Bryceland, Ben Kingsley, Celia Quicke and Paul Scofield.

1977

Once a Catholic by Mary O'Malley at Wyndham's Theatre; directed by Mike Ockrent; designed by Poppy Mitchell; with John Boswall, Jane Carr, Kim Clifford, Daniel Gerroll, Mike Grady, Pat Heywood, Anna Keaveney, Doreen Keogh, June Page, Rowena Roberts, Lillian Rostkowska, John Rogan, Sally Watkins and Jeanne Watts.

1978

Gloo Joo by Michael Hastings at the Criterion Theatre; directed by Michael Rudman; designed by Poppy Mitchell; costumes by Lindy Hemming; with Antony Brown, Akosua Busia, Edward Halsted, Dave Hill, Oscar James and Heather Tobias.

1980

Juno and the Paycock and *Shadow of a Gunman* by Sean O'Casey. For this great writer's centenary I arranged for the presentation of these two plays by the Royal Shakespeare Company. *Juno* was directed by Trevor Nunn at the Aldwych with Judi Dench as Juno, Norman Rodway as Captain Boyle and John Rogan as Joxer Daly; *The Shadow of a Gunman* was directed by Michael Bogdanov with Michael Pennington as Donal Davoren and Norman Rodway as Seamus Shields and played at the Other Place and The Warehouse.

Appendix II

Films produced by Oscar Lewenstein

1961

A Taste of Honey (assisted the Producer on the preparation but not credited); directed and produced by Tony Richardson; with Dora Bryan, Paul Danquah, Murray Melvin, Robert Stephens and Rita Tushingham.

1962

The Loneliness of the Long Distance Runner (assisted the Producer on the preparation but not credited); directed and produced by Tony Richardson; with Avis Bunnage, Tom Courtenay, Julia Foster, James Fox, Topsy Jane, Peter Madden, Alec McCowen and Michael Redgrave.

1963

Tom Jones (Associate Producer); produced and directed by Tony Richardson; with Peter Bull, Diane Cilento, Edith Evans, Albert Finney, Hugh Griffith, Joan Greenwood, Joyce Redman, David Tomlinson, David Warner and Susannah York.

1964

. *The Girl with Green Eyes* (Producer); directed by Desmond Davis; Executive Producer Tony Richardson with Peter Finch, Julian Glover, Marie Kean, T.P. McKenna, Lynn Redgrave and Rita Tushingham..

1965

One Way Pendulum (Executive Producer); directed by Peter Yates; produced by Michael Deeley; with George Cole, Graham Crowden, Julia Foster, Allison

Leggatt, Jonathan Miller, Peggy Mount, Eric Sykes, Douglas Wilmer and Mona Washbourne.

The Knack (Producer); directed by Richard Lester; with Ray Brooks, Michael Crawford, Donal Donnelly, and Rita Tushingham.

1967

Mademoiselle (Producer); directed by Tony Richardson; with Ettori Manni, Jeanne Moreau, Umberto Orsini and Keith Skinner.

The Sailor from Gibraltar (Producer); directed by Tony Richardson; with Ian Bannen, Eleanor Bron, Hugh Griffith, John Hurt, Zia Mohyeddin, Jeanne Moreau, Umberto Orsini, Vanessa Redgrave and Orson Welles.

The White Bus (Executive Producer); directed and produced by Lindsay Anderson; with Patricia Healey and Arthur Lowe.

Ride of the Valkyries (Executive Producer); directed and produced by Peter Brook; with Julia Foster and Zero Mostel.

1968

The Bride Wore Black (Co-Producer); directed by François Truffaut; with Michel Bouquet, Jean-Claude Brialy, Charles Denner, Michel Lonsdale, Jeanne Moreau and Claude Rich.

1969

The Bed Sitting Room (Co-Producer); directed by Richard Lester; with Peter Cook, Jimmy Edwards, Marty Feldman, Ronald Fraser, Michael Hordern, Arthur Lowe, Spike Milligan, Dudley Moore, Ralph Richardson and Harry Secombe.

1986-87

Rita Sue and Bob Too (Executive Producer); directed by Alan Clarke; produced by Sandy Lieberson; with George Costigan, Siobhan Finneran, Kulvinder Ghir, Michelle Holmes, Patti Nicholls, Willie Ross and Lesley Sharp.

Appendix III

*Plays produced at the Royal Court Theatre
and in the Theatre Upstairs during Oscar Lewenstein's
period as Artistic Director*

*Performances in the main theatre are indicated in **bold italic** type, the Sunday night productions without decor in SMALL CAPITALS and all productions in the Theatre Upstairs in italic.*

1972

The Old Ones by Arnold Wesker; directed by John Dexter; designed by Douglas Heap; with Amelia Bayntun, Terry Burns, Patience Collier, Susan Engel, Leonard Fenton, Stephen Grives, James Hazeldine, Rose Hill, George Pravda, Wanda Rotha, Martin Skinner, George Tovey and Max Wall.

Brussels (YPTS) written and directed by Jonathan Hales; designed by Harriet Geddes; with Peter Armitage, Sylvia Carson, Lorraine Hill, John Ringham and Geoffrey Wearing.

Richard's Cork Leg by Brendan Behan and Alan Simpson; directed by Alan Simpson; designed by Wendy Shea; music by The Dubliners; with Ciaron Bourke, Eileen Colgan, Ronnie Drew, Olu Jacobs, Luke Kelly, Fionnuala Kenny, Barney McKenna, Dearbhla Molloy, Angela Newman, Joan O'Hara and John Sheanan.

ENGLAND'S IRELAND by Tony Bicat, Howard Brenton, Brian Clark, David Edgar, Francis Fuchs, David Hare and Snoo Wilson; directed by David Hare and Snoo Wilson; designed by John Halle; with Peter Adair, Tim Curry, Timothy Davies, Denis Lawson, Stanley McGeagh, Walter Monagle, Fidelma Murphy, Wesley Murphy, Dennis O'Neal, Fianuala O'Shannon and Jeremy Wilkin.

Eye Winker, Tom Tinker by Tom MacIntyre; directed by Robert Kidd; designed by John Bolton; with Philip Donaghy, John Dunn-Hill, Donal McCann, John McKelvey, Oliver Maguire, Gerard Murphy, Frances Tomelty and Harry Webster.

A Pagan Place by Edna O'Brien; directed by Ronald Eyre; designed by Sean Kenny; with Dave Allen, David Burke, Donal Cox, Angela Crow, Sheelagh Cullen, David Daker, Patrick Dawson, Avril Elgar, Kitty Fitzgerald, Brenda Fricker, Diane Holland, Declan Mulholland, Colette O'Neil, Veronica Quilligan, Sally Tavers and Dermot Tuohy.

State of Emergency written and directed by David Edgar; with John Cudmore, Brian Hubbard, Alan Hulse, Janet Kelly and Michele Ryan.

Owners by Caryl Churchill; directed by Nicholas Wright; designed by Di Seymour; with Stephanie Bidmead, Kenneth Cranham, Lucinda Curtis, Eileen Devlin, Richard O'Callaghan, Anne Raitt and David Swift.

A Sense of Detachment by John Osborne; directed by Frank Dunlop; designed by Nadine Baylis; with Jeni Barnett, Denise Coffey, Terence Frisby, Hugh Hastings, Nigel Hawthorne, David Hill, Peter Jolley, Rachel Kempson, Ralph Michael and John Standing.

Pilk's Madhouse by the Ken Campbell Road Show with Bob Dermer, Andy Jones, Philip Schreibam and Jennifer Watts.

1973

A Fart for Europe by Howard Brenton and David Edgar; directed by Chris Parr; designed by Di Seymour; with Alun Armstrong, Jeremy Child, Louis Haslar and Hugh Hastings.

Krapp's Last Tape and *Not I* by Samuel Beckett; directed by Anthony Page; designed by Jocelyn Herbert; with Albert Finney, Brian Miller and Billie Whitelaw.

Jose Pigs / Cattle Show (The People Show 48) with Laura Gilbert, Mike Figgis, Mark Long, Jose Nava and Derek Wilson.

The George Jackson Black and White Minstrel Show with the Pip Simmons Theatre Group.

Wimbo the Wonder Dog and *The Weekend After Next* (Hull Truck) written and directed by Mike Bradwell; with Joolia Cappleman, Steve Halliman, Cass Patton and Alan Williams.

Wholesome Glory written and directed by Mike Leigh; with Geoffrey Hutchings, Roger Sloman and Alison Steadman.

Mothers and Others written and directed by Anne Raitt; with Amjula Harman, Rosamund Nelson and Cass Patton.

The Freedom of the City by Brian Friel; directed by Albert Finney; designed by Douglas Heap and Harriet Geddes (costumes); with Peter Adair, David Atkinson, Raymond Campbell, Peter Frye, Matthew Guinness, Catherine Harding, Louis Haslar, Nicholas Llewellyn, Alex McCrindle, Carmel McSharry, Anthony Nash, Michael O'Hagan, Stephen Rea and George Shane.

THE FOURTH WORLD by David Caute; directed by Buzz Goodbody; with Yvonne Antrobus, Lois Baxter, Ben Bazell, John Biggerstaff, Julian Curry, Norman Ettlinger, Richard Kane, Maureen Lipman and John Shrapnel.

The Unseen Hand by Sam Shepard; directed by Jim Sharman; designed by Brian Thomson; with Warren Clarke, Clive Endersby, Christopher Malcolm, Richard O'Brien and Tony Sibbald.

Beowulf (Freehold) dramatized by Liane Aukin; directed by Nancy Meckler; with Marty Cruickshank, Michael Harley, Dorinda Hulton, Neil Johnston, Wolf Kahler, Christopher Ravenscroft, Dinah Stabb, Paddy Swanson and Rowan Wylie.

Savages by Christopher Hampton; directed by Robert Kidd; designed by Jocelyn Herbert and Andrew Sanders; with Rona Anderson, George Baizley, A.J. Brown, Terence Burns, Tom Conti, Lynda Dagley, Glyn Grain, Leonard Kavanagh, Thelma Kidger, Donna Louise, Eddi Nedari, Geoffrey Palmer, Michael Pennington, Paul Scofield, J.C. Shepherd, Frank Siguineau and Gordon Sterne.

Captain Oates' Left Sock by John Antrobus; directed by Nicholas Wright; designed by Harriet Geddes; with Margaret Brady, Oliver Cotton, Gabrielle Daye, James Donnelly, Geoffrey Edwards, Matthew Guinness, Charles Kinross, Carol Macready, Judith Paris, Stephen Rea, Jill Richards, Nicholas Selby, Martin Skinner, Jenny Tomalin and Janet Webb.

Coming Attractions (late night) written and performed by Lizette Kocur, Neil Johnston and O Lan Shepard; music by Marty Cruickshank.

The Orange Balloon (late night) by Andy Phillips; directed by Robert Fox; with Warren Clarke and Lois Daine.

Give the Gaffers Time to Love You by Barry Reckord; directed by Pam Brighton; designed by John Halle; with Jonathan Adams, Paul Angelis, Tim Curry, Alan Ford, David Leland, Petra Markham and Peter Straker.

The Sea by Edward Bond; directed by William Gaskill; designed by Deirdre Clancy; with Coral Browne, Adrienne Byrne, Simon Cord, Ian Holm, Anthony Langdon, Margaret Lawley, Mark MacManus, Gillian Martell, Barbara Ogilvie, Diana Quick, Simon Rouse, Alan Webb, Susan Williamson and Jeremy Wilson.

MILLENNIUM by Jeremy Seabrook and Michael O'Neill; directed by Roger Croucher; designed by Harriet Geddes; with Betty Alberge, James Aubrey, June

Brown, Anthony Douse, Diane Fletcher, Philip Jackson, Norman Jones, Pamela Moiseiwitsch, Jill Richards, David Rintoul, Gwyneth Strong and Leon Vitali.

The Rocky Horror Show written and composed by Richard O'Brien; directed by Jim Sharman; designed by Brian Thomson and Sue Blane (costumes); with Jonathan Adams, Rayner Bourton, Julie Covington, Tim Curry, Christopher Malcolm, Little Nell, Richard O'Brien, Paddy O'Hagan and Patricia Quinn.

Magnificence by Howard Brenton; directed by Max Stafford-Clark; designed by William Dudley; with James Aubrey, Geoffrey Chater, Kenneth Cranham, Robert Edison, Leonard Fenton, Carole Hayman, Michael Kitchen,Peter Postlethwaite, Nikolaj Ryjtkov and Dinah Stabb.

The Removalists by David Williamson; directed by Jim Sharman; designed by Brian Thomson; with Brian Croucher, Ed Devereaux, Darlene Johnson, Mark MacManus, Carole Mowlam and Struan Rodger.

Sweet Talk by Michael Abbensetts; directed by Stephen Frears; designed by William Dudley; with Alister Bain, Lee Davies, Mona Hammond, Joan-Ann Maynard, Don Warrington and Sally Watts.

Cromwell by David Storey; directed by Anthony Page; designed by Jocelyn Herbert; with Alun Armstrong, Conrad Asquith, John Barrett, Colin Bennett, Kenneth Colley, Forbes Collins, Jariath Conroy, Brian Cox, Colin Douglass, Anne Dyson, Albert Finney, Alan Ford, Mark MacManus, Michael Melia, Peter Postlethwaite, Diana Rayworth, Martin Read and Frances Tomelty.

Bright Scene Fading by Tom Gallacher; directed by Nicholas Wright; designed by John Macfarlane; with Road Beacham, Adrienne Hill, Roderic Leigh, Andrew McCulloch, Paul Seed and Robert Trotter.

Sizwe Banzi is Dead by Athol Fugard, John Kani and Winston Ntshona; directed by Athol Fugard; designed by Douglas Heap; with John Kani and Winston Ntshona.

The Farm by David Storey; directed by Lindsay Anderson; designed by Hayden Griffin; music by Alan Price; with Lewis Collins, Meg Davies, Prunella Gee, Frank Grimes, Patricia Healey, Bernard Lee and Doreen Mantle.

The Porter's Play written and directed by Anton Gill; designed by Keith Cheetham; with Rod Beacham, Brian Croucher, Derek Deadman, Arthur English, John Fahey, Roderic Leigh, Andrew McCulloch, Don McKillop, Stanley Meadows, Anthony Nash and George Shane.

Elizabeth I by Paul Foster; directed by Walter Donohue; designed by Robin Don; with Charlotte Cornwell, Michael Feast, Carole Hayman, Paul Moriarty, Peter Postlethwaite, David Sands and Stuart Wilson.

The Merry Go Round by D.H. Lawrence; directed by Peter Gill; designed by William Dudley and Sue Plummer (costumes); with Anthony Baird, David Daker, Gabrielle Daye, Patricia Doyle, Anne Dyson, George Howe, Margaret Lawley, Alex McCrindle, Oliver Maguire, George Malpas, Michael Melia, Derrick O'Connor, Susan Traby and Marjorie Yates.

The Pleasure Principle by Snoo Wilson; directed by David Hare; designed by Harriet Geddes; with Julie Covington, George Fenton, Ann Firbank, Neil Fitzwilliam, Brenda Fricker, Stewart Harwood, Dinsdale Landen and Bob Sherman.

Dick Whittington written and directed by Mike Leigh; with Lavinia Bertram, Paul Copley, Julia Coppleman, Peter Godfrey, Philip Jackson, Roger Sloman and Tim Stern.

1974

The Island by Athol Fugard, John Kani and Winston Ntshona; directed by Athol Fugard; designed by Douglas Heap; with John Kani and Winston Ntshona.

Sizwe Banzi is Dead by Athol Fugard, John Kani, Winston Ntshona; directed by Athol Fugard; designed by Douglas Heap; with John Kani and Winston Ntshona.

Statements after an Arrest under the Immorality Act written and directed by Athol Fugard; designed by Douglas Heap; with Yvonne Bryceland, Wilson Dunster and Ben Kingsley.

Two Jelliplays (YPTS) comprising: *Clever Elsie, Smiling John, Silent Peter* and *A Good Thing or a Bad Thing* written and directed by Ann Jellicoe; designed by David Short; with Colin Bennett, Judy Buxton, Janette Legge, Stephen Mackenna and Tony Robinson.

Geography of a Horse Dreamer written and directed by Sam Shepard; designed by Bettina Reeves; with Bill Bailey, Kenneth Cranham, Alfred Hoffman, Bob Hoskins, Neil Johnston, Stephen Rea, Raymond Skipp and George Silver.

Runaway by Peter Ransley; directed by Alfred Lynch; designed by Hayden Griffin; with Bill Dean, Kim Moreton, Cherry Morris, Bill Owen, Peter Robinson, Simon Rouse and Susan Tracy.

Six of the Best comprising: *Liberation City* by Michael Belbin; directed by Joan Mills; designed by Bettina Reeves; with John Dicks, Michael Harbour, Guy Standeven and Maggie Wells; *Errand* by Jim Irvin; directed by John Barlow; designed by Bettina Reeves; with Patrick Murray and Guy Standeven; *Big Business* by Mark Edwards; directed by Joan Mills; designed by Bettina Reeves;

with Angela Crow and Michael Harbour; *Maggie's Fortune* by Sheila Wright; directed by Ann Jellicoe; designed by Bettina Reeves; with Angela Crow, John Dicks, Michael Harbour and Maggie Wells; *Fireman's Ball* by Stephen Frost; directed by Ann Jellicoe; designed by Bettina Reeves; with John Dicks and Michael Harbour; *Event* by James Clarke; directed by John Barlow; designed by Bettina Reeves; with Michael Harbour, Patrick Murray and Guy Standeven; and *Zoological Palace* by Conrad Mullineaux; directed by Joan Mills; designed by Bettina Reeves; with John Dicks, Patrick Murray, Guy Standeven and Maggie Wells.

Life Class by David Storey; directed by Lindsay Anderson; designed by Jocelyn Herbert; with Alan Bates, Stephen Bent, Brenda Cavendish, Brian Glover, Frank Grimes, Gerald James, Paul Kelly, David Lincoln, Gabrielle Lloyd, Rosemary Martin, Bob Peck, Stuart Rayner and Sally Watts.

Bird Child by David Lan; directed by Nicholas Wright; designed by David Short; with James Aubrey, Geoffrey Bateman, Jumoke Debayo, Nigel Hawthorne, Douglas Heard, Marjie Lawrence, Janette Legge and Jacqueline Stanbury.

Johnny by Robert Thornton; directed by John Tydeman; with John Biggerstaff, Adrienne Byrne, Ronald Forfar, Gabrielle Hamilton, Terence Hillyer, Robert Keegan, Paul Rosebury and David Sterne.

Shivvers (Joint Stock) by Stanley Eveling; directed by Max Stafford-Clark; designed by Poppy Mitchell; with Deirdre Costello, Tony Haygarth and Bill Stewart.

Tooth of Crime by Sam Shepard; directed by Jim Sharman; designed by Brian Thomson and Sue Blane (costumes); music by Richard Hartley; with Jonathan Adams, Kenneth Cranham, Paul Freeman, Diane Langton, Christopher Malcolm, Richard O'Brien and Mike Pratt.

A Worthy Guest by Paul Bailey; directed by Ann Jellicoe; designed by David Short; with Tom Durham, Martin Fisk, Jimmy Gardner, Gordon Gostelow, Pat Keen, Eve Pearce, William Russell, Robin Summers, Angela Thorne and Jean Warren.

THE WATERGATE TAPES edited by Sam Wanamaker; with Larry Alder, Frank Dux, Weston Gavin, Bill Hootkins, Bob Sherman and Sam Wanamaker.

The Sea Anchor by E.H. Whitehead; directed by Jonathan Hales; designed by Sue Plummer; with Peter Armitage, David Daker, Alison Steadman and Marjorie Yates.

Play Mas by Mustapha Matura; directed by Donald Howarth; designed by Douglas Heap and Peter Minshall (costumes); with Norman Beaton, Ed Bishop,

Tommy Eytle, Mona Hammond, Stefan Kalipha, Robert LaBossier, Lucita Lijertwood, Mercia Mansfield, Charles Pemberton, Frank Singuineau, Trevor Thomas and Rudolf Walker.

Bingo by Edward Bond; directed by Jane Howell and John Dove; designed by Hayden Griffin; music by Martin Duncan; with John Barrett, Hilda Barry, Oliver Cotton, Yvonne Edgell, Derek Fuke, John Gielgud, Ewan Hooper, Paul Jesson, Arthur Lowe, Gillian Martell, and Joanna Tope.

X (Joint Stock) by Barry Reckord; directed by Max Stafford-Clark; designed by Douglas Heap; with Margaret Burnett, Libba Davies, Terence Frisby and Roderic Leigh.

Taking Stock by Robert Holman; directed by Chris Parr; with Susan Blake, Brian Deacon, Gerald James, Ian Marter and John Normington.

Action by Sam Shepard; directed by Nancy Meckler; designed by David Short; with Stephen Moore, Stephen Rea, Jill Richards and Jeanne Stoller.

The Great Caper by Ken Campbell; directed by Nicholas Wright; designed by Bob Ringwood; with Katie Allan, Judith Blake, Ken Campbell, Simon Coady, Eddie Davies, Lisa Harrow, Aharon Ipale, Mark Jones, Richard O'Callaghan and Warren Mitchell.

In Celebration by David Storey; directed by Lindsay Anderson; designed by Jocelyn Herbert; with Alan Bates, James Bolam, Constance Chapman, Brian Cox, Gabrielle Daye and Bill Owen.

Lord Nelson Lives in Liverpool 8 by Philip Martin; directed by Joan Mills; designed by John Macfarlane; with Jane Anthony, James Broadbent, Chris Cregan, Brinsley Ford, Richard Forde, Stephen Pacey, Gordon Reid and Guy Standeven.

Fourth Day Like Four Long Months of Absence (Joint Stock) by Colin Bennett; directed by Max Stafford-Clark; designed by Diana Greenwood; with Mike Griggs, Carole Hayman, William Hoyland, Caroline Hutchison, Malcolm Ingram, Tony Rohr and Toby Salaman.

The City written and directed by Yutaka Higashi; designed by Yutaka Higashi; with Mitsko Fukami and Baby, Tsutomu Hori, Toshiko Inoue, Fumiko Kunyia, Hidehiko Okazako. Shoichi Saito, Megumi Shimanuki. Ryusako Shinsui, Sansho Shinsui and Paul Waki.

Remember the Truth Dentist by Heathcote Williams; directed by Ken Campbell; designed by William Dudley; music by Bob Flag; with Paola Dionisotti, Philip Donaghy, David Hill, Roy Martin, John Prior and Demelza Val Baker.

1975

Objections to Sex and Violence by Caryl Churchill; directed by John Tydeman; designed by David Short; with Anna Calder-Marshall, Sylvia Coleridge, Michael Harrigan, Rose Hill, Rosemary McHale, Stephen Moore and Ivor Roberts.

Innocent Bystanders (Sunday) by Gordon Graham; directed by Denise Coffey; with Sam Kelly, Nicholas Loukes, Paul Nicholas, Deborah Norton and Max Phipps.

SAND by Michael Almaz; directed by Peter Stevenson; designed by Rita Fuzzey comprising: MOMENTS ON JAFFA BEACH with Jack Chissick, Phil Emanuel, Jon Flanagan, Philip Jackson and Patricia Leventon; and THE PORT SAID PERFORMANCE with David Arthur, Jack Chissick, Richard Crane, Tim Davis, Michael Deacon, Dominic Jepcott,Lesley Joseph, Harry Landis and Timothy Peters.

Moments on Jaffa Beach with Jack Chissick, Phil Emanuel, Jon Flanagan, Philip Jackson and Patricia Leventon.

The Port Said Performance with David Arthur, Jack Chissick, Richard Crane, Tim Davis, Michael Deacon, Dominic Jepcott, Lesley Joseph, Harry Landis and Timothy Peters.

Mrs Grabowski's Academy by John Antrobus; directed by Jonathan Hales; designed by Sue Plummer; with Richard Beckinsale, Simon Callow, Ian Charlson, Patience Collier, Cheryl Hall, Denis Lawson, Beth Morris and Philip Stone.

NUMBER ONE ROOSTER by David Throsby; directed by William Alexander; with Barbara Angell, Michael Balfour, Ed Bishop, Joan Holken, Bob Hornery, Stephen Moore, Raymond O'Reilly, John Pine, Ken Shorter and Michael Staniforth.

Don's Party by David Williamson; directed by Michael Blakemore; designed by Alan Pickford; with Ray Barrett, Barbara Ewing, John Gregg, Tony Haygarth, Briony Hodge, Veronica Lang, Ginette Macdonald, Carole Macready, Stephen O'Rourke, Max Phipps and Barry Veryton.

Loud Reports written and performed by John Burrows, John Harding and Peter Skellern; directed by Mark Wing-Davey; music by Peter Skellern.

The Doomduckers Ball (Joint Stock) written and performed by Carole Hayman, Neil Johnston, Mary Maddox, Dinah Stabb and Jeff Teare; music by Free Money.

Entertaining Mr Sloane by Joe Orton; directed by Roger Croucher; designed by John Gunter; with Ronald Fraser, Malcolm McDowell, James Ottaway and Beryl Reid.

Paradise by David Lan; directed by Tessa Marwick and Nicholas Wright; designed by William Dudley; with Scott Antony, Jonathan Bergman, Jean Boht, Derek Carpenter, Robert Gillespie, Roger Lloyd Pack, Angela Phillips and Roger Rees.

Echoes from a Concrete Canyon by Wilson John Haire; directed by Roger Croucher; designed by Anne-Marie Schone; with Nicholas Ball, James Grant, Judy Parfitt, Leslie Sarony and Gwyneth Strong.

Loot by Joe Orton; directed by Albert Finney; designed by Douglas Heap and Harriet Geddes (costumes); with James Aubrey, Jill Bennett, Michael O'Hagan, Arthur O'Sullivan, Philip Stone and David Troughton.

Homage to Bean Soup (lunchtime and late night) by David Lan; directed by Tessa Marwick; with Jean Boht and Emma Williams.

Moving Clocks Go Slow (Sunday) by Caryl Churchill; directed by John Ford; costumes by Chris Bowler; with Nicholas Ball, Diana Barrett, Ronald Fraser, Aviva Goldkorn, Rose Hill, David Howey, Roger Rees, Paul Roylance, Jennie Stoller and Nigel Wilson.

Heroes by Stephen Poliakoff; directed by Tim Fywell; designed by John Macfarlane; with Lynsey Baxter, Peter Bennett, Phil Daniels, David Dixon, Christine Noonan and Jonathan Pryce.

Black Slaves, White Chains (lunchtime and late night) by Mustapha Matura; directed by Rufus Collins; with Eddy Grant, Mark Heath, Olu Jacobs, Saul Reichlin and Jean Warren.

A 'Nevolent Society (Sunday) by Mary O'Malley; directed by Henry Woolf; with Leonard Fenton, Patricia Franklin,Edward Kelsey, Mary O'Malley and Henry Woolf.

What the Butler Saw by Joe Orton; directed by Lindsay Anderson; designed by Jocelyn Herbert; with Jane Carr, Valentine Dyall, Brian Glover, Kevin Lloyd, Betty Marsden and Michael Melvin.

Sex and Kinship in a Savage Society by Jeremy Seabrook and Michael O'Neill; directed by William Alexander; designed by David Short; with Tom Bell, Lynn Farleigh, Doreen Mantle and Robert Putt.

Index

Abbensetts, Michael 157, 168
Abrahams, Doris 99
AC/DC 141
Acquart, André 102
Adams, Jonathan 156
Addison, John 105, 114
Adelphi Theatre 29
Adrian, Max 6
Advance 56,57
Airs On a Shoestring 6, 7, 8, 9
Alberts, The 141
Albery, Donald 23, 90, 93, 98, 110, 147
Albery Theatre 88
Aldwych Theatre 23, 179
Alexander, William 168
Allan, Elkan 80
Allan, Ted 107
Allen, Dave 149, 175
All God's Chillun Got Wings 68
All Things Bright and Beautiful 112
Almost a Gentleman 106
Alpha Beta 161
Altona 101, 107
Anderson, Lindsay 36, 38, 39, 40, 91, 92, 93, 94, 99, 100, 120, 146, 148, 156, 158, 160, 161, 162, 167, 168, 169, 170-171, 172-173, 174, 175
Andrews, David 92
Andrews, Harry 113
Anna Lucasta 73, 78
Antigone 131, 132
Antrobus, John 128
Apollo de Bellac, The 35
Apollo Theatre 142
Appleby, Brigitta 2
Arbor, The 179
Arden, Jane 87

Arden, John 38, 39, 93
Ardrey, Robert 68
Arms and The Man 80
Army Bureau of Current Affairs 54
Arnold, Helen 20
Arnold, Tom 20
Art of Living, The 98
Arts Council 30, 39, 70, 94, 138-140, 173
Arts Theatre 5, 23, 107, 118
Arturo Ui 115-116
Ashcroft, Dame Peggy 13, 14, 29, 117, 142, 170
Askey, Arthur 48
Astor, Michael 138, 139
Atkins, Eileen 110
Awake and Sing 77, 78, 79

Baal 113
Babes in the Wood 19-20, 53
Baldick, Robert 142
Ballantine, Sheila 120
Barke, James 71
Barker, Felix 179
Barker, Howard 151
Barnes, Peter 142
Baron, Alexander (Alec Bernstein) 56, 66, 68, 69, 80, 81
Baronova, Irina 35
Barrault, Jean-Louis 95, 142
Bass, Alfie 7, 17, 53, 77, 78, 83
Bates, Alan 15, 162
Bates, Michael 120, 175
Baxter, Stanley 128
Baylis, Peter 83
Beatles, The 127
Beaton, Norman 165
Beaumont, Binkie (Hugh) 10, 126-127, 129
Beck, Julian 116, 131, 133, 135, 136

Beckett, Samuel 34, 39, 40, 109, 141, 147, 152-153
Bedales School 44-45
Bedford, Patrick 121
Bed Sitting Room, The 119, 128
Behan, Brendan 90, 91, 148-149
Bennett, Jill 106, 112, 124, 175
Bentley, Eric 29
Bernstein, Lord 87, 138
Berry, John 101, 107
Bespoke Overcoat, The 7, 17, 99
Beuselinck, Oscar 31, 98, 106, 114
Bevan, Aneurin, M.P. 57
Beyond the Fringe 98
Biggar, Helen 77
Billington, Michael 148, 151-152, 159
Billy Liar 99, 100, 103, 105
Bingo 154
Birmingham Repertory Theatre 87
Birthday Party, The 25, 88
Bishop's Bonfire, The 178
Blacks, The 102
Blacksell, Edward (J.E.) 10, 11-12, 170
Blakemore, Michael 160
Blane, Sue 156, 164
Blick, Newton 110
Blin, Roger 34, 102
Blitzstein, Marc 20
Blond, Mrs. Elaine 170, 173
Blond, Neville 11-13, 14, 27-28, 39, 40, 140, 141, 145, 170
Bloom, Claire 101
Boesman and Lena 157
Bogdanov, Michael 179
Bolan, James 110

Bond, Edward 145, 146, 147, 154, 155
Bond, Ralph 80
Bonnes, Les 5
Bouchier, Arthur 43
Bourton, Rayner 156
Boychick, The 8
Boy Friend, The 8, 20
Boyle, Sir Edward, M.P. 139
Boy Meets Girl 68, 78
Braden, Bernard 107
Brecht, Bertolt 12, 15, 20-21, 23, 24-25, 26, 29, 40, 89, 113, 115, 117, 131
Brenton, Howard 141, 146, 149, 151, 155, 158, 168
Bresslaw, Bernard 142
Brickman, Miriam 17, 24
Bride of Denmark Hill, The 4
Bride Wore Black, The 135
Brien, Alan 106
Brig, The 116, 131
Brighton Combination, The 139, 141
Brisley, Stuart 141
Bristol Old Vic 12, 15, 92, 94
Britten, Benjamin 9, 20,
Brook, Peter, 80, 94, 135
Brown, Georgia 23, 94
Brown, June 5
Brown, Kenneth 116
Browne, Coral 154
Browne, E. Martin 13, 26
Bruce, Ian 139
Bryceland, Yvonne 157, 163, 164, 177
Bryden, Ronald 121, 132-134
Buchwald, Art 98
Bull, Peter 105, 114
Burge, Stuart 142
Burke, Patricia 80

Café Crown 16, 79
Café La Mama 165
Cairncross, James 105
Cambridge Theatre 100
Campbell, Ken 141, 155
Caplan, Isadore 11, 170
Cards of Identity 15, 27, 28
Carr, Jane 175
Cascando 141
Casey Jones 68
Casson, Lewis 66
Catty, Jon 169

Caute, David 54
Celebration 111
Chairs, The 27, 31, 35, 36, 97
Challenge 52
Chambers, Colin 67
Chappell, Billy 17, 86
Chater, Geoffrey 159
Charge of the Light Brigade, The 119, 123
Cheeseman, Peter 167
Chekhov, Anton 117
Chelsea Palace 118, 173
Chetwyn, Robert 128
Christie In Love 141, 158
Churchill, Caryl 151, 168
Cilento, Diane 101, 109
City, The 165
Clancy, Deirdre 154
Clarke, Alan 179, 180
Cloud Nine 151
Clynes, J.R., M.P. 43
Cockade 118
Cock-a-Doodle Dandy 76, 178
Cocteau, Jean 9
Codron, Michael 107, 120, 170
Coe, Peter 37
Cole, George 112
Collins, Norman 170
Come and Go 141
Comedy of Errors, The 4
Comedy Theatre 23, 83, 109, 137, 153, 178
Come Together 140-141
Connection, The 116
Conti, Tom 153
Cookson, Harry 94
Cooper, George A. 23, 99-100, 114
Copley, Peter 80
Corbett, Harry H. 37, 119
Correspondence Course, The 37
Costigan, George 179
Country Wife, The 15, 29, 30
Cox, Brian 160
Courtenay, Tom 100, 101, 103
Coventry Repertory Theatre 110
Covington, Julie 156
Cox, Constance 5
Cox, Sir Reginald Kennedy 11, 12
Craigie, Jill 80

Cranham, Kenneth 159
Crawford, Neil 86
Craxton, John 139
Creighton, Anthony 39
Cripps, Sir Stafford, M.P. 57
Criterion Theatre 90, 121
Croft, Michael 167
Cromwell 160-161
Croucher, Roger 168, 174, 175
Crucible, The 12, 15, 28
Crutchley, Rosalie 15
Cummings, Constance 38
Curran, Paul 153
Curry, Tim 156

Daily Express 107, 112, 116
Daily Herald 46-47
Daily Mail 53, 107, 109, 111, 116
Daily Worker 52, 53, 66
Dance Dress 7
Dancing at Lughnasa 123, 150
Dankworth, John 175
Dean, Basil 81
Death of Satan, The 12, 15
Delaney, Shelagh 89, 90
Delfont, Bernard 78, 82, 114, 117
Dench, Judi 178-179
Dent, Alan 74
Deserters, The 84
Dennis, Nigel 15, 28, 35
Devine, George 13-15, 20, 26-29, 31, 34, 35, 38, 39, 80, 91, 96, 105, 114, 117, 118, 124, 145, 153, 157, 173, 179
Dexter, John 38, 40, 109, 112, 148
Diamond, Gillian 168
Dignam, Mark 17
Dimetos 177-178
Dingo 119
Dockley, Peter 141
Donelly, Donal 121
Don Juan 10, 12, 15
Don's Party 159-160, 174
Doone, Rupert 4
Dove, John 154
Dublin Theatre Festival 121
Dudley, William 159
Duguid, Peter 105
Duke of York's Theatre 18, 38, 124, 125, 175
Dunbar, Andrea 179, 180

Duncan, Ronald 9-13, 15, 20, 24, 26, 35, 170
Duncannon, Lord 11
Dundy, Elaine 109
Dunhurst School, Bedales 44, 45
Dunlop, Frank 167
Dunster, Wilson 164
Duras, Marguerite 142
Dyall, Valentine 176

Eagle Has Two Heads, The 9
Ebb Tide 5
Eddison, Robert 83, 159
Edgar, David 149, 155
Edinburgh Festival 177
Edwards, Hilton 17, 121, 122
Elliott, Michael 138, 167
Elstein, Noah 7
Embassy Theatre 2, 6, 7, 16, 17, 24, 38, 75, 77, 78, 79, 82-83
Emery, Dick 114
Encore 81
Endgame 34,102
End of Day 109
England's Ireland 149
English Opera Group 10
English Stage Company 11, 13, 17, 20, 23, 24, 26, 27, 29, 31-32, 33, 35, 37, 40, 93, 94, 101, 102, 103, 105, 117, 119, 123, 140, 141-142, 163, 172, 173, 180
Entertainer, The 33, 34, 95, 101, 103
Entertaining Mr. Sloane 1/4, 178
Epitaph for George Dillon 39
Erpingham Camp, The 121
Esdaile, Alfred 2, 3, 4, 6, 11, 13, 14
Evans, Graham 38
Evans, Jessie 83
Evening News 179
Evening Standard 9, 98, 99, 100, 111, 112, 135
Evening Standard Drama Awards 93, 121, 124, 165, 178
Expresso Bongo 86, 98, 99
Eye Winker, Tom Tinker 149
Eyre, Richard 137, 140, 167, 171

Fading Mansions 79
Farm, The 160, 161
Fart For Europe, A 155
Fase, Berkeley 53
Faulkner, William 38, 40
Feldman, Marty 152
Fenn, Bob 87
Fennemore, Hilda 86
Ffrangçon-Davies, Gwen 15
Fielding, Fenella 114
Field, Shirley Ann 94
Fill the Stage with Happy Hours 119
Financial Times 109, 150
Finch, Peter 117
Fin de Partie (see Endgame) 34
Findlater, Richard 138, 171, 173
Fings Ain't Wot They Used To Be 93
Finneran, Siobhan 179
Finney, Albert 87, 88, 89, 91-92, 94, 99, 100, 103, 105, 114-115, 147, 150, 152, 153, 160, 168, 172, 173, 174
Flamm, Donald 99
Flowers o'Edinburgh, The 77
Forbes Robertson, Jean 5
Ford, Ruth 38
Fortescue, Kenneth 110
Foster, Julia 142
Fox, John 139
Fox, Robert 168
Fox, Robin 139, 140, 141-142
Frankau, Ronald 48
Frankenstein 131, 132
Fraser, Moyra 6
Fraser, Ronald 92, 175
Frears, Stephen 157
Frechtman, Bernard 5
Freedom of the City 150
French, Philip 180
Fricker, Brenda 149
Friel, Brian 121-123, 150
From the City, From the Plough 81
Fugard, Athol 157-158, 163-164, 177-178
Furze, Elizabeth 31-32
Future is in Eggs, The 101

Gabel, Martin 18, 19
Gabriel (cartoonist) 66
Galileo 89

Garley, John 5
Garratt, Evelyn 7, 72
Garrick Theatre 74, 137
Gaskill, William (Bill) 39, 40, 113, 119, 135, 140, 142, 145, 146, 147, 148, 149, 151, 154, 155, 158
Genet, Jean 5, 6, 102
Gentle People, The 78
Ghosts 79, 80
Ghost Writers, The 107
Gibbens, Howard 167
Gielgud, John 29, 81, 140, 154
Gilder, Rosemary 81
Gill, Anton 168
Gill, Peter 121, 146, 147, 163
Giraudoux, Jean 35
Girl with Green Eyes, The 114, 120, 149
Giveaway, The 137
Glasgow Unity Theatre 1, 2, 5, 7, 16, 17, 37, 68, 70-77, 79, 80
Gloo Joo 178
Glover, Brian 176
Glover, Julian 105
Goddard, Renée 21, 23, 87
Goetschius, George 147
Golden Boy 69
Golden Door, The 77, 78
Golding, Louis 38
Gollan, John 56
Gollancz, Victor 54
Goodman, Lord 140
Good Woman of Setzuan, The 15, 25, 27, 29, 40, 89, 142
Gorbals, Story, The 1, 70, 71, 73, 74, 75, 76, 77, 78
Gorki, Maxim 70
Granville-Barker, Harley 1
Gray, Charles 86
Great Caper, The 155
Griffin, Hayden 161
Grimes, Frank 161
Grimond, Griselda 139
Grindea, Miron 70, 72
Group Theatre 4
Guardian, The 122, 151-152, 159
Guinness, Alec 81
Gunter, John 174
Guthrie, Tyrone 80
Gwynn, Michael 15

Hackman, Helen 67
Hackney Empire 19
Haigh, Kenneth 15, 31, 101
Hall, Peter 23, 167-168, 170, 178, 179
Hall, Willis 91, 92, 93, 99, 100, 111, 112
Halliwell, Kenneth 125, 128, 129
Hampshire, Susan 86
Hampstead Theatre Club 101, 125
Hampton, Christopher 147, 153-154
Hancock, Sheila 91, 119
Happy As Larry 73
Hare, David 146, 149, 151
Harewood, George (Lord Harewood) 10-11, 34, 170
Harper, Gerald 142
Harris, Jenny 139
Harris, Richard 120
Harris, Sophie 27, 29
Harrison, John 167
Hartley, Richard 164
Harvey, Laurence 29, 87
Hastings, Michael 38, 117, 178
Hawthorne, Nigel 83
Hawtrey, Anthony 7, 75, 82
Hayes, Helen 81
Hayman, Carole 159
Haynes, Jim 135
Hazell, Hy 86
Healey, Patricia 161
Heap, Douglas 164, 174
Hedda Gabler 13
Hell and High Water 71
Hello Dolly! 83
Helpmann, Robert 37
Heneker, David 86, 91, 98
Henry, Victor 124
Herbert, Jocelyn 27, 34, 36, 40, 104, 113, 114, 152, 153, 156, 160, 162, 168, 169, 170, 174
Herbert, Victor 135
Higashi, Yutaka 165-167
Hill, John 71, 72
Hobson, Harold 25, 90-91, 100, 108, 109, 122, 149-150, 178
Hodge, Herbert 53
Holm, Ian 154
Holmes, Michelle 179
Hooper, Ewan 167

Hope, Vida 8, 19, 53, 98
Hoskins, Bob 140
Hoskins, George 136, 144
Hostage, The 90-91, 94
Hotel in Amsterdam, A 32, 123
Howarth, Donald 147, 157, 165, 168, 179
How Can We Save Father? 35
Howell, Jane 154
How I Won the War 119
How to Succeed in Business Without Really Trying 116
Hudd, Roy 137
Hughes, Catherine 164
Hulbert, Claude 5
Hylton, Jack 1, 6, 20, 29, 31, 73-74, 77, 83

Ibsen, Henrik 79
Inadmissible Evidence 123
Inside the Royal Court Theatre 1956-1981 181
International Times 135
Ionesco, Eugene 19, 31, 35, 40, 95, 97, 101
Island, The 163
Israel in the Ktchen 7
Israel, Steven Ben 136

Jackson, Freda 77, 83
Jackson, Gordon 17
Jacques 101
James, Peter 167
Jazz Train, The 30
Jeanetta Cochrane Theatre 120
Jellicoe, Ann 39, 137, 147, 168, 170
Jenkins, Anne 147, 169
Jesus Christ Super Star 156
Jewish Institute Players 77
John Bull Puncture Repair Outfit 139
Joint Stock Theatre 151
Joll, James 139
Judd, Edward 92
Juno and the Paycock 67, 74, 76, 178, 180

Kalipha, Stefan 165
Kani, John 157, 163
Kanter, Ben 78
Karlin, Miriam 17, 107
Kay, Charles 105
Kelly, Eamonn 121

Kempson, Rachel 13, 15, 152
Kenny, Sean 94, 101, 149
Kidd, Robert 153, 160, 171, 172
Kid for Two Farthings, A 99
King Lear 29
King of the Schnorrers, The 5, 78, 79
Kingsley, Ben 164, 177
Kingsway Theatre 3, 14
Kinnear, Roy 91
Kinsay, Tony 94
Kipling, Rudyard 46
Kiss for Adèle, A 6
Kitchen, Michael 159
Klausner, Arnold 2
Knack, The 119, 137, 138, 146
Kossoff, David 7, 17
Kotcheff, Ted 109, 114
Kraft, Hy 16, 17, 79
Krapp's Last Tape 152
Kulukundis, Eddie 160, 174, 177, 178

Labour Party League of Youth 56
Lahr, John 126, 129, 130
Laine, Cleo 175
Laird O'Torwatletie, The 70, 76, 77
Lambert, Jack 95, 135, 138, 139
Lambs of God, The 77
Lanchester, Elsa 88
Lansbury, Angela 103-104
Lansbury, Nelly 54
Lark Rise 143
Laski, Harold 54
Laughton, Charles 87-89
Lawrence, D.H. 163, 174
Lawson, Wilfrid 23
Lay By 158
Lear 155
Lee, Bernard 161
Lee, Jennie 140
Leeson, Sylvia and George 37
Left Book Club 54
Lehmann, Beatrix 79, 80, 81
Leigh, Mike 155
Lennon, Peter 122
Lenya, Lotte 20
Le Sage, Bill 94
Lessing, Doris 109

Lester, Richard 119, 127, 128, 155
Levin, Bernard 22, 107, 108
Lewenstein, Arthur (father) 41-42, 47-51, 61-62
Lewenstein, Clare (first wife) 8-9, 51-52, 55, 65
Lewenstein, David (brother) 43
Lewenstein, Eileen (second wife) see Mawson, Eileen
Lewenstein, Mark (son) 6, 7, 176, 181
Lewenstein, Mary (Mary Convisser, mother) 41-44, 47-48, 49-50, 55
Lewenstein, Natalie (sister) 43
Lewenstein, Paul (brother) 43
Lewenstein, Peter (son) 22, 114, 176, 181
Lewis, Arthur 116
Lieberson, Sandy 179
Life Class 162
Lily White Boys, The 94, 95
Lindsay, Jack 53
Lister, Laurier 6, 7, 9, 98
Little Nell 156
Littlewood, Joan 24-25, 83, 89, 90-91, 93-94, 143, 167
Living Theatre 116, 131, 135-137
Lloyd, Kevin 176
Logue, Christopher 94
Loneliness of the Long Distance Runner, The 103
Long and the Short and the Tall, The 92, 93
Long Mirror, The 5
Look Back in Anger 15, 25, 26, 28, 30, 33, 35, 37, 92, 100, 102, 106, 124
Loot 120-121, 125, 126, 128, 174, 175
Lord Arthur Savile's Crime 5
Lovers 122
Lovers of Viorne, The 142
Lowe, Arthur 126, 128, 154
Lower Depths, The 70, 72
Lowndes, Alan 87
Lulu 143
Luther 100, 104, 105, 114
Luv 114
Lynch, Alfred 92, 153
Lynn, Ann 87, 94, 120

Lyric Theatre, Hammersmith 13, 88
Lysistrata 38

McAlpine. Alistair 170
Macbeth 87
MacColl, Ewan 23, 24, 83
McCullers, Carson 29, 40, 115-116
MacDiarmid, Hugh 81
McDowell, Malcolm 175
McEwan, Geraldine 30
McGoohan, Patrick 17, 92
MacGowran, Jack 109, 153
McIntyre, Peter Colin Blair 72
McIntyre, Tom 149
McKenna, James 109
McKenna, Siobhan 13, 79, 109, 117-118
McLeish, Robert 70, 71, 74
McLellan, Robert 77
MacLiammoir, Micheal 121
McMillan, Roddy 37
Macrae, Duncan 96, 97
Mademoiselle 145
Magee, Patrick 152
Magnificence 158-159
Magnolia Street 38
Major Operation 71
Make Me an Offer 91, 93, 98, 99
Making of Moo, The 35
Malcolm, Christopher 156
Malina, Judith 116,135, 136
Mankowitz, Wolf 7, 8, 16-20, 24, 40, 84, 91, 94, 98-99, 107
Marcus, Frank 129, 150
Margolis, Henry 18, 19
Markham, Kika 124
Marks, Ruth 139
Marowitz, Charles 120, 121, 134-135, 167
Marsden, Betty 6, 176
Martin, David 68
Martin, Millicent 86
Massey, Daniel 91
Match Maker, The 83
Matura, Mustapha 157, 165, 170
Mawson, Eileen (Mrs. Oscar Lewenstein) 1, 2, 3, 6, 67, 82, 84, 88, 91, 95, 152, 176
May, Val 111
Mayfair Theatre 162

Meaden, Dan 105
Meals On Wheels 118
Medwin, Michael 175
Melia, Joe 142
Melly, George 175
Member of the Wedding, The 29, 37
Men Should Weep 71, 76
Merchant of Yonkers, The 83
Mercury Theatre 5, 9, 101
Mermaid Theatre 116
Merrick, David 30-31, 104, 115, 122
Merry-Go-Round, The 163, 174
Metropolitan Theatre, Edgware Road 173
Michell, Keith 15
Midsummer Night's Dream, A 89
Miles, Bernard 116
Miller, Arthur 12, 15, 33, 40, 81
Miller, Martin 37, 83, 91
Milligan, Spike 128, 152
Milton, Ernest 5, 79
Miss Hargreaves 4
Mitchell, Robert 1, 7, 53, 70, 72, 75, 77, 79, 80
Mitchell, Warren 23, 155
Mnouchkine, Ariane 143
Moby Dick 17, 86, 92
Modisane, Bloke 102
Moffatt, John 105, 114
Montague, Helen 147, 169
Montgomerie, John 170
Montgomery, Douglas 79
Montlake, Fli 77
Moon is in the East, The Sun is in the West, The 165
More, Julian 86, 98
Moreau, Jeanne 135
Morley, Robert 142
Morley, Sheridan 153-154
Morning Star 77
Mortimer, John 138
Moscow Arts Theatre 35
Mostel, Zero 95, 96
Mother Courage 24, 25, 89
Mother's Day 148
Mount, Peggy 112
Muggeridge, Malcolm 19
Mulberry Bush, The 15, 23
Muller, Robert 107, 109, 111
My Place 109

Mysteries and Smaller Pieces
131-132

National Theatre 25, 38,
110, 137, 143, 145, 167,
178, 180
Neher, Caspar 21
Nekrassov 37
New Statesman 135
New (later Albery) Theatre
88, 90, 91, 92, 124
New Theatre (magazine) 2,
65, 68, 80, 81, 89
Nichols, Dandy 137
Nightingale, Benedict 135,
154, 161, 162
Norman, Monty 86, 91, 98
No Room at the Inn 73, 75
Not I 152
No Trees in the Street 81
Nottingham Playhouse 91,
111, 142, 171, 178
Ntshona, Winston 157, 163
Nunn, Trevor 178

Objections to Sex and Violence
151
O'Brien, Edna 149
O'Brien, Richard 156
Observer, The 39, 75, 121,
132, 180
O'Casey, Sean 69, 76, 178
O'Connor, Garry 150
Odets, Clifford 53, 69, 77,
78, 80, 83
O'Hagan, Paddy 156
Oh, les Beaux Jours! 153
Okoli, Felicia 102
Old Ones, The 148
Old Vic, The 172, 173
Olivier, Laurence 14, 17, 33,
34-35, 95, 96, 97, 110,
142, 145, 168, 172, 173
O'Malley, Mary 178
Once a Catholic 178
O'Neill, Eugene 68
On Guard for Spain 53
Onikoyi, Rashidi 102
Orton, Joe 120-121,
125-130, 174, 176
Osborne, John 15, 31, 32,
35, 38, 39, 92, 99, 100,
103, 105, 106-107, 114,
118, 123, 124, 147, 151,
176
Oscar Lewenstein Plays Ltd.
99

O'Sullivan, Maureen 121
Othello 96
O'Toole, Peter 92, 93, 113
Ottaway, James 175
Owen, Bill 23, 105
Owners 151
Oxford Playhouse 38

Pagan Place, A 149, 151
Page, Anthony 23, 123,
124, 146, 152, 153,
160-161, 168, 169, 172,
174
Palace Theatre 34
Palmer, Geoffrey 153
Paradise Now 131, 132-135
Parsons, Geoffrey 20, 53
Party, The 87, 88, 103
Pasco, Richard 30
Patch, Wally 91
Patriot for Me, A 27, 145
Pearson, Noel 149
Peck, Bob 154
Penhorn, Maggie 139
Pennington, Michael 153
People Show, The 48, 155
Periton, Leslie 11
Perl, Arnold 16
Philadelphia, Here I Come
121-122, 123
Phillips, Andy 159
Phoenix Theatre 106, 112,
165
Piece of Milarkey, A 71
Pinter, Harold 25, 88, 129
Philanthropist, The 153
Pioneer Corps 59-62
Pithey, Wensley 7, 17
Plant in the Sun 53
Play 141
Players Theatre 8
Playfair, Giles 3, 41
Playhouse Theatre 77
Plays and Players (magazine)
134
Play with a Tiger 109
Pleasence, Donald 5, 128
Play Mas 165
Plough and the Stars, The 76
Plowright, Joan 15, 17, 29,
31, 35, 96, 97, 103, 110
Plummer, Christopher 115
Poke, Greville 10-11, 169,
170, 173
Pollock, Patsy 168
Porter, Eric 93
Postlethwaite, Peter 159

Price, Alan 161, 175
Prick Up Your Ears 125
Priestley, J.B. 5, 80
Prince, Arthur 43
Prince of Wales Theatre 3
Pringle, Bryan 92
Progressive Players 91
Punch Revue, The 19, 98
Purgatory 35
Purple Dust 178

Q Theatre 7
Queen's Theatre 118, 129
Queen's Theatre, Glasgow
70
Quick, Celia 177
Quilligan, Veronica 149
Quinn, Patricia 156

Rabelais 142
Raffles, Gerry 24, 83, 39, 94
Ramsay, Margaret (Peggy)
35, 94, 95, 120, 127,
128
Ransley, Peter 155
Rape of Lucretia, The 9
Rayman, Sylvia 83
Rayne, Sir Max 138
Rea, Stephen 150
Reading, Bertice 30, 38
Redgrave, Michael 13, 14,
80, 83
Redgrave, Vanessa 117, 124
Red Roses for Me 176
Regan, Sylvia 77
Reid, Beryl 175
Reisz, Karel 103, 120
Removalists, The 159, 160
Remusat, Maria 24
Renaud, Madeleine 142, 153
Requiem for a Nun 38
Resounding Tinkle, A 38
*Restoration of Arnold
Middleton, The* 160
Rhinoceros 19, 95, 97, 98,
111
Richard, Cliff 87
Richard's Cork Leg 148-149,
151
Richardson, Ralph 126,
128-129
Richardson, Tony 13, 14,
15, 26, 27, 28, 30, 31,
32-33, 34, 35, 36, 38,
40, 99, 101, 102-103,
105, 110, 114-115, 117,
120, 123, 145, 170, 171